G000278831

Platform Strategy

During the last decade, platform businesses such as Uber, Airbnb, Amazon and eBay have been taking over the world. In almost every sector, traditional businesses are under attack from digital disrupters that are effectively harnessing the power of communities. But what exactly is a platform business and why is it different?

In *Platform Strategy*, Laure Claire Reillier and Benoit Reillier provide a practical guide for digital entrepreneurs and executives to understand what platforms are, how they work and how you can build one successfully.

Using their own "rocket model" and original case studies (including Google, Apple, Amazon), they explain how designing, igniting and scaling a platform business requires learning a whole new set of management rules. *Platform Strategy* also offers many fascinating insights into the future of platforms, their regulation and governance, as well as how they can be combined with other business models.

Laure Claire Reillier and Benoit Reillier are co-founders of Launchworks, a leading advisory firm focused on helping organizations develop and scale innovative business models.

Laure Claire Reillier has worked for a number of high-growth start-ups and established tech firms. Before co-founding Launchworks, Laure Claire was a senior executive at eBay Europe. She studied computer sciences and telecommunications at Telecom SudParis (France) and holds an MBA from the London Business School.

Benoit Reillier has been advising the management teams of platforms and digital and technology companies for the past 20 years. He studied information systems, management and telecommunications at Telecom Management and economics and competition law at King's College, London. He holds MBAs from both Columbia University in New York City and London Business School.

Platform Strategy

How to Unlock the Power of Communities
and Networks to Grow Your Business

Laure Claire Reillier
and Benoit Reillier

Routledge
Taylor & Francis Group

LONDON AND NEW YORK

First published 2017
by Routledge
2 Park Square, Milton Park, Abingdon, Oxon OX14 4RN

and by Routledge
711 Third Avenue, New York, NY 10017

Routledge is an imprint of the Taylor & Francis Group, an informa business

© 2017 Laure Claire Reillier and Benoit Reillier

The right of Laure Claire Reillier and Benoit Reillier to be identified as authors of this work has been asserted by them in accordance with sections 77 and 78 of the Copyright, Designs and Patents Act 1988.

All rights reserved. No part of this book may be reprinted or reproduced or utilized in any form or by any electronic, mechanical, or other means, now known or hereafter invented, including photocopying and recording, or in any information storage or retrieval system, without permission in writing from the publishers.

Trademark notice: Product or corporate names may be trademarks or registered trademarks, and are used only for identification and explanation without intent to infringe.

British Library Cataloguing-in-Publication Data
A catalogue record for this book is available from the British Library

Library of Congress Cataloging-in-Publication Data
A catalog record has been requested for this book

ISBN: 978-1-4724-8024-8 (hbk)
ISBN: 978-1-315-59894-9 (ebk)

Typeset in Bembo and Gill Sans
by Florence Production Ltd, Stoodleigh, Devon, UK

Printed and bound by CPI Group (UK) Ltd, Croydon, CR0 4YY

To the memory of Philippe Reillier

Contents

Figures

Tables

About the authors

Benoit Reillier is managing director and co-founder of Launchworks and specializes in helping businesses design and execute winning strategies to harness the power of communities and platform ecosystems. For the last 20 years he has been working for and advising the boards and top management teams of many blue-chip companies, as well as regulators and governments.

Prior to founding Launchworks, Benoit was director at the management consulting firm KPMG, where he focused on strategic assignments for telecommunications, media and technology (TMT) clients globally. He was previously TMT practice director of expert firm LECG Europe (now FTI), and also worked as business development director of Telia Mobile International UK, the leading Nordic telecommunications group.

Throughout his career, Benoit has had the opportunity to work on and lead key strategic assignments that shaped the communications, payments and technology sectors. He participated in large-scale strategic assignments for a number of Fortune 100 companies and provided expert advice on several multibillion-dollar transactions, high-stakes litigations and arbitrations.

Benoit started his career working for the French government as a special advisor on telecom-related issues and was part of the team preparing the liberalization of the French telecom sector in the 1990s.

Benoit is a guest lecturer at leading European business school ESCP-Europe.

He holds an MSc in management sciences, a master's degree from Institut National des Telecommunications (now Telecoms & Management ParisSud), an MA in economics and competition law from King's College London and MBAs from both London Business School and Columbia University in New York City.

Benoit can be reached at benoit@launchworks.co.

Laure Claire Reillier is a director and co-founder at Launchworks and specializes in helping platforms ignite and scale their businesses through innovative strategic marketing and product development. She also manages the global expert network of Launchworks. Laure Claire has 20 years' experience in developing, managing and marketing products and services for e-commerce, telecom and software companies and has deep expertise in B2B, B2C and C2C marketing.

Before joining Launchworks, Laure Claire worked at eBay, where she was head of proposition development for sellers in Europe. In this role, she was responsible for product strategy and roadmap, positioning, customer experience (online and offline), pricing and marketing communications.

Before eBay, Laure Claire managed the P&L and development of VoIP and e-commerce services at BT Retail in the UK. She was responsible for the commercial development and launch of new services and the management (strategy, marketing and pricing) of existing services. She also worked as marketing and business development director of Goodman Blue, a VoIP software start-up, where she repositioned the company and its suite of products prior to its acquisition by American investors in 2006.

Laure Claire started her career in 1996 at innovative software start-ups Metrica and WatchMark. Both were later acquired by IBM, where Laure Claire worked as a consultant, product manager and later head of marketing for Europe, where she worked closely with many international telecom operators on performance management solutions for mobile services.

She is a regular guest lecturer at ESCP Europe and board member of their marketing master's degree. She has also been a guest lecturer at London Business School.

Laure Claire holds a Master's degree in Computer Science and Telecoms (Ingénieur Télécom, Paris) and a MBA from London Business School.

She can be reached at laure@launchworks.co.

Preface

Why we wrote this book

We were students when we met in the early 1990s just outside Paris, France. We were very fortunate to study networks and computer sciences as the World Wide Web was being invented (literally between our first and second year of graduate studies). We discovered a small – yet global – interconnected village of a handful of websites that could *all* be visited within a single day. It was a mesmerizing experience. Previous text-based tools for searching files and displaying information, such as Archie and Gopher, were largely aimed at academics and didn't stand a chance against an easy-to-use tool such as the Web. Like many early users, we intuitively understood that this new connectedness would have a profound impact on the world economy. We knew that the linear production model, at the heart of our economies and largely unchanged since the Industrial Revolution, was about to be challenged.

Much has changed since we graduated, and we have observed first-hand how large and small firms, as well as societies, have been transformed by this digital revolution.

At the same time, we also noticed that a deeper and probably more disruptive force was impacting an increasing number of markets. Successful firms were not simply becoming digital, but also transforming their business model to fully harness what the Internet enabled in terms of new interactions. It was not about newspapers having a website or even offering an online edition, but about new businesses using communities of contributors and readers. It was not about simply selling online rather than in shops, but about allowing people to interact as part of communities, to list items, to connect, to exchange and to transact through largely centralized platforms, such as eBay. This was in stark contrast with the way firms had been organized since the Industrial Revolution. The linear view of the firm, with its inputs (labour, raw material, etc.) transformed in an increasingly efficient manner into valuable outputs (products and services) was no longer able to explain how these particular firms were operating. A case study of Ford, which would have provided powerful management insights into how firms operated only 15 years ago, no longer provides the insights it once did. Firms such as Apple, Amazon, Google, Airbnb and Uber have grown at an unprecedented pace while operating in ways that have very little to do with traditional firms such as Ford.

We also noticed that many of these disruptive platforms were in fact cleverly combined with traditional business models to create powerful self-reinforcing ecosystems. Amazon, for example, used eBay's open marketplace model and combined it with its own digital retail model. Apple is focused on manufacturing and selling beautifully designed products – and this generates more than 80% of its revenues – but these devices are often bought because of the unique apps provided by the community of external developers and available on its App Store platform. Google's advertising and search platforms are also supplemented by a range of other products and services developed by Google as part of its fast-growing ecosystem.

Our fascination and interest for these new business models, whose power we experienced first-hand, led us to set up Launchworks, a new breed of advisory company dedicated to helping firms unlock value by leveraging these new platform-based business models. At the time, books on platforms simply didn't exist beyond a few, often quite narrow, academic publications.[1] As we developed our thinking and frameworks to help platform businesses, we realized that many firms could benefit from our experience and insights.

Who is this book for?

This book is aimed at everybody interested in better understanding the new business models powering our economies. Business and management students will find valuable references, frameworks and case studies to better understand how platform business models work. Platform executives will be able to step back from the day-to-day management to look more holistically at the unique challenges they face as they scale their business. Lastly, business executives working for traditional companies will gain unique insights into the inner workings of platform-based business models, their disruption potential, and possible strategic responses.

What is new about this book?

We noticed that platform businesses were generally treated as 'black boxes' by outsiders and therefore decided to shed light on how they were operating.

This encouraged us to define what platform businesses were doing and how their activities were different from traditional ones, and led to the platform rocket model presented in this book. We also realized that being a platform was not a binary question and that many businesses, such as Amazon, were in fact combining different business models. This led us to develop the platform-powered ecosystem framework that shows at a high level which portfolio of activities are undertaken by a company and their underlying business model. We have seen first-hand how important it is for firms to have clarity on these issues before they formulate their 'platform strategy'.

Lastly, we used our experience, greatly enriched by many discussions with friends, academics and colleagues with experience at platform firms such as eBay, PayPal, Uber, Airbnb, Facebook and Google, to develop a practical guide for those interested in designing, igniting, scaling and defending a platform. Clearly, each platform is different, but we describe at a high level the generic questions that platform businesses need to answer at various stages of their development.

This process confirmed the scale of the disruption that was taking place and gave us some further insights into the emerging field of platform strategy.

Over an astonishingly short time frame, platforms such as Uber and Airbnb grew at a frenetic pace and society as a whole started to take notice. In some cases, platforms attracted the ire of established players that were being disrupted. How many times have we heard stories of hotel representatives or taxi companies complaining about the 'unfair competition' of these new innovative entrants? Yet the convenience and flexibility of the innovative and cost-effective offerings of platforms have been too attractive to resist. Customers have been voting with their feet and wallets – or with their mobile phones, to be more accurate! Customer demand has fuelled the arrival of a new breed of start-ups positioning themselves as 'the Uber of X' or 'the Airbnb of Y', with X and Y being used for a wide range of industries and categories, including 'planes', 'holidays', 'boats', etc. Yet igniting and scaling platforms to critical mass is a notoriously difficult exercise, and we have tried to document some of these unique challenges, as well as offer some tips and tools to address them.

Standing on the shoulders of giants

Academics have recently redoubled their efforts to research platforms, a relatively new field of economics known as 'multisided markets' only first formalized in 2003 by French Nobel economist Jean Tirole. We are most definitely standing on the shoulders of giants, and this book would not have been possible without the insights and stories from countless platform executives, academics, students and clients who taught us so much over the past few years. We acknowledge the contribution of all those who shared their views with us, sent us their research, invited us to seminars and workshops, participated in some of our lectures or simply retained our firm, Launchworks, to advise them.

Note

1   The possible exception is an early book on multisided markets by D. Evans and R. Schmalensee, *The Catalyst Code: The Strategies Behind the World's Most Dynamic Companies*, Boston, MA: Harvard Business School Press, 2007.

Acknowledgements

While all errors and omissions are our own, we would like in particular to thank the following individuals for sharing their insights with us as we worked on the book.

In alphabetical order, we would like to thank: Ken Ardali, Jean-Jacques Arnal, Andrin Bachmann, Nicolas Bailleux, Charles Baron, Matthew Bennett, David Brackin, Verena Butt d'Espous, Sangeet Choudary, Jean-Marc Codsi, Richard Davies, Carlos Eduardo Espinal, Richard Feasey, Jean-Marc Frangos, Anshu Goel, Barbara Gray, Jonathan Hall, Tim Hilpert, Rob Hull, Stéphane Kasriel, Spyros Katageorgis, Monroe Labouisse, Terence Lim, Elisabeth Ling, Claude Lixi, Rodrigo Madanes, Frédéric Mazzella, Antonio Nieto-Rodriguez, Keyvan Nilforoushan, Natasha Osborne-Geurts, Nilan Peris, Didier Rappaport, Fred Reillier, Annemie Ress, Paul Ress, Ramsey R. F. Sargent, Joe Schorge, Marie Taillard, Aude Thibaut de Maisières, Mike Walker, Chris Webster, Taylor Wescoatt, Caspar Wolley, André Haddad, Pascal Isbell and Albin Serviant.

Please note that while many of the people mentioned above work for, advise or regulate some of the platform businesses we talk about in this book, many spoke to us in a personal capacity rather than as representatives of their employer. A small number of individuals asked to remain anonymous, and we thank them as well.

We would also like to thank all the academics, including in particular Marshall Van Alstyne, Annabelle Gawer, Thomas Eisenmann, Ray Fisman, Geoff Parker, David Evans and Peter Evans, who have done much to improve our understanding of platforms over the years. Many of them also kindly provided feedback and/or shared their thoughts with us at a number of research symposia and conferences.

Special thanks also go to Jonathan Norman, our publisher at Routledge, as well as Emma Redley and Alex Atkinson, his assistants, for believing in the project and providing ongoing support, to Philip Stirrup, our production manager, to the people at Florence Production, Laurence Paul and Andrew Craddock for their help, to Ian Koviak and Alan Dino Hebel at the Book Designers for designing the book cover, to Nirosha Fernando, who designed the illustrations, to Sue Seabury, a dear friend and talented writer who patiently reviewed a previous version of the manuscript, and to Justin Coutts, one of our colleagues at Launchworks, who volunteered to help up with this endeavour in general and made a very substantial contribution to the pricing chapter in particular.

Chapter 1

Introduction to platform businesses

Uber, the world's largest taxi company, owns no vehicles. Facebook, the world's most popular media owner, creates no content. Alibaba, the most valuable retailer, has no inventory. And Airbnb, the world's largest accommodation provider, owns no real estate. Something interesting is happening.

Tom Goodwin

In 2007, designers Brian Chesky and Joe Gebbia struggled to pay their rent in San Francisco when they noticed that the city's hotels were fully booked for an upcoming design conference. They came up with the idea of renting out three airbeds in their loft and cooking breakfast for their guests. The next day, they designed a website, originally called airbedandbreakfast.com. In less than a week, they had three guests, paying $80 each a night. When the guests left, thinking this could become a big idea, they asked a former roommate of Joe's, engineer Nathan Blecharczyk, to help them develop the site that we know today as Airbnb.

For the first few years, the team failed to raise money. The vision of a trusted community marketplace for people to list, discover and share private accommodation around the world did not appeal to venture capitalists (VCs), who couldn't see a big enough market. But Brian, Joe and Nathan persisted and found ingenious ways to keep going. In 2008, the company ran out of cash, so they had to find creative ways to make money quickly. As the presidential campaign was in full swing and both sides were keen to show support for their favourite candidates, the Airbnb team decided to sell special edition Cheerios cereal boxes for both presidential candidates called 'Obama O's' and 'Cap'n McCains' for $40 each. They made $30,000 in a few weeks.

By early 2009, they were invited to join the Y Combinator, one of the leading incubator programmes in San Francisco, and got $20,000 of funding from well-known angel investor Paul Graham. A seed round of $600,000 led by Sequoia Capital followed shortly afterwards.[1] Even so, the business did not take off. The Airbnb team realized that the photos of places advertised on their website were not appealing. According to Brian Chesky, 'A web startup would say, "Let's send emails, teach [users] professional photography, and test them." We said, "Screw that."'[2] They rented a $5,000 camera and went door to door, taking professional pictures of as many New York listings as possible. Revenues doubled quickly to $400/week and the site started to grow. Brian knew at this point that it was not just about pretty pictures, but that Airbnb first had to 'create the perfect experience [. . .] and then scale that experience.' In April 2012, the team started monetizing the service by charging up to 15% on the bookings. More funding rounds followed,[3] which enabled Airbnb to hire more staff to focus on the customer experience and market the platform in order to scale the business.

Their success came down to three things: ease of joining for host and guest; effective matching of hosts and guests; and safe and easy transactions for all.

Since then, Airbnb has grown exponentially (see Figure 1.1), from 50,000 listings in 2011 to more than 2 million in April 2016.[4] And this is not just inventory. It is estimated that roughly half a million people around the world sleep in an Airbnb rented accommodation at peak time.

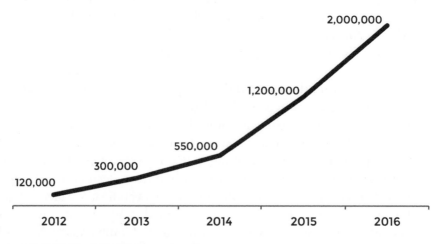

Figure 1.1 Airbnb global listing growth

Source: VentureBeat, Airbnb website, Launchworks analysis

Airbnb is currently active in 34,000 cities in 190 countries, and has had 35 million nights booked.[5] Airbnb raised $1.5 billion in June 2015, which is one of the largest private funding rounds ever. The company is estimated to be worth $30 billion,[6] which means that in less than 10 years, the travel accommodation platform has become one of the most valuable privately owned start-ups, worth more than the largest hotel chains Wyndham, Intercontinental and Hyatt, who own extensive portfolios of prime real estate globally.

And Airbnb owns no property.

While there's been an overwhelming response from customers, Airbnb's high-growth success story has not been without resistance from hoteliers, who claim that individuals renting their rooms or entire homes to visitors represents an 'unfair competition' to their trade. There is emerging evidence[7] that Airbnb is not only growing the market, but also increasingly competing against hotels, who have to respond with new services and lower prices. Interestingly, these lower prices benefit all consumers, and not just Airbnb clients. Yet Airbnb has also been under growing pressure from city authorities regarding housing regulations and tax laws. We'll come back to these issues in Chapter 13 on platforms and regulation.

Table 1.1 Comparison of the largest hotel groups vs Airbnb

Company	Market capitalization of private valuation[8] ($ billions)	Number of hotels managed	Number of rooms provided	Year of launch
Airbnb	30 billion	0	2,000,000	2007
Hilton Worldwide (including Conrad, Waldorf Astoria)	23.3 billion	4,726[9]	775,866	1919
Marriott[10] (including The Ritz Carlton, W Hotels, Sheraton, Le Méridien	17.8 billion	5,700	1,200,000	1927
Accor Group[11] (including Raffles, Sofitel, Novotel, Mercure)	11.2 billion	3,942	570,000	1967
Intercontinental Hotels Group[12] (including Crowne Plaza, Holiday Inn, Holiday Inn Express)	8.3 billion	4,921	722,575	1946
Wyndham Worldwide[13] (including Ramada, Travelodge, Super 8, Days Inn)	7.56 billion	7,670	667,000	1981
Hyatt Hotels[14] (including Hyatt Park, Regency, Place, House, Ziva, Andaz)	6.87 billion	679	172,587	1957

UNLOCKING ECONOMIC VALUE WITH EBAY

Using eBay as an example, let's say that you have a large table with matching chairs that no longer fits with your newly redecorated flat. For you, this second-hand furniture almost has a negative value; it takes up space, and given the very reasonable price you paid for it at IKEA several years ago, you don't want to spend time trying to find somebody to take this set off your hands. Conversely, think about a nearby student who has a tight budget and is looking for a table and chairs for her new pad. She wants to save money and doesn't care about 'new' stuff. The student is prepared to pay £50 for the entire set. eBay can match you and this potential buyer, with very limited friction. Let's say the student's bid of £30 is the highest and that she is the happy winner of the auction. The value created by the platform intermediation is then £20 (£50 willingness to pay minus £30 winning auction bid) for the buyer plus £35 for the seller (that's the £30 plus the negative price you were attaching to the no longer adequate table set that was taking up space: say £5). So out of 'thin air', the platform managed to create £55 of economic value. Now scale this by millions of transactions every day across all the platform companies (including car and house rental companies, e-commerce marketplaces, etc.) and you get a sense of the transformational potential of platform businesses.

Platform models have become mainstream

Airbnb epitomizes the rise of digital platform businesses. In the same way as eBay connects buyers and sellers, Airbnb creates communities of hosts and guests and enables them to transact globally. Unlike traditional businesses, platforms don't *produce* anything and don't just *distribute* goods or services. What they do is *directly connect different customer groups to enable transactions*. eBay, a well-known company, creates value by simply connecting buyers and sellers.

For thousands of years, markets have been physical and local. Connecting groups of buyers and sellers has played a big part in the fabric of human society. Farmers' markets and matchmakers have been around for thousand of years. But something extraordinary has happened in the last 20 years: technology has enabled these business models to scale to a global level. The very first platforms that scaled globally were the credit cards companies such as Discover,

Visa, Mastercard and Amex. But no one scaled as quickly or as globally as new technology-focused players such as Apple, Google and eBay, all underpinned by digital platforms.

Many more have followed suit, reinventing entire parts of consumer industries, from media (Facebook), retail (Amazon), transport (Uber), telecoms (WhatsApp), payments (PayPal), music (SoundCloud), accommodation (Airbnb) and many other sectors.

This platform colonization extends to the enterprise domain as well in an increasing number of verticals: wholesale goods (Alibaba), talent platforms (Upwork), operating systems (Windows), etc.

In most business literature, platforms are either considered as 'black boxes' serving what economists call 'multisided markets', or assumed to operate like traditional firms. Unfortunately, neither approach provides much insight into platform businesses themselves. Many commentators use the generic term 'platform' to describe a 'technology platform' that encompasses processors, access devices such as mobile phones, PCs and tablets, software applications, etc. These loose definitions often lead to vague notions of platforms that encompass firms with very different business models. We'll come back for more detailed definitions of digital platforms in Chapter 3, but for the time being we'll use a simple definition for platform businesses as those *connecting members of communities and enabling them to transact*. We'll also define platform-powered businesses as firms that have parts of their business underpinned by platforms.

Table 1.2 Examples of digital platforms

Digital platforms connecting communities of users and producers and enabling them to transact	Users	Producers
eBay, Alibaba	Buyers of goods	Sellers of goods
Airbnb, Onefinestay	Guests	Hosts
Uber, Lyft	Passengers	Taxis
Turo, Drivy	Car renters	Car owners
BlaBlaCar, Waze Carpool	Passengers	Car drivers
YouTube, Facebook	Viewers	Content producers and advertisers
Amex, Visa, Mastercard	Card owners	Merchants
Upwork, Hired	Businesses	Freelancers
Tinder, Match.com, Happn	Single guys dating	Single girls dating
UberEATS, Deliveroo	Buyers of meals at home	Restaurants
AngelList, Seedrs	Investors in start-ups	Start-ups seeking capital
TaskRabbit, Stootie	Buyers of services	Providers of services
Kickstarter, Indiegogo	Buyers of new products	Providers of new products

Since many platform businesses are digital in nature, we use the term digital platform for businesses *digitally* connecting members of communities to enable them to transact.

Platform business models can be tailored to meet a wide range of needs. They include:

- Marketplaces, which attract, match and connect those looking to provide a product or service (producers) with those looking to buy that product or service (users).
- Social and content networks, which enable users to communicate with each other by sharing information, comments, messages, videos and pictures, and then connect users with third parties such as advertisers, developers and content providers.
- Credit card and payment platforms, which attract users on one side to pay for goods and services, and merchants on the other side to be able to take their payment.
- Operating systems for computers, mobiles, game consoles, VR equipment and associated app stores, which match users with software applications produced by developers.

Some platforms can combine different aspects. For example WeChat is a social network combining an app store with payment functionality.

Why platform models are different

A closer examination of these businesses suggests that they all share features unique to platforms, and do not follow traditional management principles. These new companies are made of powerful platform ecosystems uniquely able to *attract, match and connect people to enable them to transact*. These platforms often use 'open' business models that do not require stocking or manufacturing anything, but harness the power of communities to enable transactions. This is very different from traditional organizations, which tend to run as 'linear pipes'. Traditional organizations use their linear 'value chains' – a term famously coined by 1980s strategy guru Michael Porter – to buy and transform raw materials (inputs) into products or services (outputs) before selling them at a profit.

This 'input/output' view of the world and associated management frameworks have provided helpful insights into many traditional firms' operations. Indeed, it is the value chains of car manufacturers, oil companies, hotel groups and utilities that have powered the growth of our economies since the

Industrial Revolution. But for many twenty-first-century platform businesses, this framework lost much of its usefulness.

While platforms and open business models are not new, their 'mathematical formalization' is very recent. The underlying economics of such businesses were first set out in a 2003 scholarly article by 2014 economic Nobel Prize winner Jean Tirole.[15] His seminal work was primarily focused on market dynamics and antitrust concerns rather than the management of platform businesses themselves. Since then, new platform-powered challengers have emerged, and have been disrupting entrenched competitors with their meteoric rise. More importantly, these new model companies have revealed that some markets, once thought to be 'traditional', such as taxis and hotels, could in fact be served more efficiently with innovative and open platform business models enabled by digital technologies. In many cases, platforms are able to bring to bear the power of communities to become real competitors to established companies. Ride-sharing, for example, used to be a marginal activity, often seen as unsafe. BlaBlaCar has managed to redefine this market by creating a vibrant and trusted community with more than 20 million members over 18 countries in 2016. It is now seen by Guillaume Pepy,[16] CEO of French Railways SNCF, as a key competitor.

Companies didn't wait for academics to rewrite the rules of management, and early platforms mostly proceeded through trial and error. However, we are now in a position to observe many successful (and less successful) platforms and review their past experiments so that we can learn from them and derive useful management principles for those that will follow. New platforms need not suffer through all the mistakes of early platform pioneers. Additionally, traditional companies faced with platform competition are looking for ways to stay in the game, and much can be learned from the reactions of established players disrupted by platforms. We will also show how old and new business models can be combined to create entire self-reinforcing platform-powered ecosystems. We will use a range of platform examples, such as eBay, Amazon, Google and Apple, as case studies throughout the book to guide us and provide illustrations of key business insights behind the success of these platform-powered businesses.

- Chapter 2 explores the meteoric rise of platform business models over the past decade.
- Chapter 3 reviews platform definitions in the academic literature, looks at the various types of platforms and proposes basic characteristics common to most platforms.
- Chapter 4 reviews the key economic characteristics of platforms, including network effects, externalities, critical mass and tipping point.

- Chapter 5 compares and contrasts traditional business 'value chains' such as manufacturing, service provision and distribution with various platform business models. It then proposes a typology based on the Launchworks platform rocket framework and its various core components: acquiring, matching, connecting, transacting and optimizing functions.
- Chapter 6 examines how successful companies such as Google, Apple, Amazon, Facebook and Microsoft have been able to design unique organizations – and self-reinforcing ecosystems – powered by platforms.
- Chapter 7 looks at the key life stages of platforms businesses and provides insights into the pre-launch phase of platform businesses.
- Chapter 8 focuses on the issues associated with platforms at launch and the strategies to successfully ignite the two sides of platform businesses.
- Chapter 9 addresses the key questions faced by the high-growth challenges of scaling platforms.
- Chapter 10 looks at the management challenges associated with established platforms that need to nurture and defend their ecosystem.
- Chapter 11 examines the unique pricing and incentive challenges faced by platform companies throughout their development.
- Chapter 12 discusses how trust needs to be nurtured by platforms and supported by the right governance principles, community management frameworks and brand attributes.
- Chapter 13 looks at the interplay between platforms, regulations and competition law, and discusses the complex balance that governments and regulatory authorities need to strike to unlock value creation while protecting consumers.
- Chapter 14 examines the challenges faced by traditional firms being disrupted by platforms and possible responses. It reviews past failures, highlights the relative strengths and weaknesses of existing business models competing against platforms and offers insights into strategic options.
- Chapter 15 provides a broader perspective into the future of platforms and their interplay with work, management, technology and the emergence of the sharing economy. It highlights some of the changes we are likely to see in the years to come and the extent to which platform ecosystems will both create new markets and continue to colonize existing ones.

Notes

1 *Telegraph*, 7 September 2012, www.telegraph.co.uk/technology/news/9525267/Airbnb-The-story-behind-the-1.3bn-room-letting-website.html.
2 Fast Company, www.fastcompany.com/3017358/most-innovative-companies-2012/19airbnb.

3   Following the Sequoia round, Airbnb went on to raise a series A round of $7.2 million in 2010. *Wall Street Journal*, 25 July 2011, http://blogs.wsj.com/venturecapital/2011/07/25/airbnb-from-y-combinator-to-112m-funding-in-three-years/.

4   VentureBeat, 19 June 2014, http://venturebeat.com/2014/06/19/uber-and-airbnbs-incredible-growth-in-4-charts/ and Airbnb website at www.airbnb.co.uk/about/about-us.

5   www.airbnb.co.uk/about/about-us.

6   CB Insights, 1 August 2016, www.wired.com/2015/12/airbnb-confirms-1-5-billion-funding-round-now-valued-at-25-5-billion/. By the end of 2014, Airbnb had raised over $800 million. 'Airbnb Is Raising a Monster Round at a $20B Valuation', *TechCrunch*, 27 February 2015, http://techcrunch.com/2015/02/27/airbnb-2/.

7   G. Zervas and D. Proserpio, 'The Rise of the Sharing Economy: Estimating the Impact of Airbnb on the Hotel Industry', Boston University, 27 January 2016.

8   As of 23 September 2016.

9   http://news.hiltonworldwide.com/assets/HWW/docs/brandFactSheets/HWW_Corporate_Fact_Sheet.pdf.

10 www.marriott.com/marriott/aboutmarriott.mi.

11 As of 30 June 2016, www.accorhotels-group.com/en/brands/key-figures.html.

12 www.ihgplc.com/files/pdf/factsheets/factsheet_worldstats.pdf, 31 March 2015.

13 www.wyndhamworldwide.com/category/wyndham-hotel-group, June 2015.

14 Hyatt Hotels Q3 2016 earnings, available at http://investors.hyatt.com/files/doc_financials/q3_2016/Q3-2016-Earnings-Release.pdf

15 See J. Rochet and J. Tirole, 'Platform Competition in Two-Sided Markets', *Journal of the European Economic Association*, 1(4), 2003, 990–1029. While Rochet and Tirole's contribution formalised the economics of two-sided markets, academics before them also made significant contributions to the field. See for example G. Parker and M. Van Alstyne, *Internetwork Externalities and Free Information Goods*, New York, NY, *Proceedings of the 2nd ACM Conference on Electronic Commerce*, 2000, pp. 107–16. See also M. Katz and C. Shapiro, 'Network Externalities, Competition and Compatibility', *The American Economic Review*, Volume 75, Issue 3, June 1985, pp. 424–40. And J. Farrell and G. Saloner (1988), 'Coordination through Committees and Markets', *RAND Journal of Economics*, 19, issue 2, pp. 235–52.

16 http://business.lesechos.fr/directions-generales/strategie/business-plan/0203024730098-guillaume-pepy-imagine-la-sncf-de-demain-9282.php, September 2013.

Chapter 2

The meteoric rise of platform businesses

Over the past 20 years or so, platform businesses have grown at an unprecedented pace and have been able to overtake many traditional businesses. Often, this significant shift in business models and value creation has been overshadowed by the much broader digitalization trend. Not only have platform businesses grown at a faster pace than traditional ones, but they have also created more shareholder value and attracted more venture capital (VC) investment. It is therefore not a surprise to see that platforms are now powering many of the best-known brands in the world and are at the heart of most sharing economy initiatives.

Digital transformation and new platform business models

Over the last 20 years, digital technologies have significantly disrupted traditional businesses. Their physical assets – think bricks-and-mortar stores – are no longer a source of competitive advantage. Harnessing digital distribution models has become a must. In fact, the digital transition has been high on board agendas of most traditional businesses trying to respond to and compete with digital and Internet-enabled entrants.

However, this transition from traditional offline to online (illustrated by arrow number 1 in Figure 2.1) has overshadowed a more fundamental shift in value: the evolution to new digital platform business models (illustrated by arrows 2, 3 and 4 pointing to the upper-right quadrant).

Many firms, busy with the digital translation of their existing model, may forget that the advent of digital technologies is also a key enabler of new, different and often more powerful business models such as 'platforms'. We believe it is the emergence of these digital platform models that has been the most disruptive in many sectors, including retail (eBay, Amazon), travel (Uber) and accommodation (Airbnb). This shift is far from over, and many

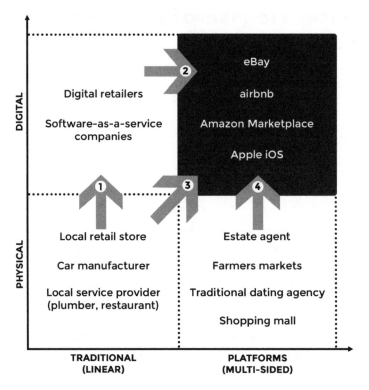

Figure 2.1 **Digital transformation from linear to non-linear**

Source: Launchworks

new industries are now being disrupted by these digital platforms (for example, healthcare, recruitment, professional services and energy).

Of course, some traditional businesses have realized that the digital transition (arrow 1) was not enough and have started to develop platform capabilities to compete (arrow 2). For example, retail giants are now going beyond their initial e-commerce offerings and are trying to harness the power of platforms (top arrow), where merchants can directly sell to customers. The recent acquisition of digital marketplace Jet.com by Walmart for $3.3 billion can be seen in that light. An increasing number of retailers who had only made limited digital investments early on are now investigating digital platforms as add-on businesses (arrow 3).

Amazon is also an interesting example, as while it started as a pure e-commerce reseller with a curated but limited range of goods for sale, it quickly added a marketplace platform to complement its reseller model. The latter now represents well over 50% of its total e-commerce revenues.[1] Zalando, the successful e-commerce fashion company, is also turning itself into a fully fledged platform business.[2]

Lastly, a number of traditional platform businesses, such as estate agents, have further developed their online presence (arrow 4), although in many cases faster and more agile platform competitors such as Zoopla managed to enter the market and are now ahead of the game. Many traditional dating agencies also found themselves replaced by native digital dating platforms such as Happn, Match.com, eHarmony or Tinder.

Of course, many firms also combine different business models, such as platforms and traditional businesses, in order to create what we call platform-powered ecosystems. We will explore their business models, as well as Amazon's, in more detail in Chapter 6.

Platform growth and market capitalization

In the third quarter of 2016, the five largest companies in the world were platform-powered: Apple, Google, Microsoft, Amazon and Facebook (the famous GAFAMs).[3] Just 10 years ago, only one – Microsoft – made the cut.[4] The total market capitalization of platform-powered businesses in the top 10 of the FT Global 500 index went from $280 billion 10 years ago (11% of the total then) to $2.2 trillion in the third quarter of 2016 (59% of the total), as shown in Figure 2.2. And this is not just about market capitalization since recent research shows that platform businesses have significantly higher sales growth, return on assets and gross profits than traditional ones.[5]

In 2015, Apple grew by 28%, Google by 14%, Amazon by 20%, Microsoft by 7.6% and Facebook by 44%. Many of these relatively new businesses have

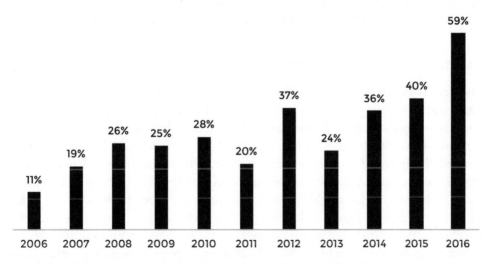

Figure 2.2 **Platform-powered businesses in top 10 FT Global 500 (market cap)**

Source: FT Global 500 list of companies, Launchworks analysis

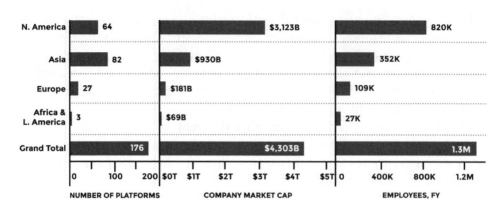

Figure 2.3 **Platform companies by region**
Source: Peter C. Evans, Global Platform Survey, CGE 2016

managed to develop complex ecosystems, often powered by a core 'platform' that acts as a catalyst for enabling transactions between different customer groups.

Peter Evans and Annabelle Gawer recently published one of the very first studies on platform businesses, aimed at identifying platforms around the world and gathering relevant data on their size and value. As Figure 2.3 shows, most of the 176 largest platforms identified are to be found in the US, followed by Asia and Europe. The estimated market capitalization of these companies is in excess of $4.3 trillion and they have more than 1.3 million employees in total. This excludes the so-called spillover effects, such as induced jobs created, impact of increased choices and reduced prices for consumers.

Platforms and brand power

Platform companies are not only creating economic value, but they have also established themselves, sometimes in only a few years, as the best-known companies in the world. When we look at which brands people value most, platform-powered businesses score particularly well. It may be surprising to see such high brand recognition since most of these firms were founded less than 20 years ago. A 2016 study from Millward Brown of the top 100 most valuable brands in the world[6] reveals that many platform businesses make the list. As illustrated in Figure 2.4, the top 10 includes Apple, Google, Microsoft, Facebook, Visa and Amazon, as well as AT&T and Verizon, which are sometimes considered as platforms.[7] In fact, the top eight brands are platform-powered companies. Only McDonald's (in 9th position) and IBM (in 10th position) do not (yet) match our definition.[8]

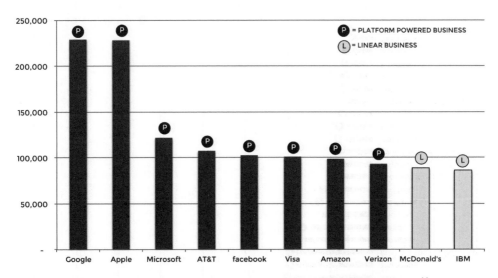

***Figure 2.4* The top 10 most valuable brands in the world (US$ millions)[10]**
Source: Milliward Brown 2016, Launchworks analysis

And platforms can, of course, be found further down in the rankings. Chinese e-commerce marketplace Alibaba, with revenues superior to Amazon and eBay combined, is now in 18th position after entering the top 100 for the first time in 2015.[9]

'Unicorn' platforms as market disruptors

While we have seen that platforms are behind many of today's largest companies and best-known brands, they are also powering many fast-growing start-ups that are attracting significant private investments (e.g. VC and private equity money). Many of these platform-powered start-ups have been able to reach very significant scale without listing on public markets. Airbnb and Uber are cases in point.[11] In only a few years, they, and others, have managed to secure market valuations in excess of $1 billion, gaining the nickname of 'unicorns'.[12]

Aileen Lee famously coined the unicorn metaphor in 2013,[13] but it looks like unicorn companies are not as rare as they once were, and perhaps should be called instead the new 'workhorses'. Today, there are no fewer than 177 such companies[14] that are worth over $1 billion each (the original definition of a 'unicorn'). As illustrated in Figure 2.5, many of them exhibit strong platform characteristics.[15]

For example, Didi Chuxing (formerly Didi Kuaidi), headquartered in China, and Lyft, in the US, are platforms matching drivers and passengers

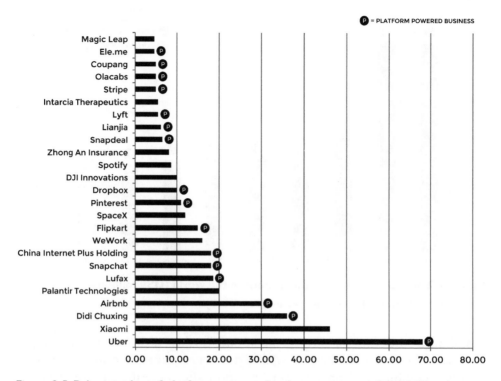

Figure 2.5 Private value of platform-powered unicorn start-ups (US$ billions)
Source: CB Insights, 1 August 2016, Launchworks analysis

like Uber, and both have raised significant private investments. Snapchat is a well-known and fast-growing communications platform that famously turned down a multibillion-dollar offer from Facebook in 2014. Stripe is a fast-growing payment platform for e-commerce merchants.

Platforms power the sharing economy movement

Lastly, platforms are at the heart of the emerging 'sharing economy' since many enable the redistribution, sharing and/or reuse of excess capacity in goods and services. The term 'sharing economy', which was first introduced in 2010, describes a 'social revolution' based on the 'sharing of resources across multiple platforms' in a way that creates values for all participants.[16]

eBay was an early precursor of this trend by allowing people to resell their little-used assets directly and easily, but many other companies have followed suit. The main categories emerging include platforms to buy, hire, share,

Table 2.1 High-level typology of sharing economy platforms (number of platforms in parentheses)

Borrow	Buy	Hire someone	Share	Swap
I can lend you some money (38)	You can buy stuff I no longer need (20)	I can help you with your chores (37)	We can drive somewhere together (22)	We can swap stuff we no longer need (11)
You can borrow my car (36)	You can buy my clothes (10)	I can teach you some skills (26)	Come have dinner at my house (13)	You can stay at my house and I'll stay at yours (9)
I can lend you money for your business (33)	I can buy something for you next time I go abroad (6)	I can show you around town (24)	You can work from my living room (6)	We can swap some clothes (5)
You can stay in my spare room (32)	You can buy currency (5)	I can deliver your parcel (22)	We can share a taxi (4)	We can swap our goods (2)
You can borrow stuff you don't want to buy (20)	You can buy my car (5)	I can cook you dinner (11)	You can camp in my backyard (3)	You can gift your old stuff (2)
Other companies (180)	Other companies (78)	Other companies (187)	Other companies (19)	Other companies (8)
Total: 339	Total: 124	Total: 307	Total: 67	Total: 37

Source: Adapted from JustPark, www.justpark.com/creative/sharing-economy-index/, with indicative number of companies identified in given category given in parenthesis, February 2016

borrow or swap a multitude of things. Seed swap exchanges are helping farmers, clothes and handbags are being shared for relevant occasions, thousands of student books are being swapped, rides and cars are now routinely shared on long and short journeys, the use of expensive real estate is increasingly optimized (flats, offices, parking spaces) and even money now changes hands directly with peer-to-peer lending or currency exchange thanks to specifically designed digital platforms. A very cursory review of sharing economy platforms[17] lists close to 900 companies and new ones are appearing every day. The categories in which the main ones are operating are shown in Table 2.1.

The new rules of management are being rewritten to allow for more powerful and innovative platform ecosystems to emerge and compete with other established businesses, as well as create entirely new markets.

And this is just the beginning.

Notes

1   ChannelAdvisor blog, www.channeladvisor.com/blog/?pn=scot/amazons-q4-results-marketplace-surges-proves-it-is-the-amazon-profit-cow.
2   See, for example, blog post of Marcel Weiß dated 19 November 2015, https://earlymoves.com/2015/11/19/zalando-we-want-to-become-an-open-fashion-platform/.
3   *Financial Times* Global 500 rankings, 30 September 2016.
4   FT Global 500 list of largest companies, 31 March 2006 and 31 March 2016, and Launchworks analysis.
5   See B. Libert, M. Beck, J. Wind, *The Network Imperative*, Boston: Harvard Business Review press, 2016.
6   BrandZ(tm) Top 100 Most Valuable Global Brands 2016, Millward Brown, http://wppbaz.com/admin/uploads/files/BZ_Global_2016_Report.pdf.
7   We recognize that telecommunications operators, such as Verizon and AT&T, operate somewhat differently than other platform-powered ecosystems. In fact, some may argue they operate more like traditional businesses than digital platforms. Yet we believe operators were an early wave of platforms that attracted users, matched them first using switchboards, then with directories and yellow pages, to connect them and allow them to transact. They also originally benefited from network effects, yet were not able to innovate as fast as the new 'Internet players'. Telecoms operators are, however, increasingly investing in digital platform capabilities to avoid commoditization (such as the acquisition of Yahoo by Verizon). We note that their exclusion from this list would still result in more than 75% of the combined value of the top 10 brands in the world coming from platform-powered businesses.
8   IBM is often seen as a platform in the technical sense of the term, and associated with both hardware standards and operating system capabilities. Yet today's business is largely run as a technology advisory company rather than a digital platform. We note, however, that the firm is investing in new capabilities that may allow it to transition to a platform-powered ecosystem model.
9   Alibaba raised $25 billion on the NYSE in September 2014.
10   This is the value of the intangible asset of the brand itself.
11   At the time of writing, neither Airbnb nor Uber are quoted on the stock market, so market valuations for these firms are based on the implied value of their last private round of financing.
12   A unicorn, a legendary animal that has been described since antiquity as a beast with a pointed horn on its forehead, is notoriously difficult to find. Private companies reaching a $1 billion mark valuation were so rare until 2010 that they were coined unicorns.
13   http://techcrunch.com/2013/11/02/welcome-to-the-unicorn-club/, 2 November 2013.
14.   Data from CB Insights, 28 September 2016, www.cbinsights.com/research-unicorn-companies.
15   As we will see later on in this book, sky-high valuation at a given point in time is in no way a guarantee of success, and even firms exhibiting strong platform characteristics are not immune to failure. In fact, 'unicorpses', defined as 'dead companies once valued at more than $1 billion', are likely to be observed soon. In the meantime, and irrespective of market volatility, it is interesting to see overall patterns of value creation around platform businesses.

16 See early definitions of the sharing economy in R. Botsman and R. Rogers, *What's Mine Is Yours: The Rise of Collaborative Consumption*, New York: Harper Business, 2010. More recently, A. Stephany, *The Business of Sharing*, London: Palgrave Macmillan, 2015.

17 www.justpark.com/creative/sharing-economy-index/, February 2016.

Chapter 3

What is a platform business?

Narrowing the search: platform definitions

The very definition of what is a platform business is fraught with difficulty. The term is widely used in a range of contexts, by academics and practitioners alike, and the generic dictionary definitions are not overly helpful.[1] At a very basic level, it appears that the term platform is often used to define 'something upon which one can build/put something else'. A physical representation could be a plank, a raised floor or a pair of shoes with thick soles, such as the ones often worn by Lady Gaga. A figurative use could be a political platform or even a technological one. This is a very generic use of the term, and we believe a more precise definition is required for what we refer to as a 'platform business model', such as eBay or others.

Defining platform businesses is not simply an academic pursuit, but a critical first step for executives to better understand how their markets are being disrupted. Too wide a definition would run the risk of overestimating the impact of these new business models while not being able to identify what is unique about them. Too narrow a definition would simply miss important firms with platform characteristics. Deciding on a definition is therefore a prerequisite to the development of any platform strategy or market response. It is so important that we almost always start our consulting projects at Launchworks with this very topic to ensure that all the senior executives have a shared understanding of what a platform business is.

In the field of academia, the term is primarily used by three different types of scholars:[2]

(a) Those concerned with the development of *products*.[3]
    A manufacturer might, for example, say that 'the Jaguar X-Type uses the same platform as the Ford Mondeo' or '74X Boeing planes share the same platform'.

(b) Those concerned with *technology*.[4]

An engineer might, for example, say that the Intel platform benefited from the replacement of DOS by Windows.

(c) Those concerned with *economic transactions*.[5]

Economists might, for example, say that eBay is a platform operating in a multisided market and enabling transactions between different consumer groups.

PLATFORM

A business creating significant value through the acquisition, matching and connection of two or more customer groups to enable them to transact.

Examples: eBay, Airbnb, Uber

While there is some overlap in terms of usage across these different definitions, we believe it is very important to be clear about what we mean by the word 'platform' from the outset. We propose to define platform businesses as 'businesses creating significant value through the acquisition and/or matching, interaction and connection of two or more customer groups to enable them to transact'.[6]

Since much of the academic work on platforms has been done in the context of competition economics or antitrust,[7] we will review some of this work and discuss its implications for management. We will then review more recent definitions against our own definition based on the activities of platform businesses, as well as the characteristics of the underlying markets they serve. We will also see that platforms are not all equal, but come in a range of shapes, colours and sizes. They may allow you to buy, rent, swap and borrow products, services or currencies. They may be open to third parties or closed, have direct distribution to consumers and producers or indirect ones and they may have a broad selection of differentiated goods or a narrow one with homogeneous products and services. All these differences call for different types of governance and business architecture within the overall platform framework. Lastly, we will see that many companies are not pure platforms, but 'platform-powered ecosystems' mixing different business models.

Economics of platforms and multisided markets

The concept of 'multisided markets' is a relatively recent one. As previously mentioned, we owe to the world of antitrust law the earliest detailed economic analysis of businesses operating as platforms. Visa and Mastercard may not have used the term multisided markets when they launched, but their operations – of connecting card users and merchants – clearly exhibited the economic characteristics of platform businesses.[8]

The concept of multisided markets started to be formalized by academics in 2000. Geoff Parker and Marshall Van Alstyne were among the first economists to look closely at platform business models while trying to understand how firms such as Microsoft could sustainably offer free software.[9] Shortly after, Jean-Charles Rochet and Jean Tirole published a seminal paper on the economics of card platforms in 2002. Their research proposed a new economic model of the price relationships used on both sides of a multisided market to better coordinate demand.[10] While the main focus area of the paper was credit cards, the analysis and key findings apply more widely. The key insight of Rochet and Tirole was that the price paid by clients of the platform on one side of its market (the commission merchants paid for cards to be accepted at their shops) enabled very attractive subsidized pricing on the other side of the market (free cards for consumers).[11] This was a significant departure from traditional markets, where pricing below costs for a service is not sustainable and may even be anticompetitive if designed to force competitors out of the market.

Platforms need to design their pricing strategies in such a way that *overall* value for the platform is maximized. Note that many different equilibria could have been reached in the cards market (fees for merchants and free cards for consumers, or expensive card fees for consumers and no fees for merchants, or anything in between), but that the current payment schemes ended up with a heavily subsidized consumer side as an equilibrium (e.g. merchants tend to pay for the bulk of card payment system costs). We note that regulators have also invited themselves to the debate and are in some markets, such as the EU, starting to regulate some of these platform fees. We will discuss some of these aspects in more detail in Chapter 13 on the regulation of platform businesses.

Some of the principles that can be used to help determine the price structure, level and dynamics of platform businesses are discussed in Chapter 11.

A review of existing definitions

A number of other economists built upon the work of Rochet and Tirole to propose slightly different economic models and apply the emerging corpus of work on platforms to different industries and market sectors.[12]

Evans and Schmalensee subsequently offered a broader definition using the notion of 'economic catalyst' with (i) two or more groups of customers; (ii) who need each other in some way; (iii) but who cannot capture the value of mutual interactions on their own; and (iv) rely on the catalyst to facilitate value-creating interactions between them.[13]

Evans has since written extensively about multisided markets and catalyst businesses in the context of payment networks and cards,[14] as well as in broader antitrust contexts.[15] His definition of 'catalyst' businesses[16] also has the merit of decoupling the underlying economics of the markets being served and the business model of the companies serving them. For example, previous definitions of platforms that focused on the features of the market served, rather than the platform businesses themselves, would not have considered the taxi market as a multisided market (since it was initially served by traditional non-platform businesses). It is, however, undeniable that Uber uses a platform-centric business model to disrupt a market that previously operated in a traditional manner. We therefore prefer to refer to these as platform businesses (or platform-powered ecosystems) rather than platform markets.

Platforms as 'catalysts'

Evans also proposed a broad classification of 'catalysts' consistent with his original definition. The three main business types identified were: (i) market makers; (ii) audience builders; and (iii) demand coordinators.

Although Evans considers all of these businesses as platforms, the distinctions between them are important:

(i)   *Market makers*: eBay has created a unique global marketplace where sellers and buyers of an incredibly wide range of goods meet. eBay is valued at more than \$35 billion[17] and generated in excess of \$83 billion of Gross Merchandise Value (GMV)[18] in 2016 without offering any product whatsoever, but simply by connecting buyers and sellers through its online platform and being paid a small percentage of the transaction[19] for this facilitation. Uber and Airbnb are in the same category.

(ii) *Audience builders*: Some platforms focus on allowing users to share and/or consume content. This in turn attracts advertisers who need 'eyeballs' for their campaigns. Evans argues that media firms, and many publications, operate in such 'audience building' multisided markets.

(iii) *Demand coordinators*: A third type of platform business focuses on coordinating demand within a given ecosystem. Unlike market makers, demand coordinators often have a broader group of stakeholders and ecosystem participants. Operating systems (OS) fall into this category since they are designed for users, licensed by hardware manufacturers and used by application developers. The more applications available for a given OS, the higher its utility or value. At the same time, app developers are only able to invest in the development required if there are either currently or prospectively enough users of the OS to cover their costs and eventually make a profit.

Economists also showed that since platforms were connecting two markets, they had a unique ability to price differently from traditional businesses. In fact, they noticed that platform businesses were able to offer free services not simply on a temporary basis or during promotions, but on a *sustainable basis*.[20] This has far-reaching implications, since it means that the very basis of competition can be dramatically changed by platforms and that non-platform businesses may find themselves 'priced out' of the market. This phenomenon will be discussed in more detail in Chapter 14, where we will examine why existing firms struggle to compete against platform businesses and what options are available to them.

Hagiu and Wright also proposed a focused definition of 'multisided platforms' (MSP). Their proposed definition is:

> Multisided platforms (MSPs) are organizations that create value primarily by enabling direct interactions between two (or more) distinct types of affiliated customers.[21]

This is a significant departure from previous market-based definitions. In our view, it provides a helpful starting point for analysing platform businesses because it deals with some of the 'over-inclusiveness' implied by broader definitions. For example, it excludes supermarkets or traditional consulting organizations that were sometimes wrongly considered to be platforms with earlier definitions.

This definition is more circumspect regarding the platform nature of many media companies: only media firms whose primary source of value creation is the direct interaction between customer groups would strictly be included. With that definition, many traditional newspapers don't make the cut.

The recent global platform survey initiative[22] led by Peter Evans and Annabelle Gawer also dealt with the definition conundrum by using a high-level typology of platforms, including transaction platforms, integrated platforms, investment platforms and innovation platforms.

This is also consistent with the most recent definition proposed by Parker, Van Alstyne and Choudary:[23]

> Platform: A business based on enabling value-creating interactions between external producers and consumers. The platform provides an open, participative infrastructure for these interactions and sets governance conditions for them. The platform's overarching purpose is to consummate matches among users and facilitate the exchange of goods, services or social currency, thereby enabling value creation for all participants.

Building on these definitions, we believe that platforms should include organizations that create value by enabling interactions, direct or indirect.

For us, platform businesses are 'businesses creating significant value through the acquisition, and/or matching, interaction and connection of two or more customer groups to enable them to transact'.

This definition is consistent with platforms as marketplaces, as well as with some types of information platforms matching consumers of content with content contributors. Platforms can connect consumers, or businesses, or a mix.[24] Target groups on both sides of the platform often have different characteristics, although in some cases, such as eBay, the overlap between buyers and sellers can be significant.[25] Our definition also includes businesses where the connection between consumer groups is indirect, such as credit card companies like Visa or Mastercard,[26] where banks often act as intermediaries on the consumer side (by distributing cards) and on the merchant side (by selling card services to merchants).

However, our definition excludes businesses such as Netflix, considered to be digital resellers. It also excludes companies such as Intel, which makes computer chips, and IBM, which provides consulting services. However, we recognize that these firms shape the development of key standards and technologies – alone and in partnership with others – and have the potential to become platform-powered ecosystems.

These differences in terms of definitions also highlight the fact that platform businesses are not binary in nature, but can be placed on a 'continuum' depending on their underlying economics at a given point in time and how much value the business derives from the transactions it enables. For example, companies such as IBM did try to become fully fledged platforms by developing their own operating systems (OS/2) to attract both application developments and enterprise users. Since this initiative failed, IBM developed alternative business models (hardware sales initially later abandoned in favour of high-value technology consulting).

These notions will be revisited when we discuss platform ecosystems and their governance in more detail. We will further explore how platforms often power entire ecosystems and what the competition implications of such models are. For example, the online resale model of Amazon (a linear business) and its marketplace (a platform) are both crucial elements of the firm's ecosystem. A review of these platform-powered ecosystems will provide interesting insights into the competitive dynamics of platforms and help us understand the interplay between platform business models and traditional ones.

Platforms compared to other business models

Table 3.1 summarizes our proposed definitions of platforms and other traditional business models such as distributors and 'input/output' businesses.

The proposed definition focuses on the businesses serving these markets as opposed to the market themselves, since the demand on the various sides of the market can also sometimes be served by traditional businesses.

As a platform, eBay acquires, matches and connects buyers and sellers and allows them to transact directly. Also, we note that eBay doesn't set the price of the goods that are being exchanged on its platform.[27]

As a UK retailer and a distributor, Tesco (like Walmart in the US, Metro in Germany, Carrefour in France, etc.) resells goods from a selected range of suppliers and distributes them through its network of shops, its online site[28] and delivery services. Tesco owns the customer relationship, the pricing and product placement of goods and services sold. It stocks the products, pays its staff at the tills and (hopefully) makes a margin on its operations as a result of all these activities. However, it doesn't connect different communities to allow them to transact. It is a distributor/reseller.

Honda produces a range of cars and motorbikes globally. In order to do so, it acquires raw materials, as well as parts from suppliers, and assembles them into cars that meet their Honda design specifications. Once the vehicles are manufactured, they are distributed by a 'reseller', in this case the dealership network. Honda's business is essentially an 'input'/'output' business.[29]

It is, however, worth noting that traditional firms can transform themselves into platforms or even in some cases add platform capabilities to their existing business models, as we will discuss in later chapters.

Table 3.1 Simplified typology of platform and non-platform business models

Platform	Retailer/reseller	Input/output business
Acquires, matches and/or connects different customer groups and enables transactions	Buys goods and/or services from selected producers and runs a value-added distribution business	Buys inputs (e.g. raw materials, energy, services) and combines them to produce a product/ service sold at a margin
eBay	Tesco	Honda

Platform-powered ecosystems

As we have seen, companies such as Apple, Google, Amazon, Microsoft and Facebook are among the largest in the world. Yet very few are pure platform businesses. Instead, these successful companies are underpinned by a mix of business models, including platforms, and are therefore 'platform-powered'. The term 'ecosystem' is often defined in a business context as a group of interdependent organizations collectively providing goods and services to their customers.[30] A platform-powered ecosystem can then be defined as a group of organizations – under the same ownership or strategically linked – that derives significant value from at least one platform business.

These platform ecosystems leverage the interplay between the various business models that are part of the ecosystem to reinforce customer propositions and create stickiness, often with spectacular success. These ideas will be further explored in Chapter 6.

With the definitions out of the way, we can examine management principles in more detail and look under the hood of platforms.

PLATFORM-POWERED ECOSYSTEM

A business comprising of a mix of business models, including platforms.

Examples: Amazon, Apple, Google, Alibaba, Microsoft

Notes

1   The *Oxford English Dictionary* states that a platform is 'a raised level surface on which people or things can stand, usually a discrete structure intended for a particular activity or operation'.

2   See A. Gawer, *Platforms, Markets and Innovation*, Cheltenham: Edward Elgar, 2009, p. 45, as well as Y. Baldwin and J. Woodard, *The Architecture of Platforms: A Unified View*, Cambridge, MA: Harvard Business School, 2009, for a discussion of the architecture of platforms across disciplines.

3   S. Wheelwright and K. Clark, *Revolutionizing Product Development: Quantum Leaps in Speed, Efficiency and Quality*, New York: Free Press, 1992.

4   T. Bresnahan and S. Greenstein, 'Technological Competition and the Structure of the Computer Industry', *The Journal of Industrial Economics*, 47, 1999, 1–40.

5   J. Rochet and J. Tirole, 'Platform Competition in Two-Sided Markets', *Journal of the European Economic Association*, 1(4), 2003, 990–1029.

6   Strictly speaking, businesses need not be Internet-enabled to have a platform business model (e.g. shopping malls or estate agents), but many of the platform businesses we

will review in this book are digital platforms that have harnessed the power of the Internet and big data to develop their offerings, often globally.

7   Also called antitrust, competition economics is concerned with competition between firms and potential abuse of market power justifying market intervention.

8   See, for example, W. Baxter, 'Bank Interchange of Transactional Paper: Legal and Economic Perspectives', *Journal of Law and Economics*, 26, 1983, 541–88, for an early discussion of pricing considerations in card markets (interchange fees).

9   Geoffrey Parker and Marshall van Alstyne, 'Information Complements, Substitutes, and Strategic Product Design', ICIS 2000 Proceedings, Paper 2, 2000.

10   We will see in Chapter 11 how important these new 'platform equations' are for pricing strategies.

11   This meets the definition of Rochet and Tirole: 'A market is two sided if the platform can affect the volume of transactions by charging more to one side of the market and reducing the price paid by the other side by an equal amount; in other words, the price structure matters, and the platform must design it so as to bring both sides on board'.

12   See B. Caillaud and B. Jullien, 'Chicken and Egg: Competition among Intermediation Service Providers', *RAND Journal of Economics*, 34(2), 2003, 309–28, who departed from the payment cards industry to explore and model in more details the expected market equilibrium of competing platforms (including estate agents, dating agencies and marketplaces) under a range of scenarios. G. Parker and W. Van Alstyne, 'Two-Sided Network Effects: A Theory of Information Product Design', *Management Science*, 51(10), 2005, 1494–504, subsequently developed a model of 'two sided network externality' capturing network effects, price discrimination and product differentiation. Mark Armstrong, 'Competition in Two-Sided Markets', *RAND Journal of Economics*, 37(3), September 2006, 668–91, also proposed a model of multisided markets built upon similar theoretical foundations (but focused on membership externalities, as opposed to usage ones, as originally modelled by Rochet and Tirole) and offered a generic definition based primarily on the scale of the benefits derived by one side of the market depending upon the size of the other side.

13   Richard Schmalensee and David S. Evans, 'Industrial Organization of Markets with Two-Sided Platforms', *Competition Policy International*, 3(1), Spring 2007.

14   D. Evans and R. Schmalensee, *Paying with Plastic: The Digital Revolution in Buying and Borrowing*, Cambridge, MA: MIT Press, 2005, for a review of the economics of card payments.

15   D. Evans, R. Schmalensee, M. Noel, H. Chang and D. Garcia-Swartz, 'Platform Economics: Essays on Multi-Sided Businesses', *Competition Policy International*, 2011, for competition issues arising in multisided businesses.

16   Also referred to as 'matchmakers'. See D. Evans and R. Schmalensee, *Matchmakers: The New Economics of Multisided Platforms*, Cambridge, MA: Harvard Business School Press, 2016.

17   As of 26 September 2016.

18   GMV stands for gross merchandise value and is used in online platforms to indicate a total sales value for merchandise sold through a particular marketplace over a certain time frame.

19   Typically final value fees are between 5% and 11% on eBay.

20 In fact, prices could even be negative on one side of the business on a sustainable basis. See David S. Evans and Richard Schmalensee, 'The Antitrust Analysis of Multi-Sided Platform Businesses' (Coase-Sandor Institute for Law and Economics Working Paper No. 623, 2012).

21 Andrei Hagiu and Julian Wright, 'Multi-Sided Platforms', Harvard Business School Working Paper 12-024, October 2011.

22 P. Evans and A. Gawer, 'The Rise of the Platform Enterprise', Center for Global Enterprise, January 2016.

23 G. Parker, M. Van Alstyne and S. Choudary, *Platform Revolution*, New York: W. W. Norton & Company, 2016.

24 What marketers call B2B (business to business), B2C (business to consumer) and C2C (consumer to consumer).

25 By targeting communities that are both buyers and sellers, such as stamps or rare coin collectors in the early days of eBay, some platforms have been able to ignite their platform more quickly and overcome some of the friction caused by the 'chicken-and-egg' problem, discussed in Chapter 8.

26 Card companies connect merchants and card users indirectly through merchant acquirers and card issuers (usually banks).

27 While many platforms let their producers and users set the price themselves, some try to internalize supply and demand to set uniform prices (e.g. Uber).

28 Many ecommerce sites today operate under a retailer/reseller model.

29 Please note that we are of course simplifying business typologies in order to illustrate the differences between business models. For example, while Honda's core business is manufacturing 'input' and 'output' business for cars and engines, it also has significant R&D activities in artificial intelligence and robotics.

30 'Business Ecosystem', *Palgrave Encyclopedia of Strategic Management*, London: Palgrave Macmillan (2014).

Chapter 4

Economic characteristics of platforms

This book is not an economics text, but knowledge of some economics concepts is useful to understand how platforms differ from more traditional firms. This chapter reviews some of the key economic principles underpinning platform businesses. If you're already familiar with the concepts of externalities, demand- and supply-side economies of scale, network effects, critical mass, tipping point, pricing elasticity, substitutes and complements, feel free to move straight to the next chapter.

Externalities

We can all benefit from and be harmed by things that are not within our control. When people join networks (be it social networks or telecoms networks), all the other network users benefit since the network's reach – and therefore overall value – is increased. This is a positive externality since all network users are better off as a result.

If a company were to dump toxic waste in the water next to a village, the villagers would suffer a strong negative externality. Villagers are not responsible for the behaviour of the firm, yet their lives are impacted by it. This is a negative externality, and the company is not incurring the real cost of its actions (unless it is caught).

An externality occurs when individuals or firms are impacted, positively or negatively, by an economic transaction that is independent of them. Many examples of externalities can be found in everyday life. Things as simple as the pleasant scent of a perfume worn by a stranger in the underground can be seen as a positive externality. A negative externality has the same properties, but with a negative impact imposed by somebody else's actions. A smoker would be imposing a negative externality on people around him.

Clearly, externalities go far beyond personal inconvenience, and the toxic waste of our factory in our previous example is a strong negative externality on the people living nearby.

Externalities can also change over time. The rather disturbing noises made by the builders next door excavating a basement as these lines are being written are not helping with concentration in the short term. However, once completed, an extended and renovated house next door will have a positive impact on the valuation of the street and therefore represent a positive externality for nearby homeowners.

One reason why such negative externalities occur is that economic agents may not be able (or willing) to internalize the effect they have on third parties. If a factory were economically responsible for the well-being of the nearby population, it would have strong incentives not to pollute as much.

Positive externalities are important for platforms, since when a platform grows, both in terms of number of transactions and participants, it becomes more valuable to all. For example, the more applications available on an app store, the more attractive it becomes for users. Of course, the more users join and interact on the platform, the more attractive the platform becomes for app developers trying to reach users.[1]

As in the Apple App Store example, when positive externalities exist on both sides of a platform, positive feedback loops appear and amplify growth. Enabling and enhancing these loops with a frictionless customer experience and the right features for users is a key objective of platform businesses.

The term 'internalizing the externalities' is sometimes used, and sounds more complicated than it is. It simply means that some firms and organizations may need or want to take into account these externalities in their businesses. So a pollution tax can help firms internalize the negative externalities associated with pollution because it gives them an incentive to pollute less.

Economies of scale

Economies of scale are said to exist when the unit cost of production goes down with the volume of production. Many businesses requiring significant upfront investments benefit from economies of scale since the more units are produced by a factory or plant, the lower the unit costs. The cost of production of cars is highly dependent upon how many cars can be manufactured by a given factory/car plant. If the production is very small, say 10 cars, the total cost of the factory will have to be covered by these very few cars and result in a very high unit cost. Car production is therefore said to benefit from economies of scale, as more cars produced will allow for the shared cost of production (including R&D) to be spread across more cars and will therefore be lower on a per car basis. The logical strategic implication of industries with economies of scale is that you need to become the largest company in the sector in order to enjoy the lowest cost base per unit.

These economies of scale affect the supply side, that is to say the company producing the goods. Recently, however, the concept of 'demand-side' economies of scale has become quite widespread. In networks, the value of the service provided increases with the number of users because of the positive externalities we discussed above. Economists therefore describe these network businesses as benefiting from 'demand-side' economies of scale. Strictly speaking, this is no longer about the cost of production (supply) going down with volume, but about the value created for users (demand) going up with the number of users.

The concept of 'demand-side economies of scale' is also referred to as network effects. It is so central to the economics of platforms that we develop it further below.

Networks and network effects

Networks are characterized by nodes interconnected by links. Networks can be physical, such as telecommunications networks where copper pairs are physically connected to premises, or logical – where the connection exists as a piece of information – such as when you are connected to friends on social media. Networks have a range of properties and topologies. They can connect different types of nodes (heterogeneous), the links can be unidirectional or bidirectional, the nodes can be more or less meshed, etc.

These distinctions are important when we discuss features of platform businesses. For example, does the platform allow two-way communication between participants (e.g. friends on Facebook) or one-way communication (e.g. celebrities followed on Twitter), and what are the implications of these network rules? For our purpose, platform businesses are powered by these communities of producers and users that can be helpfully modelled and explained using network concepts.

Network effects occur when a product or service becomes more valuable as more people use it. This can be counter-intuitive, since with traditional business models the opposite can be true, and the value of an exclusive luxury car does not increase – and may actually decrease – if another one is produced (or bought by a neighbour). However, having more collectors (buyers and sellers) on eBay clearly increases the value of the overall platform since the sellers will add inventory and the buyers will provide liquidity to the platform and increase the number of transactions. Unlike traditional businesses, platforms often exhibit network effects, and these have profound competitive implications.

Figure 4.1 illustrates the number of relationships in a network with two, five and 12 connected parties. The number of links in the network increases

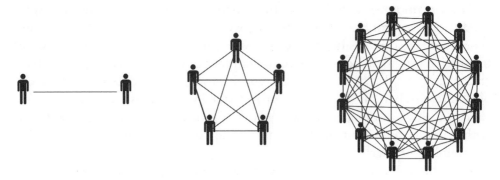

Figure 4.1 **Network effects**

'exponentially', with one, 10 and 66 relationships (and therefore possible connections), respectively.[2]

The relationship between the value of a network and its size, or between its utility and the numbers of transactions, has been modelled in a number of different contexts to help quantify network effects.[3]

Network effects can be:

(i) *Direct*: as in telecommunications, where the value of the network increases directly with the numbers of users connected to it. This is also what happens with 'peer-to-peer' or social networks, where more users tend to benefit the entire platform.

(ii) *Indirect*: as in operating systems or app stores where the value of the network increases not only with the number of users (direct), but with the number of application developers attracted by the growing user base (indirect effect). Indirect network effects result in positive feedback loops across the platform as more developers creating more apps then attract more users, and more users make the platform more attractive to developers. Games consoles, operating systems and app stores are typical platforms exhibiting strong indirect network effects.

Mature platforms such as Alibaba, eBay or Craigslist benefit from huge indirect network effects. More than 423 million active buyers[4] make an average of 58 purchases a year[5] on Alibaba; 25 million sellers[6] with 1 billion listings attract 164 million active buyers on eBay;[7] and Craigslist[8] users post well over 80 million classified ads each month.

It is worth noting that network effects can also be induced by platforms and maximized or internalized through platform design and governance decisions. For example, features that allow users to provide feedback on their experiences add value to the platform. It increases direct network effects, as the more users participate by giving feedback on books on Amazon or flats on Airbnb, the better the information to other users. By the same token, gaming platforms provide software development kits and a range of incentives for developers to select their platform over other competing ones. They do this to maximize indirect network effects since more and better games will attract more buyers of the game console itself.

Network effects are very important since they can represent a significant barrier to entry for competitors and therefore contribute to protecting a business. In certain circumstances, network effects may lead a platform to reach a 'critical mass', and even in some markets 'tip' to a 'winner takes all' natural equilibrium, where a single business ends up serving the entire market.

Network effects are not just about the number of platform participants, but about their propensity to interact on the platform as well. Inactive users contribute less to network effects on a platform than active ones that participate frequently. In real life, platforms often benefit from − and have to manage − a combination of different types of network effects. For example, Facebook started with direct network effects since Harvard students found it easier to connect to one another once their entire class had joined. These effects were later combined with indirect network effects with the addition of developers on the platform offering games and applications (e.g. *Farmville*, horoscopes, etc.). After proving that it could scale its free services, Facebook started monetizing its business by inviting advertisers to the platform and allowing them to target very specific segments of platform participants.[9] It is worth noting that while network effects may lead to viral growth, the two concepts are distinct. A new book can become very successful and be bought/ downloaded by lots of people very quickly (viral growth) but have no network effect (since new readers do not add value to previous ones).

Critical mass

A critical mass in a network is defined as the point at which the growth of the network becomes 'self-sustaining'.

In the context of platform businesses, critical mass may be required on both sides of the market and is driven by a number of variables, including the type and strength of network effects, customer behaviours and the distribution of customer tastes.[10] While scaling a nascent platform is particularly difficult, because it often has limited network effects due to its small size, reaching critical mass makes growth and participant matching much easier.

Platforms that do not reach critical mass often unravel. In the case of direct network effects, the level of participation on the platform affects the value it offers to users. Platforms without critical mass often struggle to match participants. For example, if a new dating site launches but does not have female participants on day one, male participants are unlikely to find a suitable match. If the platform is not able to match people – which is its *raison d'être* – then it unravels as early adopters leave.[11] We will see in Chapter 7 how to overcome these issues.

Tipping point

Closely related to the notion of critical mass, the tipping point is defined as the point at which a network 'shifts' from one state (e.g. competition, or normal trading activities) to another one (e.g. monopoly, or market unravelling) due to cumulative network effects. Numerous examples of markets exhibiting such effects have been widely documented in Malcolm Gladwell's book *Tipping Point*.[12] The definition offered by Gladwell is broader, but overlaps with the critical mass concept discussed above: 'the moment of critical mass, the threshold, the boiling point'.

The tipping point is therefore an inflection point that, in the case of platforms, is often synonymous with reaching critical mass. Early social networking sites SixDegrees and Friendster never found the elusive tipping point in their growth trajectory that would have allowed them to reach a critical mass. The customer experience was lacking and there was not enough for users to do, mainly because there were not enough users! Caught in a negative feedback loop, these platforms unravelled fairly quickly.

Single homing vs multihoming

Multihoming essentially means being connected to more than one network, usually for increased reliability, resilience or performance. In the context of platforms, it simply means participating in more than one platform.

For example, an application developer may decide to offer its app on both iOS and Android platforms (multihoming on the producer side), while many individuals only use one mobile phone and therefore need to commit to a given platform or 'single home' with, say, either iOS or Android. The decision to single home or multihome is typically driven by a cost–benefit analysis that will need to answer the following questions: How expensive is it to affiliate to more than one platform? What are the added benefits of doing so? How easy is it to switch between platforms?

This is an important concept since the decision between single homing and multihoming by users and producers will determine to a large extent how easy it will be for the platform to reach a critical mass and gain market power. For example, while it may be more difficult to ignite a platform when users single home, if successful the platform then becomes more valuable since a critical mass of users are committed. Of course, the platform itself can shape the decisions of its participants by trying to seek exclusivity (e.g. for game developers to single home), reducing switching costs from other established platforms (e.g. by offering a 'converter' or compatibility with other platform features) or trying to appear as the 'winning' platform, through advertising and endorsements, to make sure users don't feel the need to look elsewhere. We will also see in Chapter 13 that the extent to which multihoming is possible has implications for regulators and competition authorities.

Price elasticity

We all know that the demand for products and services changes depending on their price. If the price of baked beans goes up, people will buy fewer cans − and vice versa, if the price goes down, more baked beans are sold. The price elasticity of demand reflects this by giving the percentage change in quantity demanded for a 1% change in price. It is the quantitative articulation of the question 'How many more cans of baked beans will I sell if I decrease the price by 1%?'

A small change in price of some goods sometimes results in a large change in demand. Traditional baked beans or chocolate bars would be in this category and are therefore said to have a high price elasticity.

The demand for other types of goods doesn't change much when prices change. This is the case for cigarettes or petrol, where customers are either addicted or really need to buy in order to go from A to B. These goods have a low price elasticity.

Often, the decision to not buy something because the price has increased is driven by the fact that other, cheaper alternatives may exist. So if you are no longer buying baked beans because their prices have increased, you may be buying black-eyed beans instead. When that is the case, the products are said to be substitutes (see section below) and the relationship between the increase of price of one product and the increase of demand of the other one is called 'cross-price elasticity'. The relationships between the interplay of prices on two sides of a platform are discussed in more details in Chapter 11. This concept of cross-price elasticity is also central to understanding substitute and complement products.

Substitutes vs complements

Two products are deemed substitutes when the demand for one increases as the price of the other increases. The concept is rather intuitive, and we all review daily the characteristics of dozens of substitute products when shopping. If the price of our favourite brand of butter has increased significantly, we may want to switch to another – substitute – brand. The more substitutable the products, the more they exert competitive pressure on one another.

Complements are the opposite. Products are said to be complements if the increase in price of one leads to a decrease of demand for the other. While this may sound slightly less intuitive, complementary products abound. Printers and their cartridges (or razors and their blades) are typical complements. If the price of a printer increases (everything else being equal), it is likely to sell less, and the subsequent demand (in the aftermarket) for its ink cartridges will decrease. These products are complements.[13] In the same way, apps available on Apple's App Store are complements of its iPhone product.

This distinction between substitutes and complements is useful to better understand the disruptions brought about by platform businesses. While their operations are often very different from those of traditional businesses, the products and services they offer are often close substitutes to existing ones.

Notes

1   In the context of platform businesses, Jean-Charles Rochet and Jean Tirole, 'Two-Sided Markets: A Progress Report', *The RAND Journal of Economics*, 35(3), 2006, 645–67, made an interesting observation about the different types of externalities that exist. They distinguish between usage externalities and membership externalities. Usage externalities occur (as their name indicates) when the platform adds value through interactions and transactions (e.g. usage) by existing members. Membership externalities exist when the value received by users of the platform on one side of the market increases with the number of users on the other side of the market.

2   The total number of relationships (T) in a network of n participants is given by the formula: $T = n(n - 1) / 2$.

3   Metcalfe's law states that the value of a network is proportional to the square of its users (e.g. Facebook). Reed's law states that the increase in value is not only proportional, but exponential, due to the number of subgroups joining the network (e.g. Slack). Beckstrom's law states that the value is the net value to participants of all the transactions carried over the network. Lastly, Sarnoff's law states that the value of some networks is proportional to the number of viewers (e.g. Yahoo).

4   Alibaba.com, March 2016 numbers for Taobao and Tmall marketplaces, www.alibaba-group.com/en/ir/financial_fullyear

5   *Fortune*, 23 September 2016, http://fortune.com/2015/09/23/alibaba-says-numbers-real-not-fake/. Each package could contain more than one item.

6   eBay.com, https://static.ebayinc.com/static/assets/Uploads/PressRoom/eBay-Factsheet-Q2-2015.pdf

7   eBay.com, Q2 2016 numbers, https://investors.ebayinc.com/releasedetail.cfm?Release ID=980435

8   Craigslist website, www.craigslist.org/about/factsheet

9   Well-known venture capital firm Andreessen Horowitz, one of the early financial backers of Airbnb, knows a thing or two about network effects. See the excellent presentation and companion article of Anu Harianna et al. on their site: http://a16z.com/2016/03/07/all-about-network-effects/

10   D. Evans and R. Schmalensee, 'Failure to Launch: Critical Mass in Platform Businesses', *Review of Network Economics*, 9(4), 2010, for a discussion on platforms failing to reach critical mass.

11   Using the dating analogy, it is interesting to note that since female dating site members appear to be more difficult to attract on platforms, these have to work extra hard to ensure that they manage to reach a critical mass. This may include incentives (e.g. free service), or even in some extreme cases the creation of false profiles to 'appear' to have a critical mass! See the FTC ruling on online dating services using fake profiles, www.ftc.gov/news-events/press-releases/2014/10/online-dating-service-agrees-stop-deceptive-use-fake-profiles, or even 'female chatbots', which Ashley Madison claimed in its defence were 'widespread' in this area.

12   See M. Gladwell, *The Tipping Point: How Little Things Can Make a Big Difference*, Boston, MA: Little Brown, 2000, for a discussion on markets subject to tipping points.

13   We note, however, that platforms differ from products with an aftermarket in that, while demand is also interlinked, platform businesses involve two distinct groups of customers, as opposed to a single buyer of a product and its 'after-products'. See S. Bishop and M. Walker, 'The Economics of EC Competition Law', *European Competition Journal*, 6(1), 2010, p. 93, for examples of markets with after-products.

Chapter 5

Platforms as business models

Representation of firm activities

The linear firm

Traditional firms really took off following the Industrial Revolution around the 1800s, and thus are a relatively recent construct in historical terms. Since then, they have often been analysed by strategists, business consultants and economists in a very linear way. It is interesting to start there before comparing and contrasting traditional business models with platform ones. The overriding model of the firm historically used is predicated upon companies buying raw material (inputs) and transforming them into outputs before selling to downstream customers at a profit (hopefully). The success of these businesses is typically driven by their ability to buy efficiently (low input costs), add value (through design, efficient manufacturing, etc.) and sell resulting products and services with a high margin (through distribution networks, retail shops, etc.).

Car manufacturers take raw materials such as steel and plastic, then design and assemble parts to create vehicles. Coca-Cola combines sugar, water and other well-guarded ingredients to produce one of the world's most popular beverages. While the model is rooted in manufacturing, it also applies to services. British Airways manages its fleet of airplanes, crew, logistics, in-flight services, etc. to offer short- and long-haul flight services. In the case of British Airways, its inputs are planes, oil and personnel, and the output is the transport service provided to customers.

These firms have been described in the business literature as input/output businesses or as 'pipes' because of their linear nature.[1] We also refer to them as 'traditional' businesses in this book.

Figure 5.1 **The linear firm**

Porter's value chain

In the 1980s, Michael Porter was one of the first academic to codify and formalize how firms create value.[2] The concept of the 'value chain' was introduced and popularized in his 1985 bestseller, *Competitive Advantage: Creating and Sustaining Superior Performance*. Today, the traditional value chain is still the dominant frame of reference in business. It describes how a linear set of activities and processes are organized by a firm to maximize the value added to inputs of production.

Porter presented the concept of the value chain as the basic tool for examining the activities a company performs and their interactions to identify the sources of sustainable competitive advantage. It separates the activities of a firm into a sequential stream of activities, as illustrated in Figure 5.2. It describes the importance of the different activities in delivering the final product/service, thereby facilitating the identification of core and non-core activities:

- Core or primary activities are involved with a product's physical creation, sale and distribution to buyers, and service after sale. They include inbound logistics, operations, outbound logistics, marketing and sales, and service. These activities are termed 'primary' because they add value to the product or those involved in either producing or selling the product.
- Non-core or support activities are generic processes supporting the core activities of the firm. Procurement, technology development, human resource management and infrastructure are typical examples of non-core activities.

In this environment, a business gains 'competitive advantage' by performing these activities either more cheaply than its competitors (low cost strategy) or in a unique way that creates superior customer value and commands a price premium (differentiation).

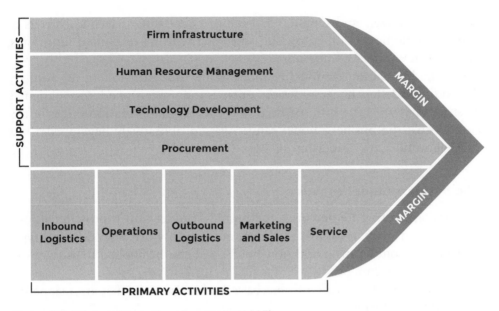

Figure 5.2 **Michael Porter's value chain (1985)**

Source: Adapted from M. E. Porter's Competitive Advantage

If we take the example of a car manufacturing business, the primary activities can be described as follows:

- Inbound logistics: receiving, storing and distributing inputs (e.g. handling of raw materials, warehousing, inventory control).
- Operations: transformation of the inputs into the final product form (e.g. car production, assembly, packaging).
- Outbound logistics: collecting, storing and distributing cars to the buyers (e.g. processing of orders, warehousing of cars, delivery).
- Marketing and sales: identification of customer needs and generation of sales (e.g. advertising, promotion, distribution).
- Service: maintain value after purchase (e.g. installation, repair, maintenance, training).

Each function can in turn be broken down into smaller components or processes for optimization. This representation of the firm goes hand in hand with Porter's five forces framework, which states that the competitive position of the firm is driven by the negotiating power of clients, the negotiating power of suppliers, the threat of substitutes, the threat of new entrants and lastly the rivalry in the sector. Within Porter's framework, a strong competitive advantage for your own value chain is predicated upon fragmented markets with lots of buyers and suppliers (unable to negotiate), as well as barriers to entry to avoid new competitors and a product with no or limited substitutes, as well as few direct competitors.[3]

The traditional linear model is under strain, though. Modern innovation-driven firms are less linear and more open as the process of adding value may be shared between the firm, partners, stakeholders and customers. It is in this context that the business model canvas was collaboratively developed a few years ago under the leadership of Alex Osterwalder.[4]

The business model canvas

Looking at existing frameworks, the business model canvas provides a good strategic management tool. It is generic enough to work with different types of business models, linear and non-linear, and can be applied to start-ups or corporate environments.

The framework is made of nine basic building blocks that are mapped in a pre-structured canvas:

1   customer segments or communities for which value is created;
2   the value proposition for each segment;

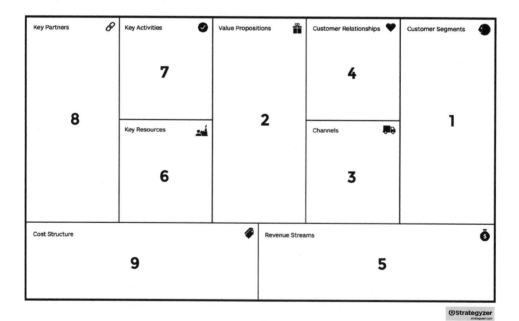

Figure 5.3 The business model canvas

Source: The Business Model Canvas, Creative Commons license, https://strategyzer.com/

3   channels needed to reach customers;
4   customer relationships;
5   the revenue streams generated by the business;
6   key resources used by the firm;
7   key activities required to create value;
8   key partners; and
9   the cost structure of the business model.

The business model canvas is less linear than the value chain model and can be applied to map out the key activities of a wide range of business models, including platforms. Let's take the example of Airbnb:

1   Customer segments: Airbnb serves two interdependent customer segments: the guests (personal and business travellers) and the hosts (residential asset owners).
2   Value proposition: A trusted community marketplace for people to list, discover and book unique accommodation around the world. For hosts, it enables them to monetize their house in a safe environment.
3   Channels: Mainly through online marketing with: (i) referrals; and (ii) paid advertising.
4   Customer relationships: hosts and guests.
5   Revenue streams: Airbnb's model is commission-based. Hosts are charged about 3% and guests between 6% and 12%.[5]
6   Key resources: Airbnb's digital and mobile infrastructure, access to capital, physical (staff and offices).
7   Key activities: Maintain and develop the online platform including key product features for hosts and guests – to match hosts and guests, connect them, enable safe payments, develop and maintain a trusted environment, manage communities and market the service.
8   Key partners: Technical partners (hosting, database and payment services), insurance companies, management service companies supporting hosts (Guesty in the US, Hostmaker in Europe), venture capital firms (VCs).
9   Cost structure: Main costs are related to marketing and sales (advertising, recruiting and opening new offices abroad), technology (platform development and maintenance) and legal.

While a very useful framework when trying to quickly map a new business model in creative sessions, this framework does not explicitly capture key success factors of platforms, but rather makes it easier to overlay traditional businesses operations onto a platform business model.[6]

The rocket model

As we worked with platforms, it became increasingly clear that the traditional management frameworks were not suitable. And that's why we developed the rocket model: a high-level functional model of platform businesses based on the core activities of firms serving multisided markets. Typically, we find that platforms need to:

- attract a critical mass of customers *on each side* of the market;
- match them;
- allow them to connect;
- enable them to transact; and
- optimize their own operations and ecosystem iteratively.

Launching a multisided platform requires a lot of energy in the same way as launching a rocket into space does. You need to recruit at least two sides of the market, and run development and marketing for each side. In a way, igniting a platform is not different from launching two companies at the same time. You also need to scale your user base in order to reach a critical mass on both sides of your platform, a challenging hurdle that doesn't exist for traditional businesses. On the plus side, once the rocket has reached a critical mass, it requires less 'power' to propel itself. It has reached 'escape velocity' and is subject to less 'gravity' thanks to network effects.

Figure 5.4 presents the rocket model and associated functional stages.

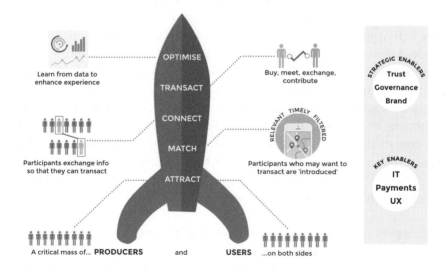

Figure 5.4 **The rocket model**

Source: Launchworks

Attract

This building block encompasses the characteristics, features and processes by which a platform is able to attract producers and users. In management literature, it is also referred to as the 'magnet'[7] or the 'catalyst'.[8] The functions performed at the attraction stage evolve over the life cycle of a platform and need to be reviewed on a regular basis. At launch, the attract function is primarily focused on acquiring and hooking new customers, but as the platform matures, retention starts to play a bigger part. While ultimately what will attract users and producers on the platform are opportunities to transact with one another, the design of the value proposition for each side is a critical driver of attraction. Since platform businesses are subject to network effects, attracting a critical mass of platform participants, on both sides of the platform, is key to its long-term success. We will review a number of attraction strategies available at ignition in Chapter 8.

The attraction – and subsequent management – of a community of users and producers on a platform (or buyers and sellers in the case of a marketplace) is quite different from the acquisition of clients in a traditional business. In fact, some of the thinking that traditional firms apply to the recruitment, management and motivation of their own employees is relevant to platform participants since they also contribute to the value delivered by the platform. Consumers will provide valuable feedback and ratings while producers will ultimately be key to the experience enabled by the platform since they will be providing their flat, their car, their content, etc. through the platform. Therefore, identifying high-potential users and producers, training them, incentivizing them and retaining them, or even 'terminating them' – terms typically used more for employees than clients – is a key part of the platform attract function. We discuss the different priorities for the attract function across the various stages of platform development, from design to maturity, in Chapters 7–9.

Match

In order for both sides to interact, they need to be introduced first. For Airbnb, that involves presenting guests with the right properties in the right locations at the right time; for Upwork, a global talent platform, it's matching companies with a specific assignment with available freelancers who have the right skill set.

The quality of the matching is critical to the success of the platform. While early adopters may be more interested by the concept and availability of relevant platform participants, matching becomes increasingly important as the platform scales. In a world of abundance, the ability to filter and present customers with the right choices creates value. For matching to be effective for participants, results must meet participant needs (relevance), be timely and present the right amount of information or depth. The latter means that the matching function should be optimized to return enough search results for the user to find a relevant match but not so many as to overwhelm the user with too much information.

The matching function can also play a key role in helping the platform maximize positive network effects. For example, Amazon Marketplace prioritizes product search results on best price but the search algorithm de-prioritizes merchants with poor feedback. This ensures that consumers are less likely to buy from merchants that provide bad customer experiences, and ultimately leave the platform.

There are different ways to match participants. Matching can be done through a search function with selected parameters for product marketplaces, such as eBay or Amazon. For service platforms, a specific graphic interface tailored to the focus of the platform (e.g. geo-localized maps for Airbnb) is often used. Sometimes, the matching function uses the information that both sides of the market have provided to the platform, such as pictures and description on a dating site.

The complexity of the matching function depends on a number of factors. Horizontal platforms, with a wide range of products and services, usually require stronger search or matching functions than vertical ones that are more specialized. In some cases, however, the matching function is almost implied rather than explicit. This is often the case with payment networks (i.e. merchants are not actively matched with cardholders, although 'Amex accepted here' signs may help).[9] The matching function can also be a mix of search and self-selection.

Ideally, the matching function is configured to provide the *optimal* level of choice required for a successful transaction. Some economists assume that maximizing choices is always a good thing, yet we find that this is not always the case and can in fact result in reduced transactions.[10] Finding the right balance between too many choices, which would confuse buyers, and not enough options, which would drive buyers away, is not an easy task. A curated, prioritized, relevant and timely selection maximizing the likelihood of transactions occurring is therefore the nirvana of platforms. This ideal matching will differ from one user to another, and therefore needs to be personalized.

Connect

Often, platform participants need to exchange additional information with their counterparty before moving on to the transaction stage. With dating platforms, the matching function may be based on a range of criteria provided by the platform, such as age, gender and location, but additional information about occupation, tastes, interests, where to meet up, etc. is also helpful to the dating process. It is the same with eBay when buyers ask specific questions to sellers before making an acquisition (Has the car been involved in any accidents?). This platform function also increases the trust of the parties and reduces the 'asymmetry of information'[11] that may get in the way of the transaction.

The connect stage will also depend upon how much information has been shared with the participants prior to the matching stage. If all the relevant information is already available and the nature of the transaction is such that there is little uncertainty as to the outcome (e.g. a basic undifferentiated product or service), then the connect stage can even be skipped altogether (although the platform may want to ensure it has the capabilities to enable it should participants need it for other types of transactions).

Platforms have to make sure their connect function minimizes the risk of 'leakages', that is to say of clients deciding to transact outside the platform after having been connected through the platform. In a way, many platforms face a self-imposed competitive constraint: if they do not add enough value, they will be bypassed and unable to recapture the value they created in matching and connecting people. In some unusually high-value/one-off purchase categories (e.g. cars, floorboards, etc.), marketplaces often suffer from significant 'leakage', with a very high percentage of transactions *initiated* but not completed on the platform. We will look at price-based mitigation strategies in Chapter 11.

Transact

Platforms enable a wide range of interactions among their ecosystem participants. In many cases, it is information, rather than money, that is exchanged with the platform and its participants. Think, for example, of a like on Facebook, a vote on Reddit, a rating on eBay or a comment on TripAdvisor. The fact that no money changes hands during these interactions doesn't mean that they are not very valuable for the platform.[12]

Out of all the interactions participants have with the platform, some really crystallize the *raison d'être* of the platform. We call these core transactions. Examples include a sale on eBay, a successful hire with LinkedIn, a date with Match.com or a click on a Google sponsored ad. These core transactions are supported by other interactions that enable the overall value proposition.

The platform should be optimized to maximize the number of core transactions and supporting interactions. It is important to note that both interactions and core transactions need to be considered from the point of view of each platform participant since they may be different for users, producers, the platform owner, the advertisers, etc. Ultimately, the value of a platform business will be driven by its ability to both maximize the total number of value-adding interactions and core transactions and to capture a share of this value through direct or indirect monetization. The platform design phase taking place before launch should be approached with this objective in mind.

Value capture at the platform level may not be directly aligned with interactions creating the most value between participants. There is direct alignment for eBay, which takes a commission on the value of each success-ful sale (a core transaction). However, dating sites rarely charge you when you go on a date, as the core transaction for participants is difficult for the platform to monitor. So dating platforms find ways to charge for other interactions that lead to dates (including membership fee, a fee per message for communicating with your matches or a fee to appear on top of searches). While pricing is often discussed as part of the transact stage,[13] it is a broad topic closely related to the overall governance of the platform and is covered in Chapter 11.

Optimize

This last optimization stage is iterative and represents an absolutely critical process for continuous enhancement of the platform. Given the dynamic nature of platform businesses, this data-driven function allows platform busi-nesses to find the right balance between the two sides of the market and to optimize all the matching, connecting and transacting functions of the platform. Google's search algorithm is constantly optimized with several A/B tests[14] a day to ensure the best and most relevant search results are provided. In fact, many platforms see their early development as a portfolio of experi-ments and hypotheses that need to be tested.

When a bottleneck forms at one of the stages of value creation, manage-ment's attention can almost immediately focus on the issue. While traditio-nal marketplaces such as estate agents are types of platforms that have existed offline for centuries, we note the technology that enables advanced use of near real-time analytics on customer data has only been available relatively recently.

Online platforms almost always capture, store and analyse vast amounts of data so hypotheses can be formed and tested. As such, data can be considered an 'input of production', as well as a 'strategic asset' and even a tradable good. Platforms increasingly use unique performance indicators and dashboards to track their progress. Selected platform success metrics can be mapped onto the rocket framework to provide a holistic way of monitoring performance and identifying bottlenecks. These metrics can apply to stages of the rocket, but also to the wider ecosystem of producers, users and partners.

The concept of 'big data' is part of the organizational DNA of most online platforms, and continuous monitoring of potential bottlenecks can unlock growth in near real time. Many platforms are so adept at these types of analytics that they are now applying these tools across their businesses to generate new management insights. Google regularly generates insights into questions such as 'What makes a successful team?' or 'What is the most efficient recruitment process?' through the use of analytics. We discuss the implication of data usage by platforms across their life stages in more detail in Chapters 7–10.

Platform enablers

A platform is supported by key enablers across all the stages of the rocket model. We typically refer to governance, trust and brand as strategic enablers, and to IT infrastructure, user interface and payment systems as key enablers.

Strategic enablers

Governance is the set of rules, norms and policies that the platform adheres to in order to build its ecosystem. Platform governance principles deal with questions such as: Who is allowed on the platform? What behaviours are rewarded? How are disputes between platform participants handled?

Trust is what makes people believe that the platform participants they engage with are reliable, credible and honest. It's a set of principles, rules, filters, processes and tools enabling participants to interact and transact in a safe environment. High trust encourages interactions and core transactions by reducing the asymmetry of information between participants. Without trust, many platforms would struggle to gain any scale. It is thanks to the trust-building features of social media that many people started to be comfortable with the idea of having a 'stranger' rent their flat (Airbnb) or use their car (Turo) while they are away.

Brand is also a key enabler that works in tandem with trust. The brand building for platforms is a slightly trickier exercise than for other business models, since much of the experience is directly influenced by other platform participants. Platforms therefore need to internalize the needs and wants of their communities and capture this in key brand attributes. Platforms such as Airbnb are taking this brand management process, in which platform participants co-create the overall experience, very seriously and use it as a way of differentiating themselves.[15]

In fact, governance, trust and brand are strategic enablers so important for platforms that they deserve their own chapter (Chapter 12).

Other key enablers

IT infrastructure is a key component of successful platform businesses. We use the term generically to capture the systems and software resources required to power platform businesses. This includes software stacks, databases, servers, apps, code, application programming interfaces (APIs), cloud access etc. These IT capabilities end up powering the platform and supporting key functions of the rocket. IT capabilities can also be leveraged for platforms to excel at some key functions such as matching. As Mike Curtis, Airbnb VP of engineering, recently declared, 'Everything that we do in engineering is about creating great matches between people'. In fact, more than 70% of Airbnb IT resources are reported to be focused on analytics and machine learning, compared to only 30% for the Web-facing part of the business.[16]

User experience. Some platforms, such as Facebook, have an online-only user experience (including mobile), while others have a mix of online and offline experience, such as Airbnb or Uber. Online, the user experience is made of user journeys and touchpoints with the platform and participants. But unlike linear businesses, which have control on the user experience end to end, a big part of the platform user experience, online and/or offline, is in fact delivered by participants themselves. Platforms have little control but can nonetheless influence positive outcomes over negative ones. Anyone can list their home on Airbnb, but Airbnb has the capacity to prioritize hosts with the highest feedback in search results. This way of operating is a significant departure from the 'value chain' model of traditional firms, where end-to-end control of the product is often taken for granted. A good way for platforms to improve the user experience is often to increase their scale to benefit from network effects and offer choice and liquidity to both users and producers.

Payments are often key to the platform function and a critical step to enabling its core transactions. The design of a 'frictionless' payment experience is therefore critical to the overall success of many platform businesses. Increasingly, solutions tailored to the needs of platforms, such as Mangopay or Stripe Connect, offer convenient ways of enabling global and secure payment capabilities.

Together, these enabling activities play a critical role in the success of the platform.

Strengths and weaknesses of platform business models

We have talked a lot so far about the success of platforms and described some of their unique features, but it would be wrong to think that platforms are superior business models in their own right. In fact, it is very important to recognize that each business model has strengths and weaknesses. Traditional business models are often better suited to serving specific groups of consumers thanks to an enhanced control of the value chain, as well as the ability to curate a product selection (or even bundle complementary products) in ways that platform businesses can't manage as efficiently. Traditional business models also enable complete control of the customer experience from end to end, something platform models cannot deliver.

Conversely, platform businesses provide a unique opportunity to manage cost effectively and provide a long tail of products or services. They enable market discovery of successful producers. They can also scale rapidly once critical mass has been reached by connecting large groups and communities of 'platform participants'. This is, however, often achieved at the cost of relatively complex management and governance decisions, trade-offs and arbitrages compared to other more traditional business models.[17]

eBay did not tightly control the various product categories that initially developed on its platform,[18] although it did orient its investments towards specific categories over time[19] to stimulate and shape its growth trajectory. This was largely based on trial and error at the beginning, but eBay learned how to kick off the development of some categories, raise awareness in relevant

Table 5.1 Economic strengths and weaknesses of selected business models

	Platform	Retailer/ Reseller	Input/Output Business
Connects several groups of customers	●	◑	○
Market discovery	◕	◑	◕
Control of value chain	◕	●	●
Control of customer experience	◑	●	●
Supports long tail inventory	●	◕	○
Potential for Hyper growth	●	◑	◕
Management complexity	●	◑	◕
Examples	eBay	Tesco	Honda

Note: In this illustrative table, a full circle means that the business has the stated characteristic, while an empty circle means the opposite.

Source: Adapted from Hagiu, A and Wright, J (2013) Marketplace or Reseller?, Launchworks analysis

communities, create a critical mass of platform participants and then move on to another relevant and complementary category for the platform. In some ways, eBay followed the 'bowling pin' strategy that we will develop further when focusing on platform ignition in Chapter 8.

Table 5.1 illustrates the strengths and weaknesses of the generic business models we previously discussed. As you can see, the different business models we discussed appear to be complementary on a number of dimensions, rather than substitutes. This is one of the powerful insights of companies such as Apple, Google or Amazon, who have been able to mix business models to develop their platform-powered ecosystems. This is the topic of the next chapter.

Notes

1 See, for example, the 'Pipes vs Platform' article in the October 2013 *Wired* magazine penned by Sangeet Paul Choudary, www.wired.com/insights/2013/10/why-business-models-fail-pipes-vs-platforms/

2 M. E. Porter, *Competitive Strategy: Techniques for Analyzing Industries and Competitors*, New York: Free Press, 1980.

3 M. E. Porter, *Competitive Advantage: Creating and Sustaining Superior Performance*, New York: Free Press, 1985.

4 See A. Osterwalder and Y. Pigneur, *Business Model Generation: A Handbook for Visionaries, Game Changers, and Challengers*, self-published, 2010.

5 Airbnb website, www.airbnb.com/help/article/384/what-are-the-service-fees.

6 It is worth noting that variants of the business canvas have been proposed to better match the requirements of different types of businesses, including multisided ones. See, for example, the Platform Design Toolkit (www.platformdesigntoolkit.com) from Simone Cicero.

7 Sangeet Choudary, *Platform Power*, 2013, http://platformed.info

8 D. Evans and R. Schmalensee, *The Catalyst Code*, Boston, MA: Harvard Business School Press, 2007.

9 Even this may change as card companies develop new advertising capabilities allowing card users to be notified of merchant promotions of interest based on their previous purchases, physical location, etc.

10 There is emerging evidence that consumers can indeed be overwhelmed by choice. See B. Schwartz, *The Paradox of Choice: Why More Is Less*, New York: Harper Perennial, 2004.

11 One side, the seller, knows everything about their products, while the buyer knows little. For the transaction to occur, the platform needs to facilitate this exchange of information by enabling both parties to communicate. Rating and reputation systems such as eBay's star system have been designed to increase the trust of potential buyers by enhancing the information to the buyer (previous buyer reviews). Trust building is discussed in more detail in Chapter 12.

12 A like on a Facebook company page was reported as being worth $173, for example. While the exact number is likely to be highly dependent upon one's own business, it

is clear that platform interactions have value not only for the community, but also advertisers. See, for example, www.wired.com/insights/2013/07/is-a-facebook-like-worth-174-probably-not/.

13 Charging sellers a sales commission fee (eBay) or members a subscription fee (Match.com) can be seen as core transactions. This is because significant value is exchanged between eBay and sellers in the first example, and Match.com and members in the second one.

14 A/B testing is jargon for a randomized experiment with two variants, A and B, which are the control and treatment in the controlled experiment, for example by sending two slightly different promotional emails while tracking responses in order to quickly select the best of the two before iterating further. See R. Kohavi and R. Longbotham, 'Online Controlled Experiments and A/B Tests', *Encyclopedia of Machine Learning and Data Mining*, pp. 1–8, 13 May 2016, for a discussion on best practices.

15 See the Airbnb rebranding exercise case study at www.wearedesignstudio.com/works/airbnb-process/.

16 Timothy Prickett Morgan, 'Airbnb Shares the Keys to Its Infrastructure', *Next Platform*, 10 September 2015, www.nextplatform.com/2015/09/10/airbnb-shares-the-keys-to-its-infrastructure/.

17 See A. Hagiu and J. Wright, 'Marketplace or Reseller', Harvard Business School Working Paper 13-092, 2013, for a discussion about the strengths and weaknesses of platforms.

18 Pierre Omidyar, founder of eBay, reported that the very first item that sold on the platform was a broken laser pointer priced at $14.83. Astonished, he contacted the winning bidder to check, just to be told by the buyer that he was 'a collector of broken laser pointers'. If evidence were needed, this strongly suggests that platforms do not tightly control their value chain.

19 eBay started with collectibles in 1995, before moving on to computers, books, movies and consumer electronics in 1997, and to cars, clothing and motors in 1999. These waves were both driven by users trying to list new products and by eBay's management trying to make it easier for people to deal with various product categories.

Chapter 6

Platform-powered ecosystems

As mentioned earlier, platform business models can be associated and combined with other business models. The aim is to ensure that the 'whole' is worth more than the 'sum of its parts', and that the resulting platform-powered ecosystem becomes stronger. In this chapter, we explore how business models can complement each other to reinforce value propositions by presenting high-level case studies on Amazon, Apple and Google.

Amazon's ecosystem

Today, Amazon is the largest e-commerce retailer in the US, as well as the world's largest provider of cloud computing services.[1] For the past 10 years, Amazon's growth rate has exceeded 20%[2] year after year, recently surpassing Walmart in market capitalization.[3] Somebody who bought $1,000 of Amazon stocks when it floated in May 1997 would now have approximately $552,700, equivalent to a yearly return of 38.6%.[4]

A bit of history

Jeff Bezos founded Amazon in 1994 as an online bookstore. So Amazon started as a traditional business model but online. The business expanded rapidly from books to new categories such as CDs, DVDs, electronics, etc. and floated three years later. In 1999, Amazon launched a separate Web auctions site to compete with eBay's fast-growing marketplace. It failed to ignite because Amazon customers were buyers who were mainly convenience-motivated. A second attempt, zShops, was based on fixed-price immediate buying but third-party sellers were in separate parts of the store, which gave buyers a disjointed customer experience. In 2000, Amazon was a third time lucky when zShops was merged with the Amazon site and repositioned as Amazon Marketplace. Deciding to let third-party sellers compete with the retail business was a very controversial decision internally. Jeff Bezos recalls:

So our buyers were extremely concerned – and rightly. They were saying, 'Let me just make sure I understand this. I might get stuck with inventory of 10,000 units of this camera that I just loaded up on, and you're going to let just anybody come in and take Amazon traffic on what is our primary retail real estate, which is the detail page, and I'm going to lose the buy box to this other person because they have a lower price than me?' And we said, 'Yeah, we are.'[5]

After difficult discussions, Jeff Bezos eventually took the bet to focus on what was best for customers, and opened its original distribution business on the producer side. As a result, a single search now returns results from both Amazon itself and the marketplace merchants. Since then, the e-commerce business has continued to expand to 15 countries in categories from clothes, furniture, toys and jewellery to fresh groceries (Amazon Fresh) and daily deal products and services (Amazon Local). Goods worth over $225 billion were sold in 2015 alone, with Amazon Marketplace representing in excess of 50% of sales.[6]

Since 2005, online merchants trading on Amazon have benefited from Fulfilment by Amazon (FBA), a service where Amazon stores, picks, packs and ships products on behalf of sellers. Amazon also launched Amazon Prime the same year, a membership service offering buyers free and fast delivery. Both FBA and Prime are traditional product lines leveraging Amazon's excellent logistics capabilities. They have been instrumental in supporting the e-commerce business.

Amazon also branched out early on into services supporting digital businesses with Amazon Web Services (AWS), a cloud computing service launched in 2006. AWS is now the largest cloud service in the world and generated $12.2 billion in 2016.

Amazon's first foray into consumer electronics started with the Kindle in 2007, supported by Fire OS, an Android based operating system. Building on the success of Kindle e-book readers, Amazon later launched the Fire Tablet, Fire Phone, Fire TV Stick, and more recently Amazon Echo. Amazon also launched the Amazon Appstore for Android devices, as well as a Mac download store with games and software for Apple computers.

In 2010, Amazon entered the entertainment and content industry with Amazon Studios, a studio that develops television shows, movies and comics from online submissions and crowdsourced feedback, and Amazon Instant Video, an Internet video on-demand service. Amazon also purchased Twitch.tv in 2014, a live streaming video platform and community for gamers. Twitch attracts more than 100 million visitors per month and 1.5 million broadcasters.[7]

The Amazon timeline (see Figure 6.1) summarizes some of the key milestones in the development of Amazon's main lines of business. Over the

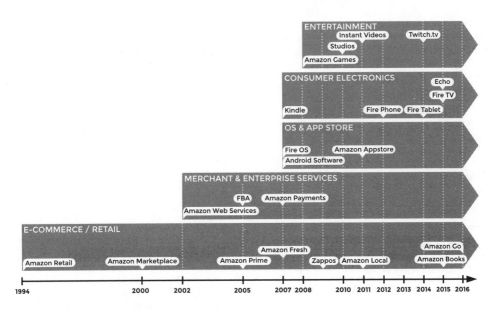

Figure 6.1 Amazon's main business lines

Source: Amazon website, Wikipedia, Launchworks analysis

last 20 years, Amazon has acquired dozens of companies and launched many services. Our purpose here is not to be exhaustive, but rather to illustrate at a strategic level how the combination of several business models has allowed Amazon to successfully develop its platform-powered ecosystem.

Amazon's business models

Mapping Amazon's key line of businesses against the three main families of business models (see Table 6.1) shows that Amazon relies on all of them.

E-commerce

Although Amazon started as a pure e-commerce reseller with a curated but limited range of goods at competitive prices, the integration of a third-party marketplace platform has been complementary to the reseller model and now represents over 50% of Amazon's e-commerce business.[8] The platform model provides many benefits, including diversity and selection of goods offered by millions of sellers. Outsourcing the risk of holding stock of new product categories has proven a cost-effective method to manage millions of different products – the so-called long tail – and scale quickly. This is one of the reasons marketplaces have the potential to grow at a faster rate than traditional retail businesses (see Figure 6.2).

Table 6.1 Amazon's ecosystem

AMAZON	Platform	Retailer/ Reseller	Input/Output Business
Amazon Retail		✓	
Amazon Marketplace	✓		
Fulfilment, warehousing (FBA), Delivery (Prime), Cloud services (AWS)			✓
Amazon Android software (OS, appstores)	✓		
Consumer electronics (Kindle, Echo, Fire Phone, Tablet & TV)			✓
Content production (Amazon Studios)			✓
On-demand video (Amazon Instant Video)		✓	
Gaming (Twitch.tv)	✓		

Source: Launchworks analysis

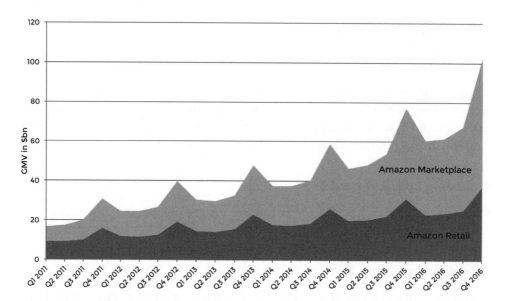

Figure 6.2 **Relative growth of Amazon retail vs Amazon marketplace (estimated split)**

Source: ChannelAdvisor and Tamebay estimates, Launchworks analysis

Amazon constantly learns from sellers and competes with them as a retailer on popular items. This hybrid model feeds the flywheel of traffic: consumers are attracted to the site because of the combination of great selection, competitive prices and customer experience. More buyers attract more sellers, which in turn add to economies of scale that can be passed along by lowering prices and reducing shipping fees.

Looking more closely at Amazon's Marketplace, the breadth of selection is a direct result of its horizontal focus and openness, as anybody, from humble one-off consumer-sellers to established merchants, can join the platform to sell. However, the right to sell on Amazon comes with the obligation to meet strict customer service standards when dealing with buyers. Indeed, merchants are responsible for a large portion of the customer experience, including shipping. Over the years, Amazon has deployed seller coaching programmes to help sellers better manage their stocks and price competitively. A number of tools and services are also available to mitigate the risk of bad customer experiences, including communications support between merchants and buyers and a dispute resolutions centre. While merchants and buyers can interact directly, communications and disputes are intermediated by Amazon for greater control of the customer experience, as well as limitation of revenue leakage.

Amazon's marketplace is a great example of a platform with many value-adding features, on the merchant side – as discussed above – but also on the buyer side. Buyers benefit from value-added services, including payment inter-mediation, independent customer reviews, a range of delivery options – including the superfast Prime delivery subscription service – a 'no questions asked' returns policy, etc. Prime subscribers can also get faster delivery of items sold by merchants using FBA.

Amazon's traffic is critically reinforced by Amazon Prime. Unlimited fast and free delivery makes Prime customers more engaged. They spend between two and four times more than non-Prime customers,[9] which has encouraged Amazon to make Prime more attractive by bundling additional services into the subscription. They include free access to over half a million e-books, ad-free music, photo storage and on-demand video, including exclusive content from Amazon Studios. The recently launched Prime Now offers Prime subscribers free two-hour delivery on tens of thousands of items or one-hour delivery for a small fee.

Finally, FBA, a service for marketplace sellers, provides the link between Amazon Marketplace and Prime. FBA leverages Amazon's own infrastruc-ture and gives Amazon greater control over the entire value chain, hence reducing the risk of bad buyer experiences. When a seller joins FBA, their goods can become Prime eligible. The Amazon fulfilment centre handles logistics, customer service, product returns and, of course, delivery in record time, alongside goods sold by Amazon. This represents a huge gain of efficiency when customers order items from both FBA sellers and Amazon. The flywheel of traffic is at play again: FBA leads to more sales for sellers,[10] more FBA sellers lead to more value for Prime customers, who then spend more, to the benefit of both Marketplace sellers and Amazon.

Amazon is getting the best of both worlds by combining the reach of platforms with the control of simple distribution models in order to be a 'one-stop shop'. The combination of the long tail marketplace with the highly efficient high-volume reseller model attracts one of the biggest audiences across the world and makes it one of the most successful e-commerce sites.

Amazon's ecosystem

When more control over the product proposition is required, Amazon uses more traditional business models. This is the case of Prime for shoppers, FBA for merchants or cloud services for website owners.

When connecting large numbers of buyers and sellers, as happens with game developers and gamers, or writers with readers, Amazon uses a platform model with its Fire OS operating system and its Appstore.[11] The launch of the Kindle (joint hardware and operating system) was instrumental to the development of the e-book market, resulting in Amazon becoming one of the largest e-book retailers.

The addition of the Echo product line and Alexa's always-on voice recognition interface is a good illustration of this self-reinforcing ecosystem strategy. Echo/Alexa gives customers access to a multitude of applications – called 'skills' – from third-party developers (a platform), as well as access to the Amazon site, Amazon Music and other services. Such an ecosystem is not only more efficient overall, but it is also 'stickier' (e.g. it is more difficult for a consumer to leave the ecosystem due to 'lock-ins' and associated 'switching costs' of having to learn a new interface and transfer all their content).[12]

Leveraging platform business models with more traditional ones was initially an organic process for Amazon. It was not designed from scratch and there were trials and errors along the way. It took a couple of years for Amazon to find the right marketplace model for its e-commerce offering.[13] And it took nearly a decade for Amazon's platform operating system Fire OS and associated hardware (Kindle, Fire Phone, Fire Tablet, Fire TV, Echo) to develop into an integrated offering. The current model is not without its challenges. Merchants on the marketplace effectively compete with Amazon's own retail activities, which creates tension, and the Fire Phone take-up has been disappointing. But Amazon is now undeniably a sophisticated global operator that manages a self-reinforcing ecosystem that uses and leverages both traditional and platform business models wherever they make sense. Amazon has recently moved into bricks and mortar retail, reinventing the shopping experience with its Amazon Books stores. Amazon Go, a new 'Just Walk Out' shopping experiment, where customers can shop with no checkout required, has also launched in early 2017.[14]

Apple's ecosystem

Apple is one of the largest companies in the world. In 40 years, it has become a leader in manufacturing computer devices and mobile phones, developing operating systems and software, and distributing music and digital apps. $1,000 of Apple stock purchased when it floated would now be worth approximately $220,287, equivalent to a yearly return of 16.3%.[15]

A bit of history

In 1976, Steve Jobs, Steve Wozniak and Ronald Wayne invented the first Apple personal computer. Sales grew exponentially and Apple publicly traded on the stock market in 1980. Over the course of 20 years, Apple released new and improved versions of its personal computer product line (Apple series, Macintosh series, PowerBook series), operating systems (System 7, Mac OS) and a suite of software applications. However, its closed approach and lack of interoperability with PCs and Microsoft software, which had by then become the market leader, almost led to its demise.

In 1997, Steve Jobs announced that Microsoft would release new versions of Microsoft Office for the Macintosh following a historic partnership. Bill Gates even appeared over a live video feed during that year's keynote speech in front of a bewildered audience to announce the new partnership. After a much-needed $150 million cash investment from arch-enemy Microsoft, Apple started a new lease of life. In 2001, the first retail store opened, and the iPod and iTunes launched, as well as Mac OS, a new operating system.

In 2007, Apple's future took a new course by extending its offering from computers to mobile electronic devices with the iPhone and its App Store, a platform selling third-party digital applications. Success was unprecedented, and by October 2008 Apple was the third-largest mobile handset manufacturer in the world.[16]

Since then, more product lines have been successfully introduced, from the iPad and iCloud, an online storage and syncing service for music, photos, files and software, to the Apple Watch.

The Apple timeline (see Figure 6.3) summarizes some of the key milestones in the development of Apple's key product lines. It is not exhaustive, but is intended to illustrate how the combination of several underpinning business models can complement and strengthen Apple's value propositions.

Apple's business models

Like Amazon, Apple manufactures its own hardware products[17] (see Table 6.2). The main benefit is higher control on design and quality of products. Through

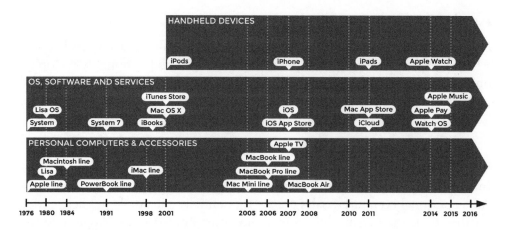

Figure 6.3 **Apple's main business lines**

Source: Apple website, Wikipedia, Launchworks analysis

Table 6.2 Apple's ecosystem

APPLE	Platform	Retailer/ Reseller	Input/Output business
Apple hardware (iPhone, MacBook, iPad, Apple Watch)			✓
Apple Operating Systems (iOS, macOS, Watch OS)	✓		
Digital Stores (iTunes, Apple Music)		✓	
App stores (iOS, Mac)	✓		
Cloud services (iCloud)			✓
Apple software (iMovie, iPhoto)			✓

Source: Launchworks analysis

its operating systems and app stores for computers, mobile phones, tablets and wearables, Apple manages a two-sided platform between consumers and software providers. This model fosters a diverse range of software applications. As of June 2016, Apple's App Store had more than 2 million applications.[18]

It is interesting to note that Apple, unlike other marketplaces, remains very keen to control the experience of its products end-to-end, and has therefore maintained strong governance around its businesses. Apple's experience is heavily mediated and curated; its App Store platform is 'regulated', with its applications selected, controlled and promoted by Apple, who reserve the right to remove apps for any reason.[19] Apple's App Store is far less open than Google's or Microsoft's in that regard.

For iTunes and Apple Music, Apple has chosen a reseller model. Apple aggregates music from a few major music labels and distributes directly to consumers. This is a very different model from SoundCloud, which enables individual artists to upload audio files and share them with friends and wider communities.

The resulting Apple ecosystem is significantly more powerful than the sum of its parts. An excellent mobile phone with features far superior to the iPhone but let down by a sub-par supporting ecosystem (with few apps, etc.) doesn't stand a chance in today's market. In order to take on the iPhone, competitors need to develop a similarly strong ecosystem of reinforcing business capabilities. Samsung has been trying to do just that. Nokia, once a mobile leader, failed to maintain its platform ecosystem and ended up selling its mobile division to Microsoft, who had been struggling to make significant inroads into the mobile market despite the strong desktop platform position of Windows.

It is also worth noting that the platform-powered parts of Apple's business are the ones growing at the fastest rate, although the positive externalities created also support the other activities, as would be expected from a self-reinforcing ecosystem. Apple's services[20] represented 11% of revenues for

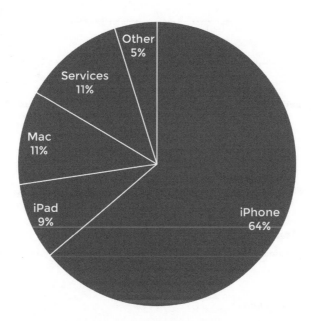

Figure 6.4 **Split of Apple's hardware vs services revenues (2016)**

Source: Apple website, Launchworks analysis

2016,[21] as shown in Figure 6.4, with a growth rate of 19% year over year for the first half of 2016.

A closer review of revenues generated by Apple's non-hardware activities since 2005 shows how apps, which were responsible for only a fraction of Apple's revenues in 2008, are now a multibillion-dollar business. In fact, Tim Cook expects that it will be 'the size of a Fortune 100 company by the end of 2017'.[22] And this, of course, excludes the amount of money that was paid to the developers of these apps (Apple keeps 30% of the price paid for the apps sold on its App Store).[23] When looking at total App Store billings (what customers actually spend), Figure 6.5 shows that they are now larger than Hollywood's US box office revenues and are likely to overtake Hollywood's global box office revenues in 2016.[24]

Apple has been able to match different business models to different activities in order to design a self-reinforcing business architecture. Apple is still committed to a unique user experience on each of its device, but it is building cross-device and cross-service experiences to offer a more unified experience to both users and developers.[25] Apple's App Stores wouldn't do as well without Apple's unique hardware offering, and vice versa.

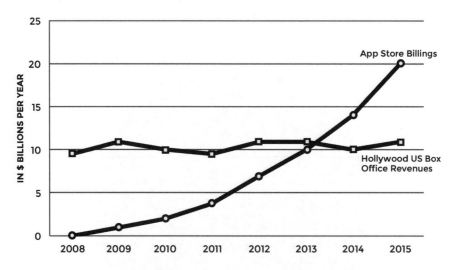

Figure 6.5 Apple App Store billings vs Hollywood US box office revenues

Source: Apple website, Horace Dediu Asymco, www.asymco.com, Launchworks analysis

Google's ecosystem

Google is one of the largest and best-known companies in the world. While the company rebranded itself at the group level as Alphabet, Inc. on 2 October

2015, with Google operating as the search engine subsidiary, we use the term Google to talk about all the group's activities in this book. A $1,000 investment in Google stock when it floated in 2004 would now be worth approximately $15,665, equivalent to a yearly return of 25.6%.[26]

A bit of history

Founded by Larry Page and Sergey Brin in 1998, Google designed its original search business around its superior ability to index what content producers were putting online, mainly in the form of websites, in order to deliver it to content seekers. Two years later, Google managed to monetize this capability by selling key search terms in order to improve the visibility of merchant sites. Advertising revenues are now at the heart of its monetization strategy,[27] with almost 90% of its $90 billion 2016 revenues derived from AdWords, an online advertising service that places advertising near the list of search results.

Google also developed a range of complementary products in key verticals as part of its ecosystem (email, maps, flight information, etc.).

YouTube, the video sharing service that Google acquired in 2007, initially launched as a two-sided platform connecting viewers and content producers. Its unique proposition at the time was to allow anyone in the world to get access to a long tail of amateur home videos, something that was not possible through traditional TV. Over time, as viewer adoption strengthened, YouTube started to attract professional and mainstream content producers,[28] improving content quality and in turn customer traction. As it reached critical mass – it's now the third most visited website in the world[29] – YouTube added advertisers as a third side to monetize the site.

Google is also behind the Android operating system, a suite of software products including the Chrome browser, associated Chrome laptop products and Android smartphones, as well as fibre access networks in the US.[30] The company also acquired the mobile division of Motorola and its extensive patent portfolio in 2013. More recently, Google has entered the 'Internet of things' (IoT) market with the acquisition of Nest (temperature control) and Dropcam (video surveillance) as well as the launch of Google Home (voice activated assistant). Google is also very active in self-driving car technology, artificial intelligence and, through its ventures arm, an investor in some of the most promising start-ups in Silicon Valley (including Uber). Although these different activities may look disparate, they actually create a powerful ecosystem with complex linkages, as well as unique antitrust challenges.

Google's main business lines are presented in Figure 6.6.

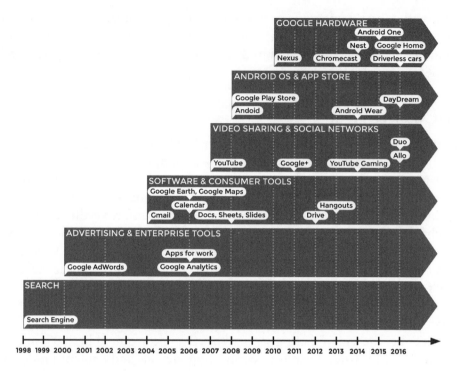

Figure 6.6 **Google's main business lines**

Source: Google website, Wikipedia, Launchworks analysis

Google's business models

Google's search platform is still at the core of the ecosystem (see Table 6.3). It connects consumers and businesses relying on Google's advertising products to achieve visibility. The search engine is constantly optimized to improve relevance, performance and efficiency for all participants. The search ecosystem is reinforced by Google's extensive range of integrated software services (also called productivity tools), such as Gmail, Calendar, Google Maps, etc., to encourage both consumers and businesses to interact within the ecosystem.

YouTube is now a platform with strong network effects. It's an open platform where unregistered users can watch videos and registered users can upload videos to their channels. Videos considered to contain potentially offensive content are available only to registered users over 18 years old. In the spirit of openness, users can make any comment they like, which can attract spammers and trolls. This has forced some superstar YouTubers such as PewDiePie, who generated more than $15 million in 2016 advertising revenues alone, to disable comments on their videos.[31] Despite cutting off

Table 6.3 Google's ecosystem

GOOGLE	Platform	Retailer/ Reseller	Input/Output Business
Search services	✓		
Software tools for enterprise (AdWords, G Suite, etc.)			✓
Software consumer tools (Gmail, Google Maps, etc.)			✓
Android OS and app stores	✓		
Video sharing and social networking (YouTube, Google+)	✓		
Google hardware (glasses, chromecast, driverless cars, etc.)			✓

Source: Launchworks analysis

his ability to interact with fans, his decision has had no impact on his 50+ million subscriber base. YouTube has since introduced better moderation tools, but the issue of moderation is still lingering, including with YouTube Gaming, its newly launched live streaming platform for video gaming enthusiasts.[32] In this category, real-time conversations are integral to the gaming experience. YouTube rebuilt the live-streaming platform with a comment system giving more control to game owners, such as chat moderation, the ability to ban users, time-out users and ban filtered words.[33]

YouTube cannot be mentioned without Google+, Google's fledgling social network. In an attempt to offer a seamless experience into the Google eco-system, Google+ was integrated directly with YouTube and the Chrome Web browser, allowing YouTube videos to be viewed from within the Google+ interface. This meant that users were forced to sign up for accounts if they wanted to use YouTube channels or accounts. We suspect this move was mainly designed to ignite and scale Google+ to critical mass and compete with already established social platforms such as Facebook and Twitter. Although Google+ claims 2.2 billion accounts, only 9% of its users are active and post public content.[34] Google announced in July 2015 that Google was scaling back the reach of its social network.[35] Services such as YouTube channels and accounts will be accessible without a Google+ account to remove unnecessary friction for customers. This decision reflects the difficulty of scaling a platform to critical mass in an already saturated market . . . even for Google!

Other platform-powered ecosystems

While we have looked in some detail at how Amazon, Google and Apple have been able to leverage platforms and combine business models to succeed, the same framework can be applied to other companies. Microsoft and Facebook deserve similar case studies. Both have made their investors healthy returns: somebody who bought $1,000 of Facebook stock when it IPO'd on 12 March 2012 would have had $4,327 four years later, equivalent to a yearly return of 40.2%, while somebody who bought $1,000 of Microsoft when it IPO'd in 1986 would have $879,343 thirty years later, equivalent to a yearly return of 24.9%.[36]

Like Apple, Google and Amazon, Microsoft and Facebook achieved these performances by adding and combining platforms with other business models to further strengthen their respective platform-powered ecosystems.

The acquisitions of Nokia's mobile phone unit in September 2013 (for $7.2 billion),[37] collaborative communications platform Yammer in June 2012 (for $1.2 billion), peer-to-peer IP-based telecoms platform Skype in May 2011 (for $8.5 billion) and LinkedIn in June 2016 (for $26 billion) were driven by Microsoft's willingness to become the leading business platform-powered ecosystem and 'recreate the connective tissue of enterprises'.[38]

The acquisitions by Facebook of messaging app WhatsApp in February 2014 (for $19 billion),[39] photo sharing platform Instagram in April 2012 (for $1 billion)[40] and virtual reality hardware company Oculus in March 2014 (for $2 billion)[41] are also key moves aimed at consolidating its platform ecosystem and gaining control of a new physical interface. Indeed, unlike Apple, Google, Amazon and Microsoft, Facebook hasn't yet got its own 'operating system', and is therefore seen by some as 'just an app' dependent upon other people's hardware and OS.

Notes

1 Synergy Group, October 2014, www.srgresearch.com/articles/microsoft-cloud-revenues-leap-amazon-still-way-out-front.

2 Amazon.com website and Statista, www.statista.com/statistics/233761/year-on-year-revenue-of-amazon-and-ebay-since-2006/.

3 Amazon's market capitalization is $354 billion and Walmart's market capitalization is $217 billion, 12 September 2016.

4 Stock returns computed using monthly price services from IPO date (15 May 1997 for Amazon until 29 September 2016) using the online stock return calculator available at www.buyupside.com/.

5 Julia Kirby and Thomas A. Stewart, 'The Institutional Yes', *Harvard Business Review*, October 2007.

6   www.channeladvisor.com/blog/?pn=scot/deep-dive-into-amazons-q4-results-for-sellers-whats-cool-100b-and-200b.

7   *Wall Street Journal*, 29 January 2015, http://blogs.wsj.com/digits/2015/01/29/twitchs-viewers-reach-100-million-a-month/

8   ChannelAdvisor blog, Scott Wingo, 1 February 2006, www.channeladvisor.com/blog/?pn=scot/deep-dive-into-amazons-q4-results-for-sellers-whats-cool-100b-and-200b.

9   http://recode.net/2015/01/28/this-could-be-the-year-amazon-finally-reveals-its-most-important-number/.

10 In a 2014 survey of US sellers, 71% of FBA merchants reported more than a 20% increase in unit sales after joining FBA, Amazon 2014 Annual Report.

11 It is worth noting that Amazon reused a lot of the open-source Android code that Google originally developed. FireOS is therefore very close to, but different from, Google Android OS. For more information, see: www.howtogeek.com/232973/amazons-fire-os-vs.-googles-android-whats-the-difference/.

12 It is worth noting at this stage that while such tying strategies may be perfectly legitimate for start-ups, competition authorities and regulators often get concerned when large established companies – with 'market power' – use these tricks. We will discuss regulatory implications of platform businesses in Chapter 13.

13 In 1999, the company launched Amazon.com Auctions, a Web auctions service that failed to make a dent in eBay's large market share. Later that year, Amazon launched zShops, a fixed-price marketplace and a now defunct partnership with Sotheby's. In late 2000, Auctions and zShops morphed into the Amazon Marketplace that we know today.

14 http://fortune.com/2016/12/05/amazon-go-store/

15 Stock returns computed using monthly price services from IPO date (12 December 1980 for Apple until 29 September 2016) using the online stock return calculator available at www.buyupside.com/.

16 *Wired*, 21 October 2008, www.wired.com/2008/10/with-iphone-app/.

17 Apple is, of course, free to select partners and suppliers, such as Foxconn in China, for the manufacturing of its products. These outsourcing decisions do not fundamentally alter the business model of the company, however, since it keeps tight control over the end-to-end production process of its devices.

18 Statista, June 2016, www.statista.com/statistics/276623/number-of-apps-available-in-leading-app-stores/.

19 If you want to better understand the nature of this 'governance', you may want to have a look at the App Store guidelines for app developers: https://developer.apple.com/app-store/review/guidelines/.

20 Apple's services include the various app stores, as well as iTunes, iCloud, Apple Music, Apple Pay, Apple Care, licensing and other services.

21 Fiscal data from Apple's website, www.apple.com/pr/library/2016/.

22 http://uk.businessinsider.com/apple-ceo-tim-cook-services-q3-2016-7.

23 Apple announced in June 2016 that this 30% figure could go down to 15% (with 85% going to developers) in some circumstances. See www.theverge.com/2016/6/8/11880730/apple-app-store-subscription-update-phil-schiller-interview.

24 Horace Dediu, Asymco (2014), www.asymco.com/, www.asymco.com/2015/08/26/much-bigger-than-hollywood/ and www.asymco.com/2015/01/22/bigger-than-hollywood/.

25 At the developer level, Apple now allows third-party developers to plug into Siri across multiple operating systems (iOS, tvOS and macOS). At the user level, the new macOS version allows users to copy something on the Mac or iPhone and paste it on the other device. And if users buy an app for the iPad, iOS's automatic app download to tvOS means that it will automatically show up on the Apple TV.

26 Stock returns computed using monthly price services from IPO date (19 August 2004 for Google until 29 September 2016) using the online stock return calculator available at www.buyupside.com/.

27 Google Investor Relations, 2016 Financial Tables, http://investor.google.com/financial/tables.html.

28 Which YouTube supported with its Partner Program, making it possible to earn a substantial living as a video producer.

29 As of June 2015, according to third-party Web analytics providers Alexa and SimilarWeb.

30 Although this may have more to do with its bargaining power with operators arguing against net neutrality than with Google's core strategy of organizing the world's information.

31 See *Guardian*, 3 September 2014, www.theguardian.com/technology/2014/sep/03/pewdiepie-switches-off-youtube-comments-its-mainly-spam.

32 YouTube Gaming launched on 26 August 2015 in response to Twitch.tv, the leading video streaming platform purchased by Amazon. YouTube Gaming is available as a website globally and has iOS and Android apps in the US and UK. Announced in June, the new portal includes a directory of more than 25,000 games, each with their own profile page collecting related YouTube videos.

33 Ryan Wyatt interview, YouTube's head of gaming, 26 August 2015, www.theguardian.com/technology/2015/aug/26/youtube-gaming-live-website-apps.

34 Business Insider, 'Nobody Is Using Google+', 20 January 2015, http://uk.business insider.com/google-active-users-2015-1

35 Google Blog, 27 July 2015, http://googleblog.blogspot.co.uk/2015/07/everything-in-its-right-place.html.

36 Stock returns computed using monthly price services from IPO date (respectively 18 May 2012 for Facebook and 13 March 1986 for Microsoft until 29 September 2016) using the online stock return calculator available at www.buyupside.com/.

37 Microsoft's intent when acquiring Nokia's mobile phone division in 2014 for $7.2 billion was to create added value by combining Microsoft's software and services with Nokia's hardware assets. It was a failure, with Microsoft writing off $7.6 billion two years later.

38 According to Benedict Evans.

39 http://newsroom.fb.com/news/2014/02/facebook-to-acquire-whatsapp/

40 www.wsj.com/articles/SB10001424052702303815404577333840377381670

41 www.facebook.com/zuck/posts/10101319050523971?stream_ref=1

Chapter 7

Life stages of platforms
Design

In the previous chapters, we covered some definitions and underlying economic principles of digital platforms. We then reviewed how they can usefully be combined with traditional business models to form platform-powered ecosystems. Finally, we reviewed a range of frameworks, including our own rocket model, to better design platform businesses.

The rocket life stages at a glance

Let's now examine in greater detail the inner workings of digital platforms across their life stages. As a platform business develops and matures, growth bottlenecks are likely to appear along the way. These bottlenecks will be different from one market to another, and the sequence we propose is by no means scientific or exhaustive since every platform is different. We have, however, seen some patterns emerge, since the same issues and bottlenecks tend to appear at similar stages of development.

We therefore propose to review the key bottlenecks and illustrate the management challenges that could present themselves for each building block of the rocket model (attract, match, connect, transact and optimize) across four main life stages of a platform, as shown in Figure 7.1:

- *Pre-launch*, when the platform is designed and built prior to its launch.
- *Ignition*, when the platform is tested and launched. The recruitment of participants may happen sequentially, on the producer side first (path A in Figure 7.1), or the user side (path B).
- *Scaling-up*, when building a critical mass of participants on all sides of the platform becomes key. The ratio of producers and users will need to be kept within an equilibrium (path C).
- *Maturity*, or how to continue to grow the business while defending against new entrants and existing competitors.

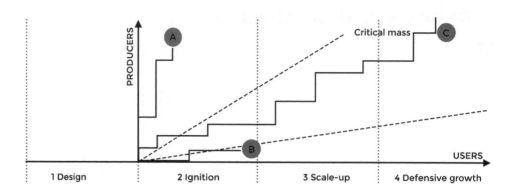

Figure 7.1 **The main life stages of a platform**

Source: Launchworks

The four life stages are presented in the next four chapters and summarized in Table 7.1. You can either read these four chapters sequentially or simply go to the section most relevant to you given the life stage of your platform. If you're not interested in life stage deep dives, you can go straight to Chapter 11 on pricing.

Pre-launch: designing the platform business architecture

The importance of this stage cannot be overstated since all the aspects of the business need to be broadly developed or hypothesized during this design phase. Having clarity over the definition of platforms and a broad understanding of how the business model is going to operate are obvious prerequisites to ignition and central to the pre-launch phase. Starting with technology questions is the wrong approach, yet we find that many would-be platforms make this initial mistake.

Questions to be addressed at this stage include the identification of the key stakeholders, the value proposition offered to them and a broad sizing of the market opportunity. Note that these relatively generic questions will also allow you to validate your critical business assumption that a platform business model really is the best way to address the opportunity in question.

Using our proposed definition, this means the opportunity would be best addressed by a business able to *attract* producers and consumers of a good or service, to efficiently *match* and *connect* them in order for a *transaction* to occur and for data to be captured so that the business can be further *optimized*.

Table 7.1 Rocket life stages

	Pre-launch	Ignition	Scale-up	Maturity
Key priorities	**Platform Design** **Market Sizing** **Prototyping**	**Platform Fit** **Build liquidity** **Raise capital**	**Customer /Transaction growth** **Balanced and relevant liquidity** **Trust and loyalty** **Team culture and recruitment**	**Business growth** **Profitability** **Platform Power** **Brand**
Attract	**Define value propositions** Who are the key participants? What is the value proposition for each side of the platform? What tools/services should the platform provide to Users, Producers?	**Build liquidity** Experiment/decide market side focus and ignition sequence i.e. which side should be recruited first Attract identifiable target communities Iterate value propositions based on market feedback to find platform fit	**Strengthen liquidity** Build liquidity whilst keeping growth balanced and within equilibrium limits Get insights into tipping point/ critical mass, network value and level of network effects Focus on participant acquisition first then retention	**New markets and sustainable growth** Extend value propositions to meet participants' needs and compete against other offers Focus on retention in existing markets and acquisition in new markets
Match	**Define matching/filter criteria** How will the matching be done? What are the key matching criteria to capture?	**Build matching effectiveness** Review matching criteria and filters	**Improve matching effectiveness** Automate and optimize matching to improve relevance, depth of results and timeliness	**Strengthen matching effectiveness** Optimize matching at mass scale Blend AI to matching/search algorithms
Connect	**Define interactions between participants** What is the nature/type of interactions? How will Users/Producers interact? Directly/indirectly?	**Remove friction between participants** Clear interaction bottlenecks Review rules and norms to encourage positive interactions and limit negative ones	**Improve Connection effectiveness** Encourage positive interactions at scale and discourage negative ones	**Strengthen Connection effectiveness** Review/simplify interactions as value propositions mature and network effects are at scale
Transact	**Define core transactions between participants** What is the nature/type of core transactions?	**Remove friction between participants** Clear core interaction bottlenecks	**Scale core transactions** Continue to clear core interaction bottlenecks	**Maximize core transactions** Continue to clear core interaction bottlenecks

Table 7.1 continued

	Pre-launch	Ignition	Scale-up	Maturity
	Which side adds the most value? How is it enabled? How to monetize? Which side(s) to charge?	Elements needed post-transaction (delivery, cancellation, etc.) Consider the range of possible price options to quickly attract most valuable customers (including freemium)	Deploy monetization when/if relevant	Monetize for profitable growth
Optimize	**Define North Star and key KPIs** What are the North Star and key KPIs?	**Monitor North Star and ignition KPIs** KPIs to track North Star, platform fit, liquidity, matching effectiveness, core interaction bottlenecks and raising capital	**Monitor North Star and scaling KPIs** KPIs to track North Star, participant acquisition/retention, liquidity and balance, matching/ connection effectiveness, trust and customer experience, brand awareness	**Monitor North Star and maturity KPIs** KPIs to track North Star, new markets and on-going growth, matching optimization, monetization/ profitability, customer success and innovation
Enablers				
UX	What is the desired level of control from the platform? What are main flows?	**Optimize UX to remove bottlenecks**	Continue to optimize UX to reduce friction	Simplify UX as more functionality gets introduced
Payments	What are the key payment flows?	Implement payment solution (if needed)	Scale payment solution (if needed)	Investigate upside of optimizing payments/ generating other revenue streams
Infrastructure	Make or buy platform infrastructure?	Infrastructure to support platform fit	**Scale IT infrastructure**	Keep infrastructure up to date
Governance	What are the rules of access and engagement for Producers, Users? Will pricing be centralized/ decentralized? How to capture/distribute value	Adjust governance principles as Producers and Users join the platform and engage Set the rules for conflict resolution	Adjust governance principles for mass scale Automate conflict resolution Community management and tools	Consolidate governance principles
Trust	What framework to establish trust?	Map key trust interactions	Deploy solid **Trust and Safety** framework and **scale customer service** teams	**Consolidate Trust and Safety framework**
Brand	What does the brand stand for and how does this translate into visual identity/design?	Ensure brand identity/design is aligned with platform fit	Consolidate **brand to appeal to mass market audience**	Consolidate **brand to appeal to new and existing audiences**

Source: Launchworks

There is no skipping a platform design phase, since it would be impossible to design a platform without having at least first hypothesized the key principles of its operations. However, staying in the platform design phase too long can result in diminishing returns, since the best type of feedback is market feedback and the cost of experimentation keeps going down.

One possible exception to this is when established businesses are keen to develop and launch a platform as an add-on to their existing operations to create a 'platform-powered ecosystem'. In such cases, a longer pre-launch phase may be considered because of the perceived sensitivity and risk of the operation and its interplay with existing business activities. Managers may be concerned about protecting a brand and an existing market position, minimizing disruption to the existing business, and leveraging current assets while acquiring new skills and capabilities.

Many business planning[1] and start-up[2] books highlight the key issues that need to be addressed at the outset when launching a new business venture. Summarizing the entire start-up literature would be difficult, so we are

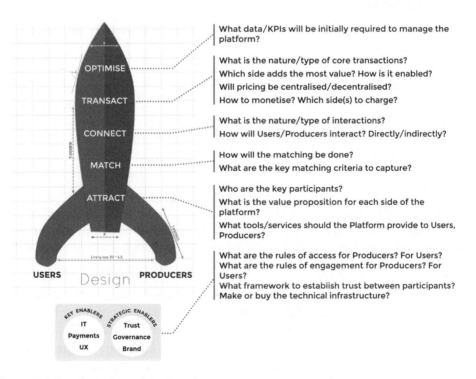

Figure 7.2 **Pre-launch rocket questions**

Source: Launchworks

focusing on the things that are *really different* for platform businesses. We will focus on business-related issues rather than technical questions. This is because a successful platform is *first and foremost* a business construct later supported by the right technical infrastructure.

The key pre-launch questions summarized in Figure 7.2 are developed below.

Before attracting anybody to a platform, it is critically important to understand *who* the key platform participants will be, and *what* kind of value proposition will be offered to them. As we will see, the concept of value proposition is an interesting one in this context since some of the platform participants are also co-creating value on the platform. While their expected contribution needs to be defined and incentivized by the platform, it cannot, by definition, be entirely controlled, but merely influenced.[3]

A good way to think about value creation is to map participants' contributions out using a simple matrix, presented in Table 7.3, to describe the value proposition to and from each stakeholder.

Identify participants

It is useful, as a preliminary step, to identify key participants involved with the platform.

Platform owner: typically the organization (business, not-for-profit or network) responsible for the development and management of the platform itself and its ecosystem. For example, eBay Inc. (commercial organization), Kiva (not-for-profit organization), Kickstarter (public-benefit corporation), Reddit (community).

Sides: the distinct and diverse groups of customers or entities being connected by the platform. For two-sided platforms, they are typically segmented into two groups: one on the supply side (often called producers) and the other on the demand side (often called users or consumers). They are jointly called 'platform participants'.

- *Producers*: individuals, communities, businesses or entities delivering value created on and/or through the platform. For example, eBay sellers, Kiva borrowers, Kickstarter creators, Reddit content contributors. The producers side can be further segmented if it is made of different customer groups. For example, eBay sellers can be segmented into consumer sellers and business sellers, and even broken down even further by product categories (e.g. professional fashion sellers, non-professional coin collectors, etc.).

- *Users (or consumers)*: individuals, communities, businesses or entities that access, consume and utilize the value provided by producers. For example, eBay buyers, Kiva lenders, Kickstarter backers, Reddit readers.

Partners: individuals, communities, businesses or entities that collaborate with platform owners and add value for the platform participants. For example, the Airbnb management companies Guesty in the US or Hostmakers in the UK, who manage listings, bookings, etc. on behalf of the hosts. In a first analysis, partners may be left blank, especially in new markets where their identity may not be obvious. But these providers of complementary products can play a key role as the ecosystem expands.

Other stakeholders: typically actors who have a specific interest in the development of platforms, and their impact on public welfare, competition, etc. Examples include governments and regulators. They are often less relevant in the early days, but their importance increases over time, so it is useful to identify them early if possible. If your platform is very disruptive to established market participants, it will be particularly important to engage with these stakeholders early to ensure a balanced debate.

Market sizing

A necessary second step is to 'quantify' the number of possible platform participants in order to get a sense for the market potential. Typically, this requires a high-level, top-down estimate of classic marketing metrics such as the total addressable market (TAM), the serviced addressable market (SAM) and the target market (TM).

Using Airbnb as an illustration, the TAM would be all days/nights where properties are empty, the SAM would be restricted to areas where it is possible to rent from a regulatory perspective, and the TM would be the segment of people who would be open to renting their home. The TM can of course be sub-segmented further by age group, geographies, risk aversion, etc.

Market sizing is a traditional step for all start-up businesses, but with platform businesses this requires some specific considerations, since:

- You need to get a sense of who in your market will be a *platform participant*. Some people will never share their flat when they go on holiday. Some people only want to go to hotels. Some platforms will require ownership of a smartphone.

- Your market sizing needs to ensure that there is a *critical mass* of participants on both sides of the platform as quickly as possible so that your proposition is 'liquid' and transactions are maximized.
- It is important to be careful when using existing market information and statistics, since, more often than not, these have been framed in the context of traditional businesses rather than platforms. For example, had Uber based its business on the size of the taxi market, it would have significantly underestimated the opportunity. In fact, 3 years after entry Uber managed to grow the San Francisco taxi market by a factor of 3.5.[4]

Business architecture drivers

In addition to market sizing, there are several drivers to consider when designing the business architecture of the platform. Some of the main ones are listed below.

Market focus

Which parts of the market do you intend to focus on first? Should you target a well-defined vertical first and then expand to other ones, and if so which ones?

Type of interactions between users and producers

Will interactions between participants be one-to-one? One-to-many? Or many-to-many?

Nature of interactions between users and producers

Will interactions be transactional or relationship-based? Will connections be asymmetric (a participant can follow another one) or bidirectional (opt-in from both sides)?

Level of intermediation

Will platform participants connect directly or indirectly? Direct platforms allow for direct connection between customers, while indirect platforms connect two or more customer groups indirectly. For example, card companies, such as Visa or Mastercard, go through banks to issue their cards and acquire the merchants that will accept cards. These intermediaries – so-called card issuers and merchant acquirers – are effectively the ones in contact with the end

Indirect platform on two sides

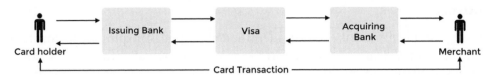

Direct platform on both sides

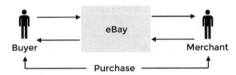

Figure 7.3 **Direct vs indirect platforms**

Source: Launchworks

clients, while Visa manages the business-to-business platform in the centre (interbank switch). As shown in Figure 7.3, platforms can be indirect on both sides (e.g. Visa), on one side or direct on both sides (e.g. eBay). When a platform is indirect, it needs to think about its value proposition to its intermediaries, as well as its end users.

Governance

What are the main rules governing the platform?

- Users and producers joining rules: Who should be allowed to join the platform? Everyone (open) or a curated few (closed)? How can the positioning of your platform encourage your target users to join (and keeps others at bay)?
- Centralized/decentralized governance: Will you keep control of management decisions? For example, will the pricing of products and services on the platform be delegated to the ecosystem stakeholders (i.e. eBay sellers setting product prices) or will it be under the platform's control (i.e. Uber setting car ride tariffs).
- User experience control: How much of the user experience should you control vs platform producers/users?
- Users and producers operating rules: What should be the rules for users and producers to keep the right to interact and transact on the platform?

The rocket model for platform design

Attract

Using the platform stakeholders identified above, it is helpful to go through the value they bring to the platform – as well as the value that the platform brings to them – to ensure that the overall architecture is consistent with the type of self-reinforcing community model that powers most platforms.

For traditional businesses, this is a fairly straightforward exercise, as shown in Table 7.2 for the Hilton Group.

Table 7.2 Hilton's value proposition

Hilton	Value proposition to hosts	How
Value proposition	'Leading brands serving virtually any lodging need anywhere'[5]	Identify prime locations, build/ acquire hotels, manage hospitality logistics, sell rooms and invest in Hilton brands

Source: Launchworks

The exercise is, however, a bit more complex for a multisided business because: (i) there is more than one value proposition to define; and (ii) several stakeholders can contribute, which is a significant difference from traditional businesses. A good way to do this methodically is to use the matrix in Table 7.3 and map each value proposition, and associated contributions from

Table 7.3 Deconstructing value propositions for multisided businesses

	User (or US for user side)	Producer (or PS for producer side)	Partner (P)	Platform (PO)
Motivation	'motivations of users for transacting on the platform'	'motivations of producers for transacting on the platform'	'objectives and vision of the partners in the context of the platform'	'objectives and vision of the platform owner'
Value proposition (target)	Contribution from PO: PS: P: US:	Contribution from PO: US: P: PS:	Contribution from PO: US: PS: P:	Contribution from US: PS: P: PO:

Source: Adapted from Simone Cicero, Platform Design Toolkit

key stakeholders. This framework was used at eBay to identify value proposition gaps and compare against competitive offers. It has been formalized by Simone Cicero in the Platform Design Toolkit.[6]

Let's use the above framework to map Airbnb's value propositions in Table 7.4.

Table 7.4 Airbnb's value propositions

	User (US) Guests	Producer (PS) Hosts	Partner (P) Hospitality service companies	Platform (PO) Airbnb
Motivation	Experience a new place like locals do	Monetize my place when I'm away	Solve admin, hospitality and cleaning pain points for Airbnb hosts/ Provide experiences to guests	Attract, match and connect guests and hosts and generate a margin
Value proposition	PO: mobile and Web access, efficient search, safe transaction and payment services, customer care	PO: listing tools, calendar, efficient matching, safe transaction and payment services, insurance, customer care	PO: access to a market of hosts in need of hospitality services and guests looking for experiences	PS: publish and manage listing(s), host guests, pay host service fee, write guest reviews
	PS: detailed listings, home hosting, guest reviews	US: guest reviews		US: search and book listing(s), pay guest service fee, write host reviews
	P: unique local experiences			
	US: reviews from other guests	P: listing and key management, meet and greet, cleaning services		PO: raise funds to support growth
		PS: reviews from other hosts		P: assist hosts, provide experiences for guests

Source: Launchworks

Users, producers and partners will need tools and services to encourage contributions. We therefore recommend mapping the likely tools and services required for each customer group to facilitate them joining and operating on the platform.

The design of tools and associated features will largely be driven by how platform owners plan to structure content from producers and users. This question is particularly important for product marketplaces, such as Amazon Marketplace or Etsy, for example. While Amazon manages a predefined catalogue template against which sellers can create listings, craft marketplace Etsy allows each listing to contain product information that is completely custom. Etsy, however, prescribes a template with required fixed attributes, such as the listing title, description, price, delivery cost and availability, in order to control the front-end experience, while allowing the seller to be relatively free-form with their supplied content. By contrast, social platforms such as community forum Reddit or Facebook allow users to post largely unstructured content in a free-form format. These considerations impact how much control the platform owner applies to producer content, and this has a direct impact on the matching, connect, trust and brand dimensions.

Match

Matching is a platform-specific activity, and key questions need to be addressed at this platform design stage:

- What will be the matching criteria that need to be captured by the platform?
- Will the matching rely on structured and formatted content or free-flow content? Will the function be automated or manual and done by the platform owner (in the early days)?
- To what extent will people self-select? For example, are people expected to apply filters themselves to access relevant content?

The more information from platform participants is captured manually at the outset, the greater the friction is. However, capturing relevant information can enable efficient matching. For example, dating platform eHarmony asks members to fill in a detailed questionnaire, and the results feed into their compatibility-matching algorithm. While the length of the questionnaire can be seen as an obstacle to joining the platform, the granularity of results allows for optimal matching and successful 'transactions' (defined here as successful dates). Dating platform Happn has a very different approach to matching, which, according to CEO Didier Rappaport, reflects how people meet in real life. Initial matching is done on where participants have been and who else has passed within an 800-foot radius, gender orientation and age. No need to fill in a questionnaire to join Happn. A simple Facebook log in is enough to populate one's profile. Over time, the matching algorithm learns form participant activity – who they've liked, sent charms to or had a conversation with.

Connect

Many platforms need to also enable peer-to-peer connection between platform participants post-matching because the combination of these enabling interactions drives the overall core transactions. Key questions at this stage include:

- What will be the type and nature of interactions between users and producers?
- How will users and producers interact on- and off-platform?
- How much structure should be applied to participants' interactions?
- How can interactions be captured in a way that will enhance the platform's matching and support core transactions?

Transactional platforms such as marketplaces typically require advanced connection capabilities between participants when one or several of the following apply:

(i) the asymmetry of information between market participants is high;
(ii) the transaction is more a 'one-off' than a 'recurring' purchase; and
(iii) the value of the transaction is relatively high.

For example, the probability of using the messaging function of eBay to ask questions to an individual car seller before making the transaction is high (the three conditions above are met), while asking many questions to a marketplace seller about napkins, notepads or pens (recurring and relatively low-value purchases of products you already know) is less likely.

Transact

The ultimate goal of platforms is to maximize the number of value-adding core transactions. Beyond defining what the core transaction actually is, clarity on the following questions will be useful:

- What is the nature/type of core transactions?
- Will core transactions be on and off the platform?
- How will supporting interactions (covered in the connect section) enable core transactions?

- Which elements will be needed to complete core transactions (payment, delivery aspects, other)? If the platform involves the physical delivery of goods, should the delivery be outsourced to producers or should it be intermediated by the platform?

While the main purpose of platforms is to enable value exchange between participants, value capture should also be discussed early on. It is critical to minimize friction in the earlier days of the platform, but it is equally important to understand monetization options:

- Which side adds the most value? How is it enabled?
- How to monetize? Which side(s) to charge?

Even platforms that ended up monetizing late in their development often experimented with revenue models very early in order to understand the implications of the various growth models available to them.

Optimize

Although there is no data available at pre-launch to optimize the platform, it is appropriate to think about the type of data that the platform could usefully capture without increasing friction too much.

Key questions at this stage include:

- What information will the platform need to gather in order to test the main hypotheses behind the business case?
- Which interactions between platform participants can be captured in a small set of key performance indicators (KPIs) to track platform developments and help identify bottlenecks as it scales?
- Which metrics can best measure platform success?

While the selection of KPIs is not an exact science, we found that the following principles were often helpful in the context of platform design.

The definition of a generic overriding growth metric, that we call a 'North Star', can be helpful to track the overall health of the platform community. Beyond encapsulating a key growth dimension, it also represents the key engagement/core transaction of the platform. The North Star metric should be fully endorsed and championed by the CEO, and remains the same through growth stages to guide all employees.

Selecting the right North Star metric depends on the type of platform you are running. It is important to note that the core transaction may take place off the platform (e.g. dates or restaurant meals), and so a proxy metric may be needed. The types of key engagement metrics include value exchanged (e.g. gross merchandise value for marketplaces such as eBay or Etsy), transaction numbers (e.g. nights booked at Airbnb,[7] messages sent for WhatsApp), activity or participation metrics (e.g. posts or monthly active users for social media[8]), expressions of interest or connections that lead to off-platform transactions (e.g. restaurant bookings on OpenTable).

Tracking of user behaviours through the various rocket stages gives a helpful picture of the platform's overall health. As we will see in the next three chapters, the key for each stage is to find relevant metrics that capture the main enabling interaction as well as core transactions.

Enablers

Like any business, it is important to sketch the type of user experience the platform will deliver, the interface it will need, how payments (if any) will be made and what type of technical architecture it may have, as well as the company's key brand attributes and culture. Pre-launch, most of the above topics are similar to traditional firms, but the following are platform-specific.

Governance and trust

Defining the rules of access and engagement for both producers and users will determine who can join the platform, how they interact and transact. This groundwork is essential to building the foundations of trust between participants. Platform governance and trust are broad subjects that will be covered more extensively in Chapter 12.

To make or to buy a technical platform solution?

As your platform concept gets defined, how should you build the technical infrastructure underlying your platform? Should you build it yourself or use an off-the-shelf solution?

There is currently a limited selection of software solutions able to support platform-based business models out of the box, although choice is improving. This means that the make-buy decision will depend upon the availability of a solution catering for the vertical market being concerned, as well as specific circumstances.

For existing businesses that may not have the right in-house development capabilities but wish to add a marketplace to their existing ecommerce offering, buying off-the-shelf software and plugging it into an existing infrastructure is likely to be the fastest and least risky solution – at least in the short term. For well-defined verticals such as marketplaces for products, some well-developed software solutions[9] do exist. Solutions are usually Software as a Service (SaaS)-based and priced on a revenue sharing model, which may be fine initially but can become fairly costly for the platform owner as the platform scales.

If you're starting from scratch, or are addressing a specific vertical that is not covered by existing software solutions, you may need to build the platform infrastructure yourself. Bespoke development will give more control and the ability to iterate quickly and customize the experience from a producer, user and owner perspective. More investment will be required up front for technical design and development. So it may be the preferred solution for founders who know how to code, or for established firms with access to quality developers.

The answer also depends upon the strategy planned to overcome the chicken-and-egg problem described in the next chapter. If the initial focus is on recruiting one side of the market first, the early technology selection needs to consider this. Many successful start-ups launched basic concept validation using off-the-shelf 'pipe' software designed for one side of the market (usually the user side), such as Shopify or Magento, while manually dealing with the back-end supply side.[10] However, this may not always be feasible if building liquidity on both sides is a really important driver early on. When possible, though, this path enables market validation on a reduced budget until you can demonstrate traction. Migration to a more scalable infrastructure later on may be painful, but this transition may be the price to pay for de-risking development costs up front.

The market for off-the-shelf platform software is changing rapidly, though. Mirakl, Izberg, Near-me, Sharetribe and Marketplace Lab offer off-the-shelf marketplace solutions for retailers, while Upwork offers white-label freelancer marketplace solutions to large corporates. As the platform market matures, we anticipate enterprise software vendors to develop platform solutions tailored to specific verticals (telecoms, health, professional services, etc.) and offer platform as a service – or PaaS – solutions.

Design a platform as an add-on to an existing business

Many established businesses now understand the impact of platforms and are keen to add or replicate platform capabilities to their own activities. In such cases, the platform design stage needs to take into account a range of additional considerations that are related to the overall strategy of the company. Leverageable assets, brand equity, resources and existing client relationships can be both a help and a hindrance in the context of a platform play. Some of the difficulties for existing firms considering a transition to a platform model or add-on will be discussed in Chapter 14.

Notes

1 Business model generation, with its previously mentioned business model canvas tool, is a good start.
2 Eric Ries's *The Lean Startup* has become a de rigueur read for any would-be entrepreneur keen to change the world on a limited budget. See E. Ries, *The Lean Startup*, New York: Crown Publishing, 2011.
3 While Hilton can manage and tightly control the experience of its guests, Airbnb can only influence the experience provided by the hosts.
4 Henry Blodget, 19 January 2015, Business Insider, http://uk.businessinsider.com/uber-revenue-san-francisco-2015-1.
5 Hilton Investor Presentation, November 2015.
6 The Platform Design Toolkit 2.0, the ecosystem's motivation matrix, by Simone Cicero, www.meedabyte.com.
7 Airbnb CEO Brian Chesky routinely tweets their nights booked milestones.
8 Alex Schultz, How to Start a Start-up, Lecture 6: Growth, Sam Altman.
9 We have seen a number of interesting implementations of Mirakl at Galeries Lafayette, Darty, Halfords and l'Equipe.
10 LoveKnitting, the marketplace for knitting yarn, patterns and needles, was initially built on Magento. Truly, a marketplace for unique experiences, was initially built on an even tighter budget, using WordPress and WooCommerce, before migrating to Magento.

Chapter 8

Platform ignition
Proving the concept

The business architecture of the platform has been designed and a technical solution has been built for ignition. The platform now needs to be launched and platform participants recruited in order to test the platform's concept.

The key challenge at this stage is typically to develop a minimum viable product (MVP) of the platform that allows you to attract enough producers and users in order to test your business hypothesis. You need to decide which side to attract first and how to go about it. Since the platform hasn't yet got many users, there will be opportunities for iterating on the proposition, testing additional features, different market channels, etc.

The main objective of this ignition stage is for your platform to pass the product/market fit test that we also call 'platform fit', since it tests whether the platform is able to attract, match, connect and enable transactions among its participants. It would be very difficult for anybody to attract significant capital to scale before showing a genuinely strong engagement from customers, at least in a given market niche/community.

Finding this 'platform fit' is not straightforward and may require many iterations of the original concept. It is, however, critical that the platform manages to find its 'fit' relatively quickly since, unlike other more traditional business models, platforms are only viable after they reach a critical mass of participants.[1] If it takes too much time for the platform to attract enough participants, the platform is in danger of losing momentum and 'unravelling'. This is what happens when users are not finding what they are looking for because the platform is subscale (e.g. imagine a dating site with only a few profiles). If the platform is free, then its perceived value may still be positive without much scale. But if the platform is already charging for its services, participants are likely to be less forgiving.

Conversely, moving to the scaling phase should only take place once the 'platform fit' is validated. Understanding any technical or product obstacles for platform participants to experience their 'magic moment' on the platform (i.e. the moment where they experience real value) is also a prerequisite. It is much easier to make changes to the value proposition with few customers than at scale.

The ignition stage is also the stage at which contracts need to be drafted and signed by platform participants. These are very important and need to clarify the responsibilities and liabilities of the parties (platform owner, producers and users). Platform contracts also need to make it clear that platform participants are not employees of the firm.

Getting the 'cookie cutter' right before scaling is therefore one of the key objectives of the ignition phase.

The key ignition questions of Figure 8.1 are developed below. There are two distinct scenarios. The first one is launching a platform from scratch. It creates a unique chicken-and-egg problem: Which side of the platform should be attracted first? The second scenario is when the platform is launched as an add-on to an existing business.

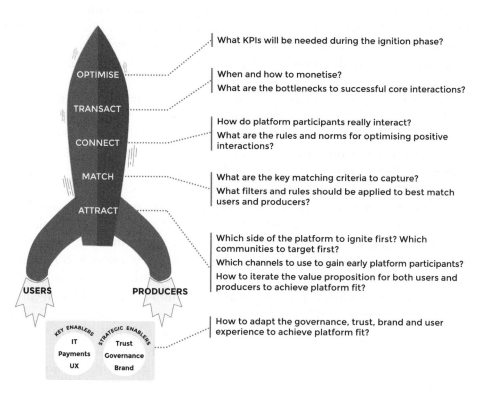

Figure 8.1 **Ignition rocket questions to achieve platform fit**

Source: Launchworks

Launching from scratch: the chicken-and-egg problem

Attract

The platform needs to attract the target participants identified during the pre-launch phase. The attraction and acquisition of customers online is a topic worthy of a book in itself and the key issues are not unique to platform businesses so we will be very brief on the 'dark arts of customer acquisition' and focus on platform-specific aspects. While customer acquisition strategies change with each wave of Internet marketing techniques, developing a value proposition for each side of the platform that resonates with targeted audiences remains a major driver of attracting and retaining customers.

At the outset, a platform is faced with a conundrum: the value it creates is predicated upon one side of the market seeking to transact with another one. Since there is nobody on board at the beginning, it is, of course, particularly difficult to attract users and producers for the purpose of transacting. This is a platform-specific problem. In terms of execution, the key tactics that have been shown to help break the chicken-and-egg conundrum fall into the following categories.

Focus on one side first

This is one way of breaking the deadlock of 'no producers and no consumers'. Simply focus on one side first – as a traditional company would do – and then once you've developed a value proposition that makes sense for your customers, pivot to start your platform play by opening the other side. Before launching its taxi booking app in London, Hailo, now MyTaxi, developed a deep understanding of a taxi driver's life by talking to many black cab drivers. Hailo addressed their main 'pain points' by offering a free mobile app to help them manage their money more effectively and get real-time traffic and speed camera information. Casper Woolley, one of Hailo's founders, acknowledges that it would have been extremely difficult to recruit taxi drivers without this.

Similarly OpenTable first focused on the needs of restaurants by offering them the tools to easily manage bookings online before opening up its listing of restaurants to customers once it had reached a critical mass.[2] The combination of deep understanding of the economics and booking dynamics of the restaurants they sold their software to, combined with a critical mass, allowed OpenTable to negotiate booking fees and in turn invest in advertising and loyalty points to attract many more customers.

Marketplaces often need to attract the supply side first. La Belle Asiette, a marketplace matching chefs with diners at home, initially focused on attracting chefs. Helping chefs to create innovative menus, coupled with financial incentives to secure availability on the platform, ensured that new diners had a wide range of options available to them from day one.

Use your producers or users to attract the other side

By enabling one side to transact, your platform may give incentives to its producers to bring in participants through their own networks. If a start-up uses a crowdfunding platform for raising money, they will tell all their potential investors about the campaign. Some may join the platform as members and invest in other start-ups, and some may even decide to use the platform to raise money for their own venture at a later stage. In the early days, Etsy courted established crafters and leveraged word of mouth through the 'Stitch 'n Bitch' movement by attending local art and craft fairs across the US and Canada. These influential artisans had established substantial followings. They had no e-commerce presence prior to Etsy and were therefore motivated to recommend potential buyers to the site. We'll see in Chapter 9 (scaling-up) that identifying and recruiting early adopters who can recommend the platform to a large following can significantly boost growth.

Seed one side to ignite traction

Sometimes the best way to get a platform going is to do what platform participants would do if they knew the platform existed . . . but by yourself. Hiring great contributors helped Medium kick-start its curated content platform and established an image of quality contributions that subsequently attracted both readers and contributors. Reddit initially submitted large amount of content using fake profiles. It gave the impression that that site was alive and in turn attracted people interested in the content.[3] Online dating sites are notoriously difficult to kick-start given the importance of having a critical mass for traction in this area (e.g. how would you feel if a site was unable to match you with anybody?). This has led to persistent rumours of fake profiles being created – often of attractive single women who play the role of producers on many dating platforms – at launch in order to seed that particular side.[4]

Focusing on meshed communities

Attracting both sides at the same time can be challenging, so it helps when early producers also happen to be users. eBay initially launched collectables categories, targeting existing offline communities of passionate collectors (coins, stamps, etc.). eBay's early focus on collectibles allowed the platform to grow a vibrant online community of people who were very often both buyers and sellers. This overlap of roles is very useful in terms of entry point for platforms, since a new platform participant will be adding value to the platform both as a buyer/user and seller/producer. Meshed communities with significant overlap are often prioritized as entry points for this reason.

The bowling pin strategy

One tested way to overcome the chicken–and–egg conundrum is what Geoffrey Moore calls the bowling pin strategy:[5] find a niche where the chicken–and–egg problem is more easily overcome and then find ways to hop from that niche to other niches, and eventually to the broader market. Typical examples are Facebook, which was first ignited as a platform at Harvard, and then slowly expanded to other Ivy League universities in the US before crossing the pond and reaching some elite universities in the UK, then spreading to all universities, and ultimately reaching almost everybody.[6]

The bowling pin strategy is also highly relevant for hyperlocal services where platform owners need to create local matching within limited geographic areas. This can be done with focused geographic targeting of relevant communities. Deliveroo, the restaurant delivery platform, initially launched in Chelsea, a relatively well-off area of London with lots of time-poor executives. It started by recruiting restaurants and diners in the neighbourhood, before successfully scaling to other parts of London and other cities in the UK and across the world.

Piggybacking on existing networks

There are many tales of platforms igniting by piggybacking on existing networks. The most famous one is Airbnb. Craigslist had many users who looked for listings other than the standard hotel experience, which was precisely Airbnb's target market. To attract guests, Airbnb developed an integration with the Craigslist platform as early as 2010.[7] It offered hosts who listed properties on Airbnb the opportunity to automatically publish them on Craigslist. To attract hosts, Airbnb also developed a hack that spammed people posting listings on Craigslist, offering them to list on Airbnb.[8] Both hacks allowed Airbnb to grow their guest and host base at almost no cost.

PayPal initially ignited (when still independent from eBay) by targeting eBay power-buyers and power-sellers, which were high growth segments at the time. Cash incentives for people to join and refer others,[9] combined with a high velocity of buying and selling, generated viral growth, and PayPal expanded rapidly to become the de facto payment solution on eBay,[10] squeezing out eBay's own in-house payment solution.

The event strategy

A variant of the bowling pin strategy is what we call the 'event' strategy (sometimes also called 'big bang launch strategy'),[11] in which the platform chooses a particular event where a critical mass of an identified target community is present in order to kick-start the platform in the hope that other communities will follow. Typical examples of such a strategy include the launch of Twitter (and then later Foursquare) at the South by Southwest (SXSW) festival, which gave the company a captive audience for exchanging short messages that were displayed in real time on stage. It also allowed Twitter to recruit a critical mass of 'opinion formers' who were subsequently instrumental in spreading the app. Similarly, Tinder, the famous dating app recently valued at more than $3 billion, was launched in 2012 at 'exclusive' University of Southern California (USC) campus student parties, where downloading the app was a condition of entry. This allowed them to sign up a significant number of young singles, and they replicated the model at other universities, using the college-by-college growth technique used by Facebook, in order to get a critical mass in each relevant campus.[12] After the parties, Tinder users told their friends, and this led to a viral growth effect, reaching over 1 million monthly active users (MAUs) within the first year.

The VIP strategy

The VIP strategy (also called the 'marquee strategy')[13] consists of attracting 'star' producers or users on the platform, who in turn attract more producers and/or users. Game console platforms often try to sign exclusive partnerships with developers to attract players with 'must-have' games only available on their console.

Tinder's successful 'hyperlocal saturation campaigns' also targeted the most popular organizations within colleges to seed the app with key influencers. Whitney Wolfe, then VP of marketing, explains: 'You need to identify social influencers in small areas, see who the influencers are, and target them . . . That's how we spread throughout college campuses and other social scenes.'[14]

In more extreme examples, some platforms sign up powerful clients who are then able to literally 'coerce' the other side into joining. A number of large corporations who use Ariba's supply management platform require suppliers to onboard Ariba's platform and answer a raft of questions before becoming an accredited supplier. The Ariba platform then uses the information provided to match the supplier with other possible work opportunities in their field across other companies.

The cultural meme

Embedding an existing cultural meme as part of the value proposition on one side can also accelerate acquisition. To grow the adoption of its peer-to-peer payment service, WeChat launched a feature called Lucky Money, later renamed Red Packets, during the Chinese New Year Holiday in 2014. Red Packets is modelled after red envelopes, a cultural tradition in China and parts of South East Asia, where a monetary gift is given during holidays such as the Chinese New Year or special occasions such as weddings, graduation ceremonies or the birth of a baby. WeChat injected lottery-like features into its digital version of red envelopes, which encouraged senders to share red envelopes with large groups of friends to win goodwill. Viral effects started to build with little acquisition costs.[15] These were further compounded by paid partnerships and advertising campaigns.[16] Red Packets has today become a new form of communication in China, with over 60 million WeChat users sending Red Packets every day.[17] *Pokémon Go*, which connects players with advertisers through augmented reality (AR) gaming, also experienced phenomenal growth at launch.[18] The app game concept is based on the original Game Boy and physical trading card game developed by Nintendo, which has inspired millions of children worldwide – now young adults – over the last 20 years. *Pokémon Go*'s growth was not sustained, but the Pokémon cultural meme has played a key role in igniting the platform.

Match

Since the platform is now live, the objective is to make sure the matching works on a small scale. Even if aspects of the matching still require manual interventions, it becomes important to start thinking about ways to automate this.

Key matching questions include:

- Is the basic matching concept working?
- What would need to be done for it to scale?
- How could the matching be improved?
- Is more data from platform participants required to improve matching relevance?
- Are matching rules improved with more participants?

Depth of results

At launch, the platform may suffer from a lack of selection/choice for both sides. As a result, the matching criteria need to be defined to maximize liquidity.

Relevance or matching quality

Relevance or matching quality is a function of matching information from both users and producers against the right set of criteria. For platforms such as product or service marketplaces, poor quality of structured information on products or services may lead to suboptimal matching. For social networks, though, it will be more about understanding users' actions so that they can be served with posts/content/ads and people they're likely to engage with.

At launch, ranking results against one criterion only may make sense until you learn more about user preferences. Stootie, the French geo-localized service marketplace initially ranked producers on their location. But as the platform grew and the choice for producers increased, Stootie started to rank on producer availability and feedback score. Producers with low feedback score were also de-prioritized from the search results. The mix of search parameters will likely evolve over time as the number of users and producers scales.

Timeliness

Many platforms try to display matching results instantly to meet participants' needs. At the ignition stage, though, matching may still be done manually for a range of platforms – say, a marketplace matching an expert consultant with a complex technical assignment.

However, when participant behaviour is well understood, timely does not always mean immediately. Carwow, the marketplace matching car buyers and dealers, discovered that conversion rates were higher when search results were not sent immediately to potential buyers, but a few hours later, as if the platform was effectively taking time to negotiate on their behalf.

Connect

At ignition, the connect function may be quite basic, but the key questions include:

*   How do platform participants really interact?
*   Is the connect function working? Is it currently a bottleneck for core transactions or is it likely to become one in the future?
*   What new interactions, communication features, rules or norms would be most relevant to deal with such bottlenecks?
*   What are the emerging patterns of communications between platform participants, and what do they reveal about customer engagement?

• Is there a need to add filters to the platform connection function (e.g. prevent email addresses from being exchanged, etc.) in order to prevent leakage or other unwanted behaviours emerging on the platform?

In its early days, the dog-sharing marketplace BorrowMyDoggy had lots of activity, but few people made the jump of transacting on the platform. BorrowMyDoggy introduced local meetups where dog owners and dog-sitters could meet locally. This new type of off-platform interaction increased trust between participants and unlocked further core transactions on the platform. Since the platform is still adding significant value to the community – in terms of access to veterinary help, insurance for both dog owners and borrowers, information sheets on different breeds, etc. – the incentives to transact off platform remain minimized.

Transact

At this stage, the main focus should be testing the proof of concept of the prototype platform. The key questions are whether or not the interactions previously identified are indeed leading to core transactions and under which conditions:

• Is the platform managing to enable core transactions between participants?
• What are the bottlenecks to successful core interactions? Which ones are on or off the platform?

Poor matching effectiveness (discussed previously) or lack of liquidity are often bottlenecks during ignition. Platform liquidity is a proxy for activity on the platform and how network effects are building. In finance, a market is said to be liquid when assets can be quickly bought or sold without their price being affected.[19] The concept applies to platforms as well since they need to ensure that transactions are as seamless as possible. For fashion marketplaces such as Depop, Vinted or notonthehighstreet, 'liquidity is the reasonable expectation of selling something you list or finding what you're looking for'.[20] For advertisers on Instagram, it will be the reasonable expectation of eyeballs from the right demographics. Defining a minimum liquidity target might be useful at this stage. For example, La Belle Asiette aims for new chefs to get their first booking within two weeks.

A freemium model can be used at launch in order to minimize friction while the platform is 'subscale.' But if participants are charged, is this creating friction or solving a commitment problem on the platform?

Building liquidity and network effects are often more important priorities than monetization at this stage. However, while the priority should be growing network effects, monetization experiments can be useful to develop organizational expertise on revenue systems and operations, and to answer monetization questions of investors in follow-up rounds. Facebook had small advertising revenues from its very beginnings. LinkedIn also started to generate revenues 18 months after launch.[21] The interplay between pricing and revenue generation is developed further in Chapter 11.

Optimize

The optimization process is quite critical during the ignition stage. In fact, the platform is likely to change quite dramatically in the early days based on participants' direct and indirect feedback. One of the unique features of platforms is that development can be shaped at least as much by participants as by platform owners. This endows the platform with some strategic flexibility that traditional businesses would only dream of, since participants can start using the platforms for a range of activities that may not have been even identified as opportunities at the outset.[22] Some key optimization questions at ignition are:

*   Are the metrics giving a good sense of bottleneck formation that prevents core transactions?
*   Is feedback from platform participants taken on board?
*   Are the key datapoints/insights needed to demonstrate traction captured?
*   Does the optimization process enable convergence towards platform fit?

In addition to the North Star metric, which was introduced in the previous chapter, several focus areas should be closely monitored during the ignition phase. They are related to achieving platform fit, creating liquidity, clearing interaction and core transaction bottlenecks and raising capital. While KPIs are likely to be industry-specific, a few generic examples are proposed in Table 8.1.

Enablers

Typically, many of the platform-enabling capabilities, from governance, trust, brand and customer experience, to infrastructure support, are in their infancy at launch. They are there to support the MVP and make sure that early traction can be demonstrated. Platform owners should be thinking about the following questions:

- What are the basic enabling capabilities needed at ignition?
- Which enabling capability is most likely to become a bottleneck in the near future and how much investment will be required to fix it?

This doesn't mean that enabling capabilities are not important, but rather that they are unlikely to be immediate bottlenecks at ignition. If early participants are tech-savvy early adopters who like the platform concept, they won't mind the imperfections and will willingly provide feedback to improve the user experience. As the number of participants is still small, the launch team should be able to be right on top of any participant issue that comes up, and update governance rules on an ongoing basis. Participants should feel

Table 8.1 Examples of performance metrics at platform ignition

Platform fit

- Engagement: % of sign-ups that search, connect, transact
- Customer feedback: particularly qualitative
- Customer retention: % of users that remain active, 'retention curves'

Clearing core interaction bottlenecks

Liquidity:
- Ratio of active users (producers) to total users (producers) and ratio of active users to active producers
- Number of active users/producers vs minimum liquidity target
- On-boarding completion rates
- Fulfilment completion rates and time (e.g. suppliers delivering goods on time), waiting times for users (e.g. Uber car waiting times)
- Utilization rate of any seeded liquidity (e.g. utilization rates of Uber drivers directly employed vs the minimum utilization to be viable)
- Ratio of nil return search queries to total search queries

Matching effectiveness:
- Ratio of searches to core transactions
- Ratio of matches to core transactions
- Quality of supplier presentation (e.g. Airbnb listings and professional photography bookings)

Metrics to raise capital

- Growth rate of active users and producers (above some defined activity level, e.g. Instagram daily active users)
- Viral coefficient and breakdown of paid vs organic viral growth
- Speed to saturation in targeted niche markets (e.g. Facebook penetration in college campuses)
- Super user segments (e.g. % of users above higher engagement level thresholds)
- Revenue proxies: metrics correlated with revenue

Source: Launchworks

comfortable interacting and transacting on the platform. Basic checks should take place, even if they are done manually at the ignition stage.

What is more important at ignition is to minimize friction for users and producers to easily join, on-board the platform, and start interacting.

Launch an add-on to an existing business

Established companies interested in harnessing the power of platforms – to become a platform-powered ecosystem – may find that they already have possible sides of platform businesses. Retailers such as Amazon or Zalando were already successful online retailers when they decided to open their business model further to merchants, stylists, designers or manufacturers. French retailer Darty had an established online and physical presence with thousands of shops before opening its online marketplace. Cloud-based team collaboration Slack built a strong user base before launching a platform and an app directory, connecting users with apps through its API.[23]

Launching a platform on the back of an existing linear business to create a 'platform-powered ecosystem' may appear easier than launching from scratch. After all, if there is an existing customer base, adding another side must be easier than launching two sides from scratch. While this may be the case, adding a platform to an existing business comes with a number of challenges, including risks of disruption, need for coordination of different business models, alignment of incentives, skills and culture. These issues are discussed further in Chapter 14.

Notes

1 www.launchworksventures.com/insights/scaling-up-a-necessity-for-platform-businesses/.
2 OpenTable was able to reach a critical mass of restaurants and diners in some cities first where it launched its platform. It still sold its online booking tools to restaurants in other markets where it was building its presence.
3 See http://venturebeat.com/2012/06/22/reddit-fake-users/.
4 There are many examples of allegations of fake profile schemes. In 2014, the Federal Trade Commission reached a settlement that prohibits JDI Dating Ltd., the British company that owns 18 dating sites, from using fake, computer-generated profiles to trick users into upgrading to paid memberships and charging these members a recurring monthly fee without their consent: www.ftc.gov/news-events/press-releases/2014/10/online-dating-service-agrees-stop-deceptive-use-fake-profiles.
5 See Chris Dixon's blog post on the topic, www.businessinsider.com/the-bowling-pin-strategy-2010-8?IR=T.
6 Facebook has in excess of 1 billion users logging in daily and monthly active users in excess of 1.7 billion at the time of writing.

7   Rishi Shah, 24 November 2010, www.gettingmoreawesome.com/2010/11/24/airbnb-leverages-craigslist-in-a-really-cool-way/.

8   Dave Gooden, 31 March 2011, http://davegooden.com/2011/05/how-airbnb-became-a-billion-dollar-company/.

9   4 May 2012, Peter Thiel's CS183: Startup – Class 9 Notes Essay, http://blakemasters.com/post/22405055017/peter-thiels-cs183-startup-class-9-notes-essay.

10 By the time PayPal was acquired by eBay, 70% of all eBay auctions accepted PayPal payments, and roughly one in four closed auction listings were transacted using the payment service. VentureBeat, 27 October 2012, http://venturebeat.com/2012/10/27/how-ebays-purchase-of-paypal-changed-silicon-valley/#8cV8y19jcBArQLfE.99.

11 G. Parker, M. Van Alstyne and S. Choudary, *Platform Revolution*, New York: W. W. Norton & Company, 2016, p. 97.

12 Bryan Hackett, 'Tinder's First Year User Growth Strategy', 3 March 2015, https://parantap.com/tinders-first-year-growth-strategy/.

13 D. Evans and R. Schmalensee, *Matchmakers: The New Economics of Multisided Platforms*, Cambridge, MA: Harvard Business School Press, 2016.

14 Bryan Hackett, 'Tinder's First Year User Growth Strategy', 3 March 2015, https://parantap.com/tinders-first-year-growth-strategy/.

15 Connie Chan, http://a16z.com/2016/07/24/money-as-message/.

16 The first prominent campaign was the Festival Gala TV show on CCTV during the annual Spring Festival. It is the largest TV show on earth, with seven times the number of viewers of the Super Bowl in the US. WeChat advertisers distributed $81 million of digital money to 36 million WeChat users.

17 Stephen Wang, WeChat senior product manager, Siyu Xiao, WeChat product manager, https://soundcloud.com/wechatpodcast/red-packets-wechats-secret-weapon-in-payments.

18 *Pokémon Go* was launched in July 2016. It is one of the most used mobile apps in 2016, having been downloaded more than 500 million times worldwide in less than two months since launch.

19 High price dispersion is often the sign of an inefficient and illiquid market.

20 Simon Rothman, 19 August 2012, https://techcrunch.com/2012/08/19/how-to-structure-a-marketplace/.

21 Matt Colher, Quora, 16 March 2016, www.quora.com/In-the-early-days-of-LinkedIn-how-much-of-a-focus-was-there-on-monetization-and-who-was-their-target-customer.

22 eBay's founder, Pierre Omidyar, was the first to be surprised when eBay's first auction revealed a buyer interested in purchasing broken laser pointers.

23 16 December 2015, Slack API, https://medium.com/slack-developer-blog/launch-platform-114754258b91#.1yrakzpuk.

Chapter 9

Platform scaling

Reaching critical mass

Congratulations, the platform has been ignited and the business concept proven. Now that you have clearly demonstrated a valid platform concept and early traction, more funding will be required to support the scaling-up phase and really take the 'rocket' into orbit. Since this growth stage can take several years and a number of funding rounds, it covers a wide range of business situations, but the key questions remain the same.

Platform fit is a prerequisite for successful scaling. Otherwise, the money spent on marketing to acquire lots of customers is unlikely to generate customer engagement and value creation. We agree with Sean Ellis, CEO of GrowthHackers, who says that 'you should survey your user base before doing growth work. At least 40% of your users should say they would be very disappointed if your service or product went away overnight'.[1] If the platform is part of an add-on to an existing business, or part of a transformation, it is also important to ensure that scaling investment is not available 'too early'. While this may sound counterintuitive, the danger for large firms keen to push their new platforms is to invest in scaling before the platform fit is achieved.

This stage is critical for the platform since it is likely to have to go through the usual 'growth pains' associated with scaling-up. This includes preserving the winning culture, introducing new scalable processes, attracting talents, looking beyond domestic boundaries, attracting significant growth investments, navigating regulatory hurdles and attracting growth capital,[2] to name a few. This critical growth phase is also a unique period of transition between the well-documented and supported start-up stage and the more traditional challenges associated with the management of large firms. There are now excellent resources[3] and tips on scaling-up that, while not always uniquely tailored to platforms, are highly relevant to inform and guide the platform owners during this important phase.

From a platform point of view, the main challenge is to grow each side to critical mass in a balanced way. The monetization question may also become important during the scaling-up stages, although in some cases this question is only relevant after a critical mass has been reached. Lastly, the existence of imitators in other countries may provide an added stimulus for some platforms to scale globally as quickly as possible.[4]

During the scaling phase, the following activities should be in focus:

- Use of marketing levers to keep growth balanced between the two sides.
- Reduce friction (improve customer experience) to increase velocity.
- Get insights into tipping point/critical mass, network value and level of network effects.
- Foster trust and safety, and scale customer service team.
- Deploy and optimize pricing model.
- Develop a distinctive brand that resonates with customers on both sides of the platform.

The key scaling questions summarized in Figure 9.1 are developed below.

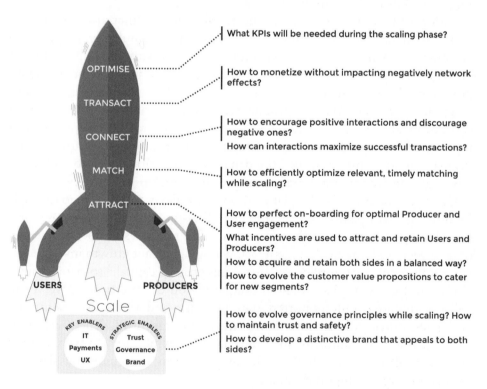

Figure 9.1 **Scaling-up the rocket to reach critical mass**

Source: Launchworks

Attract

Scaling effectively will probably require significant investment in customer acquisition not only to gain traction, but also to create a viral acquisition effect. For some platforms, often those with a social network component such as Facebook, Instagram or LinkedIn, the all-important 'viral coefficient' (also sometimes called K-factor or contagion coefficient)[5] will become critical since it will contribute significantly to the traction of the platform and the efficiency of marketing.

Perfect the on-boarding process on both sides

As more users and producers join the platform, the on-boarding process needs to be as smooth as possible for both sides. It might be acceptable to on-board producers and/or users manually at ignition to test a platform concept, but automation becomes critical prior to the scaling phase to accelerate growth and keep costs down. While many traditional businesses need to add significant resources in line with their growth (i.e. buy more raw materials, get more employees), platforms should be able to rely on significant automation of the key platform functions to scale at a minimal incremental cost.

Special attention to on-boarding can pay off not only in terms of customer acquisition numbers, but, most importantly, it can make a big difference to customer engagement and customer retention. As Facebook opened up beyond the Ivy League schools, the social network realized that the on-boarding experience for users was more than just joining the platform. Analysing cohorts of new joiners showed that users who connected to 10 friends in the first 14 days were far more engaged and were way more likely to become lifelong users. On the other hand, users making fewer friends in the first few days tended to lose interest and become inactive. This could be easily explained: no or few friends meant that customers' newsfeeds were empty, and no one would see their posts, hence limiting the number of potential interactions. So VP of growth, Alex Schultz, and his team focused on making it easy for new joiners to quickly find friends. This included collecting the most appropriate data during the on-boarding journey – such as age, school, university attended, company, etc. – so the matching function could automatically suggest the best results in terms of potential friends. Facebook found the right balance after many iterations and is now able to collect key information required to find enough relevant 'friends' quickly and without making the sign-up process too cumbersome. Alex talks about the 'magical moment' when users see their friends on Facebook. 'It is just as simple as when you see the first picture of one of your friends on Facebook, you go "Oh my God, this is what this site is about!" '.[6] Concentrating on getting that magical moment right has had a profound impact on both user retention and engagement. The on-boarding process should be designed to enable these 'magical moments'.

On-boarding can often be more complex on the producer side for two reasons. First, the platform may try to apply quality filters on the producers it accepts. For example, TaskRabbit helpers go through a screening process, including interviews, before being able to offer their services on the platform. There is a trade-off between the selectivity level of the platform towards producers and achieving critical mass as soon as possible. The dynamics between the level of openness for producers joining the platform and the joining customer experience can, however, be flexed over time as the platform scales. When Uber launched in the UK in 2012, drivers had to go through a comprehensive training before being able to register on the platform. Three years later, the on-boarding process still includes driver screening but is now much simpler and faster. The Uber 'ignite' programme offers a step-by-step process for securing the required licence and, depending on the country, get specific training, tests, medical exams, access to a car and insurance marketplace, visit of Uber offices and financial incentive to start as an Uber driver.[7] It is designed to minimize the friction and assist would-be Uber drivers with the entire process of joining the platform. It benefited from the feedback of many Uber drivers who helped identify bottlenecks on the driver recruitment side.

Second, new producers may need to familiarize themselves with tools to engage and ultimately transact on the platform. Depending on the complexity of the on-boarding process, email, phone, training or even dedicated account management resources should be allocated. The level of support should be proportionate to the effort required for producers to interact and therefore may vary across customer segments. eBay provides email support for consumer sellers registering a listing on the marketplace, a five-step process that is designed to take no more than a few minutes. For large merchants and brands, a dedicated team of account managers is on call to help with listing catalogues and integrating eBay as part of their multichannel strategy. The on-boarding process is also a unique opportunity to convey key messages about the ethos, governance principles and norms of good behaviours to new platform participants.

Acquire users and producers

There is no one-size-fits-all approach when it comes to scaling the number of producers and users to critical mass. While acquisition should be the first priority when starting the scaling process, retention should become a close second as soon as producers and users have been engaged for long enough on the platform.

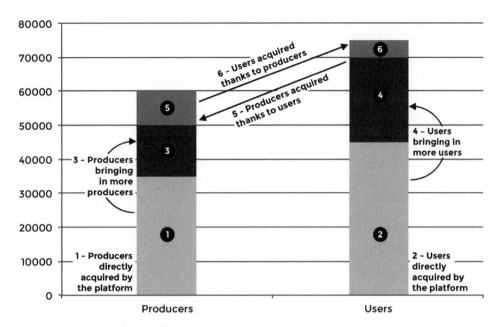

Figure 9.2 User and producer acquisition sources

Source: Adapted from T. Eisenmann, G. Parker and M. van Alstyne 'Strategies for Two-Sided Markets', *Harvard Business Review*, 84(10), October 2006

While initially designed to solve the chicken-and-egg problem, some ignition techniques that we have already discussed, such as the bowling pin strategy, can still be very useful to unlock pockets of supply and demand during scaling stages. By mapping adjacent target segments and communities, which can themselves be leveraged to win other segments, the platform may better inform the allocation of its marketing spend. Acquiring users and producers can be achieved by using resources from the platform itself but also by leveraging marketing capabilities from users and producers themselves. There are six growth dynamics at play,[8] as shown in Figure 9.2, which can all be modelled to forecast growth and funding requirements:

1 *Direct acquisition of new producers and new users by the platform.* The platform markets directly and acquires producers and users, through organic (press, SEO, email, social media, direct mail, etc.) and paid acquisition channels.
2 *Acquisition of new users through existing producers.* The producers themselves market the benefits of joining and using the platform to their customers and people in their network. This can be through word of mouth, social media or platform tools aimed at helping producers advertise. Indiegogo, Kickstarter and other crowdfunding platforms have viral invite loops enabling project owners to invite people in their network to join in and

fund their project. Eventbrite acquires new users by relying on event organizers to invite attendees to their events.

3   *Acquisition of new producers through existing users.* This is the reverse, with users themselves inviting producers to join the platform, using similar channels and/or features. We mentioned above Eventbrite's viral loop of event organizers inviting attendees to their events. After attendees buy tickets, they discover that they can also use the platform to organize their own events.

4   *Acquisition of new users through existing users.* Product features such as viral invite loops are a great way to tap into existing users' networks to acquire new users. For example, Snapchat and WhatsApp ask users to invite their friends by importing their contact books.

5   *Acquisition of new producers through existing producers.* Finally, existing producers can help acquire new ones. In addition to the techniques mentioned above, new content generated by producers can help acquire new producers and users. Knowledge platform Quora uses fresh content produced by its contributors to continually improve its search rankings. This makes Quora more visible to readers and contributors, and helps attract new readers and contributors, creating a positive feedback loop.

The above-mentioned viral loops can be very useful to maintain low acquisition costs. Instagram spent very little marketing in the first couple of years, relying instead on viral loops, brand ambassadors and great app store ratings, which all contributed to securing a top place in the app stores. Etsy also has a low cost of acquisition thanks to viral effects, with the majority of gross market sales generated from organic marketing channels (i.e. from users and sellers themselves). In 2015, 91% of Etsy's site traffic came from direct, organic and email traffic sources, with only 9% from paid traffic. The underlying strength of a large organic channel is also illustrated by Etsy's repeat purchase rate, with 81% of purchases from repeat customers in 2015.[9]

Many of the growth techniques listed above rely on several levers and not just marketing. Brian Rothenberg, VP of growth and acquisition marketing at event booking platform Eventbrite, emphasizes how growth is a cross-functional effort: 'Growth is best driven through tight alignment and coordination between marketing, product, engineering and analytics'.[10]

Retain users and producers

Once users and producers have been interacting long enough on the platform, it's time to look for those who don't come back or churn. It can be difficult to measure initially because the numbers may not be significant enough. This is especially true for transactional platforms where the frequency of interaction and transaction is low – for example, legal services platforms where a client may hire a lawyer for a one-off case. It is, however, essential to have a sense of how many users and producers are no longer engaged and why, and customer feedback is a good way to do this (Net Promoter Score[11] surveys, for example). For these reasons, retention efforts at the beginning of the scaling stage tend to focus on product and customer experience improvements, and reviews of user and producer funnels.

As the platform scales and more users and producers join, get matched, connect and transact on the platform, network effects start to kick in and the value proposition becomes richer for all participants. Such positive feedback loops may translate into more selection for users, more reviews for producers and more overall traffic, which in turn attract more users and producers.

A review of the value proposition might be useful at this stage to understand what users and producers value most in the platform, and what features/ attributes are currently missing. Tools and services can make a significant contribution to producer engagement. Beyond traffic, Amazon Marketplace offers bulk listing, editing and management tools to enable merchants to list and update listings as efficiently as possible. Sometimes important aspects of the value proposition are outside of the direct control of the platform. For example, Deliveroo, the food delivery platform, discovered that many of its drivers were joining while learning English before trying to become Uber drivers. This became an unexpected part of Deliveroo's value proposition to its drivers.

Aiming for 'balance'

Keeping the platform 'balanced' is critical to successful scaling. This requires keeping tabs on the ratio of active producers to users in order to understand where the sweet spot is, and when one side starts to become a bottleneck for growth.

Once a bottleneck has been identified – say, not enough producers – the platform needs to take action to get back into its 'sweet spot' ratio that maximizes good interactions and transactions on the platform.

This sounds simple, but many platforms are not homogeneous, meaning they have to manage different equilibria across different product/service categories, at different points in time and in different geographies. In fact, international platforms are often better represented as portfolios of platform positions, each characterized by a given level of maturity and equilibrium in a given country at a given point in time.

In some cases, platforms develop a 'centralized' or 'regional' function whose goal it is to overcome the bottlenecks that appear during the scaling–up phase. BlaBlaCar has a dedicated team focused on launching and scaling in international markets. No less than 60 people from headquarters were allocated to the project team who launched BlaBlaCar in India.[12] eBay Europe set up a centralized, dedicated team focused on optimizing search and stimulating seller growth in countries and categories where buyer demand was strongest – and sellers were becoming a bottleneck. Through targeted seller acquisition and coaching, eBay was able to nudge its platform in the right direction by improving both the quality and depth of its inventory, as well as search relevance for buyers.

In our experience working with high-growth platforms, modelling the growth of both user and producer communities is not straightforward, but can provide valuable insights into how the balance between the two sides is likely to shift over time. It also provides essential visibility on funding requirements until the platform becomes profitable.

Developing value propositions for new customer segments

While the core offering to users and producers is unlikely to have dramatically changed since ignition, the needs of early customers may evolve over time, while new types of customers may also join the platform. As a result, the value propositions will require changes to meet new and existing customer needs.

For example, while eBay started as a C2C auction marketplace, many of its most successful consumer sellers, who initially started selling as a hobby on eBay, became professional sellers with carefully managed inventories and sometimes full-time staff to deal with the logistics. As buyers also expressed the need to be able to buy new items immediately at a fixed price in many categories (fashion, electronics, home & garden, etc.), eBay saw an opportunity to update its value proposition. It gave its increasingly professional sellers the tools to list and sell in bulk new items at a fixed price. The Powerseller programme, launched in 2005, offered fee discounts proportional to sales volume, and resulted in the number of business sellers, their associated inventory and sales scaling dramatically. By 2010, the majority of items sold on eBay were offered by professional sellers. Today, eBay manages three distinct seller segments: merchants, entrepreneurs and consumers. eBay offers each of the three segments a distinct value proposition that meets their different motivations and needs. Each segment brings a different kind of inventory (unique, long tail and affordable inventory from consumer sellers and entrepreneurs, as well as popular new products from merchants), as illustrated in Table 9.1.

Table 9.1 Illustrative value proposition for a scaling product marketplace

	Merchants	Entrepreneur sellers	Consumer seller
Motivation	• Pragmatic, rational, profit driven • Sales strategy: multichannel • Motivation: *What can I do to get the most out of the marketplace?*	• Highly engaged, passionate • Sales strategy: mostly mono-channel • Motivation: *What can the market-place do more to help me?*	• Active buyers ('think' buyer) • Sales strategy: mono-channel • Motivation: *I want a secure and easy way to sell stuff for a great price*
Key needs	• Sales velocity • Profitability • Reliability/predictability	• Sales velocity • Make money • Support from the community and marketplace • Safety	• Reliable way to sell an item • Easy to list/sell and ship • Make some money (often to fund buying activity)
What each segment brings to the table	• Scalability offers growth potential • High concentration • 90% new inventory • Offer trusted, e-commerce-like experience	• Bring unique long tail inventory in fashion and collectibles • Offer unique, personable e-commerce experience	• Extremely active buyers • Provides wide range of unique inventory: 50% of used items, C2C auction inventory provides best value vs competition • Selling drives engagement and loyalty/word of mouth

Source: Launchworks

At the end of the scaling phase, it is common for platforms to cater for the needs of several consumer and producer segments. A C2C, B2C and B2B[13] skill set is often required to understand the motivations of these diverse customer segments, and how to best attract them.

Match

At this stage of development, the matching function can quickly become a real bottleneck if it does not efficiently match users with relevant producers.

Balance of supply and demand

Close monitoring of matching results allows the platform to identify pockets of missing supply (or demand) in particular verticals, locations, times of day, etc., depending on the nature of the business. This information should be fed back to the team members looking after attract and optimize activities in order to improve the targeting and recruitment of platform participants and unlock pockets of transactions. Hyperlocal marketplaces – which often require a geographically located critical mass to fully benefit from network effects – need to closely monitor the spatial distribution of their recruitment. As more producers join the platform and supply increases, the depth of the results can be controlled through the introduction of search filters. They can be search engine driven – for geo-localized services, only local producers can be shown by default – or can be user-configurable – especially when users express the need to search for a particular location or type of service/product.

Relevant and timely results

While scaling platforms often benefit from a long tail inventory generating unmatched levels of choice in selected categories, the key to maximizing transactions is to ensure that this selection is displayed in the most meaningful way to the users and that the most relevant results are listed first.

At this stage of development, the matching rules should have now been captured and automated as part of a matching algorithm. As soon as there are enough participants and interactions on the platform for meaningful A/B tests, the search or matching team can start to run experiments. Many things can be tested iteratively, from the blend of criteria used in the matching algorithm to how search results should be displayed, in order to improve relevance and ultimately conversion.

Lastly, matching results must be timely. This is often a technology design issue, and many platforms need to re-engineer their original code in order to cope with the level of activity generated at scale. BlaBlaCar started to grow rapidly in 2012, and by January 2013 the number of rides booked on the platform had hit 50 million.[14] The in-house search engine became a bottleneck. It was not scalable enough to consistently return search results in less than 200 milliseconds, and could not support more complex queries and new features beyond a basic geographical search. BlaBlaCar completely redesigned and migrated its search engine in 2013 with limited customer disruption and has been scaling aggressively ever since.

The secrets of matching algorithms

At ignition, the volume of transactions is still small so changes to the matching algorithm criteria are unlikely to have much impact on producers. However, as the platform scales, some of its producers become larger and more dependent on it. A change to the matching algorithm may have a profound impact on search results rankings and therefore producers' revenues. Platform managers need to provide enough transparency and notice for the producers to success-fully adapt to the new changes. On the other hand, providing too much detailed information on the inner workings of the platform's matching engine may encourage some producers to game the system. Platform managers need to communicate the changes in a way that will truly encourage positive interactions on the platform. We'll come back to managing this delicate balance for mature platforms in Chapter 10.

Connect

As we have seen, facilitating positive interactions – and preventing negative ones – between participants on the platform is a way to enhance positive net-work effects.

Using eBay as an illustrative example in Table 9.2, mapping the core inter-actions between the different sides of a platform can be a valuable scaling tool to identify inefficiencies, governance or trust issues that may not have surfaced during the ignition phase.

As eBay scaled to categories with fixed-priced, high-volume and low-margin items, a review of interactions between eBay sellers and buyers revealed new inefficiencies. Being able to ask questions to sellers prior to purchase made sense in categories with unique, high-value inventory such as cars and collectables. However, high-volume, low-margin items also generated a high level of questions, often making the sales process inefficient for merchants. eBay subsequently introduced new features such as product listing FAQs and product catalogues to reduce most buyers' generic queries.

Table 9.2 Mapping interactions between participants – eBay illustration

Interactions between	Buyer	Seller	eBay
Buyer	eBay forum discussions	Pre-sale questions	Customer support requests
	Community support	After-sale communications	Report seller's bad behaviour
		Seller ratings and reviews	
Seller	Answers to pre-sale questions	eBay forum discussions	Customer support requests
	After-sale communications	Community support	Report seller or buyer's bad behaviour
	Buyer feedback	Off-site meetings	
eBay	Buyer customer support	Seller customer support	N/A
	Conflict resolution	Conflict resolution	

Source: Launchworks

Transact

Enabling transactions is the *raison d'être* of platforms, so the scaling phase must ensure that transactions occur as smoothly as possible.

Since the platform is now fully operational, it is often useful to use transaction metrics in marketing and communication briefs as social proof to further increase trust. In some cases, the platform enables 'ultimate' transactions, such as weddings for dating sites. eHarmony reports being responsible for more than 2 million marriages.

The scaling phase is often the phase when monetization needs to be introduced to ensure that the platform generates enough revenues going forward.[15] The various pricing levers available in the context of monetization, and their respective strengths and weaknesses, are discussed in Chapter 11 on pricing.

Optimize

The optimization function should focus on the development of metrics that can help monitor and adjust the growth trajectory of the platform. During the scaling-up phase, the platform needs to maximize its viral impact and ensure it is focused on the needs of the marginal user so that growth continues.

The optimization function should monitor individual building blocks of the rocket model and look for bottlenecks. It should also develop a more holistic view of its ecosystem and its alignment with the platform itself. Some of the key questions at this stage are:

- Is the platform growing in a way that maximizes positive network effects?
- Are both sides of the platform growing in a balanced way?
- How much capital is required to support growth over the next few months? (See Chapter 8 on ignition for a list of metrics.)

A few generic metric examples are given in Table 9.3. Note that the 'North Star', introduced in Chapter 7, should ideally continue to act as the overarching growth metric for the business.[16]

Table 9.3 Examples of performance metrics at platform scaling

Attracting participants

- Growth rate of interactions
- Growth rate of active users and producers
- Cohort analysis of growth, % of interactions from 'new' users
- ' New/marginal' user feedback
- Viral coefficient, breakdown of paid vs organic viral growth
- Retention curves, frequency/number of interactions per user

Liquidity and balance

- Number of/ratio of active producers/users above some activity threshold (e.g. Upwork sets targets for the number of workers per posting)
- Liquidity failures (i.e. opening Uber app and finding no cars)
- Growth in listings per supplier
- % of listings that receive no interaction (e.g. eBay listings with no bids)
- Value received by each platform side to determine balance (i.e. pricing, marketing and feature development)

Matching/connection effectiveness

- Interactions: impressions, purchases per week, sales conversion rate
- Consumer side: time to book, listings viewed before booking, average time to choose listing, average number of clicks/searches for each booking, first page search result connections
- Producer side: % of listings with no views/matches
- Connect: ratio causation analysis of connections driving interactions. Frequency of connections (e.g. connections on WeChat monitored to understand user/producer relationships)

Trust, customer experience

- Ratio of reviews to core transactions
- Ratio of positive to negative reviews
- Average ratings
- Ratio of complaints or fraud to core transactions
- % of disputes successfully resolved
- % of transactions preceded by review viewings
- Net Promoter Score (NPS)

Source: Launchworks

Beyond the platform dashboard that will be focused on key functions, the platform will need to develop modelling and forecasting capabilities. This will be particularly important during the scaling phase to be able to understand the impact of growth on funding requirements and infrastructure needs.

Enablers

The supporting capabilities and infrastructure of the platform need to be able to grow and evolve to support the scaling process.

In many cases, the customer service team balloons in size to support platform operations at scale. As the customer experience keeps being optimized to remove friction, the ratio of the number of complaints over the number of new participants should ideally decrease. That is to say the platforms should have relatively less negative interactions as it scales. It's important to establish a feedback loop between the product and customer support teams for customer feedback to be embedded back into the value proposition.

The platform's brand may also need to morph into a more mainstream, and often more international, proposition. Finally, as the communities now constituting the platform are shaping its success and offering unparalleled feedback, their contributions need to be reflected in the brand attributes of the scaling platform. We will discuss some of these trust and brand aspects in Chapter 12.

Notes

1 First Round article, 'Answers to Your Tough Questions About Growth – Learned While Scaling Eventbrite's $5B+ Growth Engine', http://firstround.com/review/answers-to-your-tough-questions-about-growth-learned-while-scaling-eventbrites-5b-growth-engine/?ct=t(How_Does_Your_Leadership_Team_Rate_12_3_2015).

2 See, for example, the scale-up report, Sherry Coutu *et al.*, November 2014, www.scaleupreport.org/, for a well-documented articulation of the scale-up challenges.

3 Reid Hoffman is now teaching his own version of fast scaling strategies at Stanford: 'Blitzscaling', http://techcrunch.com/2015/09/14/reid-hoffman-to-teach-blitzscaling-at-stanford-this-fall/.

4 Rocket Internet is a VC firm well known for launching and selling copycat business models in markets when the leading player is not yet established. See, for example, 'Rocket Internet: What It's Like to Work at a Startup Clone Factory', http://thehustle.co/rocket-internet-oliver-samwer.

5 The K-factor simply represents the number of new customers an existing customer brings to the platform on average. It is often driven by social media promotions and online acknowledgement of your platform. If i is the number of invites sent by your existing platform participants and c the percentage of conversion to your platform, then $K = i \times c$.

6   Alex Schultz, http://startupclass.samaltman.com/courses/lec06/.

7   See, for example, Uber ignite programme in the UK: www.driveuberuki.com/private-hire-booking/.

8   See, T. Eisenmann, G. Parker and M. van Alstyne, 'Strategies for Two-Sided Markets', *Harvard Business Review*, 84(10), October 2006.

9   Distribution of visitor traffic to Etsy from 2011 to 2015, by channel and Etsy's repeat and first-time purchase sales 2011–2015, Statista.

10 First Round, Brian Rothenberg interview, http://firstround.com/review/answers-to-your-tough-questions-about-growth-learned-while-scaling-eventbrites-5b-growth-engine/?ct=t(How_Does_Your_Leadership_Team_Rate_12_3_2015).

11 Net Promoter Scores (NPSs) are computed using the following question: Using a 0–10 scale: How likely is it that you would recommend [COMPANY] to a friend or colleague? Respondents are grouped as promoters (score 9–10), passives (score 7–8) or detractors (score 0–6). Subtracting the percentage of detractors from the percentage of promoters yields the Net Promoter Score, which can range from a low of −100 (if every customer is a detractor) to a high of 100 (if every customer is a promoter). See www.netpromoter.com for more information.

12 Conversation with Frédéric Mazzella, 14 January 2016.

13 C2C: consumer to consumer; B2C: business to consumer; B2B: business to business.

14 'How Elasticsearch Was Deployed at BlaBlaCar', 19 June 2013, www.slideshare.net/sinfomicien/presentation-elastic-searchfeedback.

15 In some cases, this question is only relevant after a critical mass has been reached.

16 Unless, of course, the platform has pivoted since then and a new North Star metric is more appropriate for the new business.

Chapter 10

Platform maturity
Defending profitable growth

Once critical mass is reached, the energy required to sustain platform growth is proportionally smaller than the energy required at ignition due to network effects. With an established market position, barriers to entry are likely to be high for new entrants. However, competitive threats will come from numerous fronts and will need to be dealt with appropriately. Scale also comes with drawbacks. It may take longer to adjust to new market dynamics and make changes to the value proposition – at least without alienating existing platform participants. Product/market fit was a prerequisite for successful ignition and scaling, and remains essential for all subsequent growth phases. Like a rocket, the platform has some velocity and momentum, but its trajectory is now more difficult to change. If the platform is really successful, it is also likely to attract the attention of competition authorities.

As the platform matures and continues to grow (see Figure 9.2 in the previous chapter), focus is usually given to the following activities:

- Respond to competitive threats.
- Increase engagement, repeat visits, stickiness and retention.
- Enhance feature set for both producers and users.
- Extract value by lowering acquisition costs and monetizing platform services.
- Scale trust and customer service teams.
- Consolidate brand.

In this chapter, we first review aspects of defensive growth with the rocket model framework (Figure 10.1), as well as managing change in a mature platform environment. We then discuss the strategic management of mature platforms.

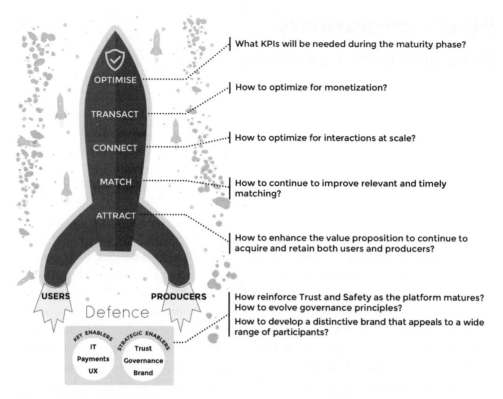

Figure 10.1 **Defending platform position and growing profitably**
Source: Launchworks

The rocket model for platform maturity

Attract

Retention is key

While acquisition is the main focus of the platform during the scaling phase, retention and engagement maximization become increasingly important as the platform matures. Acquisition remains key to the growth of the platform, but its established market position makes it much easier to attract new customers, at least until its market is saturated.

Innovation

Enhancing the platform's value proposition with new features/tools to meet platform participants' needs is an important lever for retention and to keep engagement levels high. To avoid the threat of new entrants, the platform needs to keep learning from its customers. Alibaba's proposition to merchants, 'to help small businesses grow by solving their problems',[1] has kept expanding from its basic marketplace features to an extended range of services, including analytics tools showing data trends to assist sellers' decision-making, logistical services and financing solutions. To help hosts set a price for their listings, Airbnb offers a free smart pricing tool, which automatically adjusts daily price listings based on a minimum and maximum price range and willingness to host.[2] Price listing adjustments are based on supply and demand, and the listing's features, location, amenities, booking history and availability.

Monitoring the success of platform participants is a good way to gain insights into what works on the platform and how to further enhance the value proposition for all users. Which users and producers could become more valuable with better support, tools or advice from the platform?

In some cases, platform participants themselves develop new functionalities that are so successful that they should in fact become part of the platform. In such cases, the platform needs to consider carefully how to secure strategic control of these features. When a new application on an app store becomes a 'must-have' app, the platform owner has a strong incentive to either duplicate or acquire it. If it fails to do so, the platform will be at the mercy of platform participants with a strong bargaining power and an increased ability to monetize their offering. In some extreme cases, these new great features may even end up being controlled by a competitor whose objectives are not aligned with the interest of the platform (and may want to degrade, rather than enhance, the features of an app, for example). At the same time, the platform ideally needs to ensure that it remains fair to its ecosystem participants and does not 'expropriate' them on a whim. Of course, platforms can play games but it may undermine the trust of participants. For example, Spotify, the music streaming service with over 30 million paying subscribers – twice as many as Apple Music has – recently claimed that Apple was intentionally making it difficult to update its iPhone app and was holding back new features.[3]

Paying a fair price in the context of an acquisition or giving fair warning that a feature is so strategic[4] that it will be replicated by the platform within a given timescale are two ways of ensuring that strategic control is gained without alienating platform participants. SAP gives developers visibility of its roadmap over an 18–24 month period so that they build new products without the risk of competing with SAP – for at least two years. SAP also has a policy of partnering with developers to help them financially or buy them out at a fair price.[5]

Personalization

Managing the balance between simplicity and new features is key to strengthening the platform's overall market position. One way to achieve this is through contextualization and personalization. By only showing features/choices that may be relevant for a given customer at a given moment in time, platforms can leverage their feature-rich architecture without complicating the user experience. Many Facebook features are only made visible when particular events are triggered (e.g. the option to post an album just after a user takes a series of photos).

Match

The same logic applies to marketplaces' long tail inventories. Being able to personalize a search result allows platforms to leverage their wide selection without confusing buyers with too much choice. This has allowed Alibaba to push the concept of the long tail to the limit with in excess of a billion products listed. To make the most of this unique inventory, the same search engine powers a number of consumer marketplaces owned by the group, such as Tmall and Taobao. This means that a search on one consumer site can also return search results across all other Alibaba consumer sites. This guarantees customers complete inventory discovery and access to the long tail across all marketplaces. For example, a search on Taobao for the latest Burberry tote bag may come back with few results on Taobao, but with a relevant selection on Tmall. The mix of search results displayed across marketplaces is decided at group level, based on priorities, relevance, supply gaps and merchant performance.

Optimize matching at mass scale

Search optimization should continue to be a priority, with iterative improvements of the search algorithm relying on A/B testing. Because the algorithm rules are rarely perfect, the best way to validate improvements to the matching algorithm is often to combine A/B testing with qualitative human feedback. Hugh Williams,[6] who used to run search at eBay, said:

> One of the most important ways we understand if we've improved our search engine is by asking people what they think. We do this at a large-scale: we've asked human judges questions about our search results over two million times in the past year.

This process of collecting human observations about the relevance of search results is also used by Facebook to improve what people should see first in their newsfeed.[7] It started as a feed quality panel experiment in 2014, asking people to provide detailed feedback on what they saw in their newsfeeds, which posts they liked and why, and what posts they would have liked to see instead. This qualitative human feedback exposed blind spots that data scientists, who work on improving the newsfeed algorithm, could not identify with machine learning. Facebook now runs feed quality panels across the US and international markets, and combines both quantitative and qualitative approaches to optimize its newsfeed algorithm.

Search innovation

Search is an area that is constantly evolving. In the past, the matching function relied mostly on algorithms that followed a set of rules written by software engineers. But artificial intelligence is starting to redefine how search works. Search neural networks can learn from analysing large amounts of data and build their own rules to match users and producers better and faster. RankBrain, Google's deep neural network, which helps generate responses to search queries, now handles about 15% of Google's daily search queries.[8] All major platforms, from Facebook to Microsoft, have invested in deep learning, with Amazon even having released deep learning open-source software for search and product recommendations.[9] Search technology, increasingly powered by deep neural networks, is evolving fast beyond text and geo-localized data to include voice and images. No doubt the integration of new technology such as messaging bots (automated search) and augmented reality (visual search) will redefine existing platforms' user search experience.

Connect

What defines positive interactions may change over time so it's worth revisiting these definitions on a regular basis. Mature platforms can also leverage their communities to increase the quality and quantity of relevant content available on the platform. To drive higher customer engagement, Taobao's mobile app offers new social commerce features to meet the evolving needs of how people shop. Taobao hosts over 1,000 quanzi (circles) where shopping enthusiasts talk about their hobbies and favourite products. Taobao also hosts crowdsourced Q&As. When a buyer submits a question, Taobao's algorithms identify buyers who are best qualified to answer and send them a message. 25% of all questions are answered within one minute and 60% of questions within 10 minutes.[10] Two million buyers help answer 1 million questions every day.

Transact

Maximizing the number of core transactions should remain a key objective through improvements to the customer experience to reduce friction during and after the transaction. The services added to enhance the transaction experience – from loan products to users, conflict resolution support, insurances, etc. – should be well integrated to the existing customer experience.

Now that the platform has reached critical mass and that network effects are in full swing, the platform can optimize how much of the excess value delivered to customers can be captured during the core transaction. This may translate into more refined pricing structures and levels. The key things to watch out for at this stage are disintermediation and leakage. For example, Upwork changed its pricing structure in June 2016 to reduce leakage from its most profitable freelancers. Based on their choice of payment method, clients now either pay a processing fee of 2.75% when paying by credit cards, or no processing fee if they choose a low cost payment method like an Automated Clearing House (ACH). This change enabled Upwork to rebalance their pricing and charge a fee inversely proportional to total billings, as shown in Table 10.1.[11]

Table 10.1 Upwork's new sliding fee structure

Fees paid by	Before	After
Clients	• No fees	Choice of payment options • 2.75% per transaction (if the client pays by credit card) • 0% (if using a low cost payment method like an Automated Clearing House)
Freelancers	• 10% service fee	Sliding service fee per client • 20% for first $500 billed • 10% for billings greater than $500 and smaller than $10,000 • 5% for billings greater or equal to $10,000

Platforms also need to ensure that revenues do not encourage negative network effects. A number of marketplaces have allowed sellers to purchase increased listing visibility. So-called 'promoted listings', although not always clearly labelled as such to buyers, typically appear at the top of the search result page. While this generates sizeable revenues for the marketplace, this feature also potentially weakens the relevance of items shown to buyers, which in turn impacts the number of purchases, as well as positive network effects. Many marketplaces, including eBay, eventually chose to remove this 'bad revenue' to preserve the platform. While in some cases the lost revenues in the short term were significant – and not always offset by increased sales – the long-term health of the platform ecosystem was deemed to be more important.

In order to allocate resources efficiently, mature platforms need to understand the relative price responses of platform participants on both sides of the market they serve. For example, credit card companies need to understand the extent to which lowering the price they charge to merchants (merchant fee) will result in increased coverage (more merchants will join the card network). This, in turn, needs to be contrasted against the impact of a resulting increase in card fees on users' propensity to get and use their cards.

Optimize

By now, the platform should have developed strong analytical capabilities and the challenge is the opposite of the one faced during the ignition phase. There

Table 10.2 Examples of performance metrics at platform maturity

New markets and ongoing growth

- Product/geographic market coverage (e.g. Airbnb: cities served as % of total universe)
- Growth of users switching sides
- Effectiveness of notifications for prompting transactions
- % of existing users total business (e.g. How much are users multihoming? How much do producers sell through other channels?)
- Disintermediation metrics (e.g. measures of repeat business between the same user and producer)

Search/match optimization

- Proactive and predictive search/match analytics
- Individual customization of offers, marketing, etc.

Monetization/profitability

- Revenue/profit per core transaction, customer lifetime value
- Customer acquisition costs
- Organic vs paid growth (e.g. Etsy tracks merchandise volumes from paid vs organic to understand profitability)
- Ancillary revenue growth (e.g. from premium services such as enhanced curation, premium listings, insights products)

Metrics for customer success

- Metrics to assist users/producers optimize their contribution (e.g. eBay improved pricing by providing metrics such as number of items that failed to receive a bid, those bought with buy now button, and the duration and outcome of auctions)
- % of transactions preceded by review viewings
- Net Promoter Score (NPS)

Innovation

- Understanding how users are creating new value on the platform
- Developer activity, high-growth user-created apps
- Growth in new transaction categories

Source: Launchworks

is so much data available that identifying which key metrics are really relevant for sustainable and profitable growth requires focus and discipline. We recommend continuing to develop the strategic ecosystem dashboard, including profitability and monetization metrics, as well as operational dashboards for both user and producer sides, focusing on detailed success metrics.

Financial metrics will become increasingly important, as the platform's ability to monetize becomes the critical issue for its sustainability. Finally, the self-marketing and innovation potential of the community will now outstrip that of the platform business, and so it will be critical to empower and measure the community's performance in these areas. A few examples of metrics at platform maturity are shown in Table 10.2.

Enablers

Customer experience

Improving and simplifying the experience of platform participants on both sides may not be as straightforward now that many users and producers are familiar with the platform services. But perfecting the customer experience for all participants should remain a goal.

Managing change

Traditional companies make management decisions about the development of their value proposition – such as price changes, new product introductions, new features, etc. – unilaterally and sometimes adjust them if customers do not respond well. Platforms are different. They have to take into account the impact of changes on different sides of their platforms. Some changes can be perceived as positive for one side, but not the other. They could also be positive for both, or negative for both. A mature platform will need to carefully consider the interests of its stakeholders, including producers and users, as well as employees and partners, as changes to its rules may have far-reaching consequences for its participants. A new pricing model or matching algorithm may fundamentally impact the economics of a wide range of platform participants.

Mature platforms therefore need to track the changes in their roadmap and understand which side(s) will be impacted and how. If many changes are planned at the same time – which is often the case when a new release is prepared – it is important to understand their cumulative effects and try to ensure that the overall balance of the platform is not undermined.

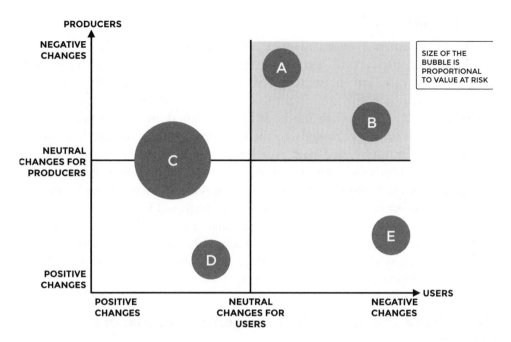

Figure 10.2 **Assessing platform changes on users and producers**
Source: Launchworks

Figure 10.2 illustrates some changes that are negative for both producers and users[12] (A and B), some important changes that are neutral for producers and very positives for users (C), as well as small changes that are slightly positive for users and very positive for producers (D) and very negative for users but positive for producers (E). The size of the 'bubble' can illustrate the value at risk for stakeholders.

Processes need to be put in place in order to both assess and mitigate the impact of changes. Advanced notice should be given and reactions carefully monitored. Ideally, a rollback plan should be available in case something goes wrong. A large platform considering changes that are both difficult to rollback and have a significant customer impact need to invest significant time and resources in ensuring these are successful, and/or develop mitigating strategies that will reduce the customer impact. Mandating free postage for media products (CDs, DVDs) generated a revolt from eBay sellers,[13] although it was a buyer need that Amazon and other competing e-commerce websites had already met. eBay had to roll the policy back, but interestingly sellers didn't revert to charging postage fees, and arguably the entire eBay ecosystem benefited as a result.

Trust and safety

The set of governance, trust and safety rules encouraging positive interactions and limiting negative ones evolve organically during scaling, as more and more new use cases are encountered. Some of these rules are embedded into automated scripts, while community or customer service managers enforce others manually. Often both methods are combined and employees act on filtered content or events brought to their attention by algorithms. After years of scaling, the resulting rules and policies defining the difference between a positive interaction vs a negative one are often so complex that they become a challenge for the customer service team to apply efficiently. A restructuring and simplification of rules and policies is often required for mature platforms. Mature marketplaces often need to rationalize and simplify their trust and safety policies. Beyond the customer benefits, this simplification of rules is often combined with increased autonomy given to first line service advisors in order to reduce customer service costs.

Optimizing the strategic management of mature platforms

One of the important long-term aspects of the optimization function is the development of a sustainable market position over time. This goes beyond metrics used to manage the actual business, but includes the analysis of internal data and market trends to identify new opportunities, seize them either directly or through partnership, and embed them into the organization. In this section, we discuss some of the strategic challenges that mature platforms may encounter and possible courses of action.

Platforms typically face three types of competitive pressures: internal ones, external ones from other platforms, and external ones from traditional players.

Competition from 'within' the ecosystem

Once mature, a platform may give rise to very successful producers who may end up having significant negotiating power and influence over the entire ecosystem. In some situations, these companies may even be in a position to establish rival platforms and take significant business away. In such cases, the platform may want to follow an envelopment strategy[14] to secure strategic control of such 'must-have' complements.

Microsoft followed such an approach when it realized that RealPlayer was becoming an important streaming app with the potential to become a platform in its own right. Microsoft famously added its Media Player to Windows to replace RealPlayer (and subsequently added the Explorer browser to replace

Netscape). While this strategy can be a very effective attack (or defence), it may also attract the wrath of the competition authorities since it involves bundling and may lead to foreclosure. If used too often, it may also deter complements from investing in the platform (and result in less apps developed for your app store, less inventory in your marketplace, etc.).

In some other cases, the complement service being developed ends up being acquired by the 'complemented' platform. For example PayPal managed to attract lots of eBay sellers (and buyers) onto its own platform, which led to its acquisition by eBay. By the same token, YouTube ended up becoming a search platform for video in its own right and this led to its acquisition by Google.

In some cases, however, the acquisition or imitation of the complement is not required. When faced with the formidable success of some of its game producers (such as Zynga when it launched the game *Farmville*), Facebook thought about its options. While buying Zynga was a possibility, the price was already high and the risks associated with follow-up games deemed significant – despite incredible early successes. Facebook decided instead to manage more closely the gaming category of its app store in order to ensure that barriers to launching apps were minimal and that whoever ended up providing the best entertainment would succeed on the platform. Other providers launched equally successful games and Facebook didn't have to face too strong a producer in follow-up negotiations.

Competition from other platforms

As we have seen, platforms increasingly compete against one another, and this gives rise to some new strategic challenges. It is useful to review some of the strategic moves that competing platforms may be considering:

- Side differentiation: Other platforms in the same space may decide to focus on the needs of the side that is 'the least looked after' by the established platform. For example, new platform entrants in the taxi market may focus more on the needs of drivers (Hailo, Juno) than Uber, which arguably was more focused on its clients.
- Challengers' mergers: Established platforms are also exposed to the merger of smaller followers, which may result in a challenger suddenly with critical mass. This may drive the acquisition of smaller competitors.
- Niche/vertical focus: Niche players may try to cherry-pick the most profitable segments that are big enough to support a critical mass on their own (e.g. fashion marketplaces such as Farfetch, Videdressing, Vestiaire Collective and Vinted compete against eBay's fashion vertical).

- Subsidized cost competitors: Platforms may copy your basic functionality but seek alternative monetization methods in order to offer low transaction costs to address the price-sensitive segments of the market. Classified sites such as Gumtree, leboncoin or OfferUp have been challenging incumbent marketplaces.
- 'Me too' imitators: Some firms may try to replicate your business model in other geographies before you can establish a footprint. You may then have to acquire them, decide not to enter in these international markets, or invest more to catch up at a later stage. Companies such as Rocket Internet are famous for such strategies.
- Creating barriers to growth: Some competitors prevent access to new markets. Tencent has repeatedly blocked the Uber app on WeChat in 2015,[15] with a ban in December 2015 days after Tencent-backed Didi Chuxing announced a global partnership with Lyft, GrabTaxi and Ola.[16] Competitive pressure was too hard for Uber, and it led Uber China to merge with Didi.[17]

Mature platforms have a range of strategic options available to deal with increased competitive pressures, but we'll focus here on two generic responses: (i) creating a platform-powered ecosystem; (ii) adding sides to their existing business models.

Creating a platform-powered ecosystem

Successful mature platforms often end up developing adjacent activities with traditional business models in order to strengthen their ecosystem. The same is true for businesses that started as linear ones (e.g. Amazon started as a digital book retailer) and then added platform elements. As we have seen in Chapter 6, the most successful platforms seem to have developed complementary activities and combined business models in ways that enhanced their value propositions. Microsoft did not shy away from entering the hardware business with its surface tablet to compete against Apple's platform ecosystem, Google is investing in fibre to reduce its dependence on telecommunications operators, Facebook and Microsoft are laying transatlantic cables for the same reason, and Alibaba ended up developing one of the largest delivery infrastructures in the world (Cainiao)[18] to deliver to any city in China in 24 hours.[19] Facebook has also realized that the next bottleneck for connecting everybody on the planet to its services is . . . Internet access. That's why it set up Internet.org[20] to provide broadband connectivity using high-altitude aircraft and satellites to the 4.5 billion people not currently connected to the Internet. All these moves result in the development of a platform-powered ecosystem where the various business models constituting the entire ecosystem are more or less integrated.[21]

Opening another or multiple sides

Opening another side is likely to require significant funding and resources, but it may provide multiple benefits from value proposition improvements, superior monetization opportunities, accelerated growth and/or stronger competitive position against new entrants and existing firms. In 2015, Etsy opened Etsy Manufacturing in the US first to match Etsy sellers with small manufacturers. In another bid to help its sellers expand their businesses, Etsy also launched Etsy Wholesale,[22] a service that allows independent retailers to buy items wholesale from Etsy sellers to sell in their bricks-and-mortar stores.

Many of the pre-launch and launch principles discussed in Chapters 7 and 8 still apply. There are, however, additional concerns to address, the main one being how network effects will change. Will opening a third side potentially strengthen positive network effects (e.g. Facebook opening to developers) or weaken them (e.g. opening to advertisers)? A negative impact on the customer experience may impact positive network effects, and this could weaken all sides as a result. When Instagram opened to businesses with its Ads API in 2015, great care was taken for ads to be as unobtrusive as possible. The 'swipe to view' posts require the user to swipe left or right on an image to see any additional content or calls to action.[23] Key to success also requires Instagram's matching algorithm and content mix to be aligned.

Opening of a new side might also impact the delicate balance between existing sides. UberEATS, the on-demand meal delivery service powered by Uber, allows users to order from local restaurants and get delivered through Uber's network of drivers and riders. Ordering a ride or a meal are different experiences, which impact logistics. Drivers cannot arrive late at the restaurant or the food might be served cold. Peak times for food delivery are also different. This will have an impact on driver supply and incentives, which Uber has solved by managing two distinct driver bases.[24] With UberEATS's launch, and its most recent UberRUSH, an online delivery service to merchants, Uber is not only competing head to head with Seamless, Postmates, Delivery.com, Deliveroo and Amazon, but also strengthening its foothold in the on-demand transport market.

Competition from traditional players outside

Established platforms have often been able to redefine the reference offer in a given market and to establish a more effective and efficient platform powered business model. Yet, traditional companies that have been outmanoeuvred can also fight back.

Established companies may decide to launch their own platforms to counter any perceived threat to their businesses. Merchants in the US have tried to set up payment alternatives to Visa and Mastercard in order to reduce their influence. For traditional players, the temptation to respond to platform disruption without fundamentally changing existing capabilities, processes and mental models often makes successful execution difficult. We discuss how traditional firms compete against platforms in Chapter 14.

Notes

1 Alibaba founder Jack Ma's open letter to the company's investors after Alibaba's IPO, September 2014.
2 Airbnb's smart pricing was launched in November 2015. There are other pricing tools on the market, such as Beyond Pricing, which charge 1% of booking earnings.
3 Peter Kafka, Recode, 30 June 2016, www.recode.net/2016/6/30/12067578/spotify-apple-app-store-rejection.
4 Platforms providing a new core features roadmap over the next 18–24 months, such as SAP, come to mind.
5 G. Parker, M. Van Alstyne and S. Choudary, *Platform Revolution*, New York: W. W. Norton & Company, 2016, pp. 174–5.
6 Hugh Williams, 'Measuring Search Relevance', eBay Tech Blog, 10 November 2010, www.ebaytechblog.com/2010/11/10/measuring-search-relevance/.
7 Will Oremus, *Slate*, 3 January 2016, www.slate.com/articles/technology/cover_story/2016/01/how_facebook_s_news_feed_algorithm_works.html.
8 Cade Metz, 'AI Is Transforming Google Search. The Rest of the Web Is Next', *Wired*, 4 February 2016, www.wired.com/2016/02/ai-is-changing-the-technology-behind-google-searches/.
9 Klint Finley, 'Amazon's Giving Away the AI Behind Its Product Recommendations', *Wired*, 16 May 2016, www.wired.com/2016/05/amazons-giving-away-ai-behind-product-recommendations/.
10 See Alibaba.com, 26 July 2016, www.alibabagroup.com/en/ir/article?news=p160726.
11 In the old pricing (where the fee was entirely paid by the freelancer), the client had no incentive to switch to a low cost payment method and often had reasons not to, e.g. because credit cards offer points and float. Conversely in the old pricing, the freelancers were always paying for the cost of payment, i.e. they were burdened with a cost that only the client could change. The idea was to charge clients for this because they can make the decision to pay by credit card despite the 2.75% fee, if they see value in doing this, or else to switch to a low cost payment method. This rebalancing enabled reducing Upwork fees to 5% for cumulative billings over $10K for a given client.
12 Of course, changes that have a negative impact on both sides would need to be justified on the basis that they benefit the platform even more than they hurt its participants. For example, this could be the case if the platform needs additional income to reinvest in new services, or wants to reposition its proposition and is prepared to 'cull' some of its existing producers and users as a result.
13 The policy was rolled out in 2009 in the UK and Germany.
14 T. Eisenmann, G. Parker and M. Van Alstyne, *Platform Envelopment*, Harvard Business School Working Paper, 2010.

15 http://venturebeat.com/2015/12/06/uber-is-still-blocked-on-wechat-in-china-and-the-situation-is-getting-worse/

16 http://venturebeat.com/2015/12/03/lyft-adds-grabtaxi-and-ola-to-its-faction-of-allies-against-uber/.

17 www.wsj.com/articles/china-s-didi-chuxing-to-acquire-rival-uber-s-chinese-operations-1470024403.

18 Cainiao was formed by a consortium of existing logistics companies to give the project a running start. Alibaba itself took a 48% stake.

19 See https://techcrunch.com/2016/03/14/alibaba-backed-logistics-firm-cainiao-lands-funding-at-a-reported-7-7b-valuation/.

20 Internet.org is a partnership between Facebook and six companies (Samsung, Ericsson, MediaTek, Opera Software, Nokia and Qualcomm). In February 2016, regulators banned its Free Basics service in India based on 'Prohibition of Discriminatory Tariffs for Data Services Regulations'.

21 Benjamin Gomes-Casseres, 15 June 2016, *Harvard Business Review*, https://hbr.org/2016/06/is-the-linkedin-acquisition-microsofts-attempt-to-build-its-own-alphabet.

22 See https://techcrunch.com/2015/09/14/etsy-opens-to-manufacturing/.

23 At the time of writing, there are no page takeover ads, no advertising video content forced viewing, and no autoplay of videos from paid posts yet.

24 See www.wired.com/2016/03/ubereats-standalone-app-launches-us/. Drivers can choose to switch between modes freely, by logging into and out of the app.

Chapter 11

Platform pricing

Pricing in traditional businesses

How much are we going to charge for our product or service? This is a fundamental question that most firms have to address early on if they want to generate revenue. For traditional businesses, pricing can be set in a number of ways. A simple approach is to set the price of a product or service on a 'cost plus' basis in order to ensure that a margin is generated on every sale. In such a model, all the relevant costs are captured before a mark-up is applied to the total. Many retail stores and small businesses use such an approach as their basic pricing strategy.

More advanced pricing methods allow firms to differentiate their pricing based on the 'willingness to pay' of various customer segments (or price elasticity, as discussed in Chapter 4). Being able to 'price discriminate', that is to say to set a price that is different from one customer group to another, often allows firms to increase revenues. This is because the propensity of one customer to pay can be higher than that of another. For example, if there is a unique market price for a product (say \$10 for a game), then customers that would have been prepared to pay more (say \$15) end up paying the lower market price and the difference (\$5 in this case) is not captured by the seller. Price discrimination can be created at the customer level with unique prices (e.g. bespoke price for a given contract), at the segment level with prices for certain customer groups (e.g. student discounts) or even at the product level where slightly different versions of the product are priced very differently and marketed at different customer groups (e.g. economy vs business class airfares). Such approaches need to be adapted depending on the market environment, the propensity of clients to compare price information, and regulatory constraints, among other things.

Because many firms compete on price in many sectors, price benchmarking is often a key input to the pricing strategy of the firm. If all your competitors

– that is to say firms offering substitute products or services – are pricing a given product between X and Y, then this is a powerful source of information for your own pricing.

So while much more sophisticated pricing approaches do exist (e.g. airline dynamic pricing, etc.), it is fair to say that most traditional businesses typically use a mixture of cost-plus, value-based and competitive benchmarked pricing approaches in the context of their pricing strategy. This pricing strategy process can end up being quite complicated for traditional businesses, yet it is often much simpler than pricing for platform businesses.

Unique challenges of platform pricing

While platform-powered businesses must consider all of the above, they also need to deal with unique features linked to their business models, including:

1   their customers create value for each other when using the platform due to *network effects*;
2   pricing on one side of the platform often impacts the other side of the platform due to *cross-elasticity of demand across the platform*;
3   a *critical mass of customers* may be required to make the platform valuable to other customers; and
4   *pricing in platforms truly shapes the behaviours of platform participants* and therefore needs to be set to enhance the overall value proposition.

It is important to reflect on how different platforms are from traditional businesses in terms of pricing decisions. Pricing strategies for platforms need to not only capture some of the value created – to generate revenue for the platform owner – but also to enhance the platform's overall value proposition. This is achieved by using pricing as a lever to encourage positive interactions on the platform – and incidentally discourage bad interactions. Given that any change in price will have both direct effects for those paying and indirect effects for other platform participants, platform pricing can only be approached holistically. For example, a decision to increase the price for sellers may lead to a reduction in inventory, which may result in less choice for buyers who may then be tempted to leave, which in turn may make the platform less attractive to sellers (or even advertisers, in the case of a three-sided platform). Pricing decisions therefore need to consider these – positive and negative – feedback loops. Lastly, platform pricing decisions stack up, that is to say a pricing decision made in the past (say, free transactions) may have attracted producers on the platform that will remain there even if the price changes again.

To develop a suitable pricing strategy, it is important to consider the distinct characteristics of the platform itself along with the following pricing design questions:

- *What is the pricing governance framework?* (e.g. are the end prices set by the platform owner or by the platform participants?).
- *Which pricing model to follow?* (e.g. charging platform users, advertising model, freemium/selling of value-added services).
- *Who to charge?* (e.g. all users, one side, third parties, specific customer sub-segments on each platform side).
- *Which pricing structures to use?* (e.g. one-off joining fees, annual membership fees, transaction fees – fixed amounts or proportional to transaction value – donations, as well as discounts and rewards).

The answers to these questions lie in the type of platform and ecosystem that need to be developed, and the extent to which pricing is a strategic enabler and lever for the platform to succeed. In this context, it is important to keep in mind that since the interactions and behaviours of a critical mass of customers are the key to platform value creation, pricing strategies need to support these objectives first and foremost. Generating revenue will (almost) always be the ultimate goal, but successful pricing architecture will also contribute to addressing broader questions, such as:

- How do platforms ensure that 'end user pricing' is efficient and creates a good customer experience for 'users' (even if producers are the ones setting the price)?
- How can platforms both support rapid user growth and generate revenues with minimum friction to maximize network effects?
- How can platforms use pricing to ensure the communities are balanced in terms of supply and demand?
- How do platforms maximize the quality of customer interactions and experiences?
- How can platforms use pricing models that minimize the risk of 'disinter-mediation' and 'leakages' (i.e. transactions moving 'off-platform')?
- How to best transition from one pricing model to another (in particular, transition from free to a paying model)?

We'll review these questions in turn. Let's start by looking at key pricing governance questions.

How to ensure 'producers' pricing creates a good customer experience for 'users'

A platform architect must consider not only the impact of the platform's own pricing strategies on interactions, but also the impact of producers' pricing structures. Two key aspects to consider are the nature of the good/service and the differentiation strategy of the platform.

Nature of the good/service

It is often argued that simple, standardized, low-cost and high-frequency services benefit from standardized pricing across all producers. This is to make the customer buying experience efficient and reassuringly predictable, while also giving suppliers greater certainty around revenues. For example, Uber does not ask each driver to set prices but standardizes its pricing, based on supply and demand conditions, to ensure a consistent experience for users.

Conversely, where the goods and services on the platform are more differentiated and consumers are more price-sensitive, it may be preferable to allow producers to signal quality and compete by setting their own price. In addition, if the platform supports a large portfolio of different goods/service categories, it may be impractical for the platform to set prices.

Platform strategy

Strategic platform design choices also need to be considered. In particular, the overall differentiation strategy of the platform and the customers it is targeting.

For many of the platforms that standardize producer pricing, there are often competing platforms offering greater pricing flexibility. The competing platform may seek to provide superior pricing innovation or competition among producers, greater flexibility for producers to differentiate their product/level of service, or improved customization and negotiation options for users. It is therefore important to ensure that the level of control over producer pricing is aligned with the overall strategy of the platform, not just the nature of its products. For example, eBay had to introduce its 'Buy It Now' option in order to compete with other platforms and e-commerce sites offering a fixed price, while also keeping its auction model to allow more price-sensitive customers a chance to secure lower prices.

Implications of open or controlled pricing governance

Where producers' prices are highly standardized, the platform architect must consider tools to help balance supply in the platform (for example, Uber's 'surge pricing' approach to demand management). Users can, however, see these dynamic pricing tools in a very negative light. As a result, platforms should ensure that users see the link between the premium price and the service while retaining control over their purchase (for example, while Uber will increase its prices during a 'surge', users can wait or upgrade/downgrade ride categories – moving between 'uber pool', 'uber X', 'uber XL' and 'EXEC' – to avoid paying a premium). It is also important to show that the surge price is not 'made up', but represents the required incentive for the platform to be able to attract producers at this particular time. In that context, behavioural economists at Uber have established that users were more likely to accept at 2.1× price multiplier (which sounds 'computed' by the platform) rather than a 2× price multiplier (which sounds 'made up').[1]

Where pricing governance is relatively open, information and rating tools take on added importance. For example, to ensure that a producer's lower prices are not being achieved through a misrepresentation of product or service quality. This can be illustrated by the importance of eBay's multi-criteria rating system in influencing purchaser behaviour vs the Uber rating system, which probably has a lesser impact on which Uber driver you use. It is also worth noting that a platform-controlled end user pricing regime may raise some regulatory concerns, which we discuss in Chapter 13.

How to support rapid user growth by avoiding 'pricing friction'

This is one of the key questions that platforms need to address, since there is often a perceived trade-off between charging for services (and running the risk of never reaching a critical mass) and offering core platform services for free (and running the risk of not generating sufficient revenues to finance the platform itself).

A range of pricing models is usually considered, each with unique strengths and weaknesses. We review the main ones below and the extent to which they may support the strategic objectives of the platform.

Not charging for services

Due to network effects, platform businesses want to encourage membership growth and maximize the number of valuable interactions occurring on their platform. The more users and the more active they are on the platform, the better. In that context, monetizing customers' participation can be difficult because charging for access or use may introduce friction and hamper the positive growth dynamics. In fact, a number of platforms decided that they would try to reach critical mass first and monetize later. Such a strategy minimizes friction, and may have some economic rationale since the value of the platform with critical mass is much higher than before, but financing that growth requires deep pockets. Once a critical mass is reached, the platform may be able to justify introducing a fee or monetize its interactions by bringing on board other participants, such as advertisers.

Not charging temporarily for services (trial period)

Another traditional method of attracting users with minimal friction while monetizing afterwards is the simple 'free trial' model, although platform users may decide not to invest too much time in joining and participating in the platform if they believe they will end up having to pay for the privilege. This can be mitigated if the trial period is long enough (WhatsApp used to offer one year of free service), but even then it may still create a barrier to adoption (WhatsApp made its app free in January 2016 and introduced some degree of advertising instead).

Charging others for financing free platform services

Monetization needs not be seen as mutually exclusive with exponential growth. In fact, pricing can also be designed in a way that strengthens – rather than weakens – the effects of positive network effects. It is possible to monetize a platform by opening it to another side (for example, like Facebook did with advertisers) rather than to charge existing platform participants. Such a model may be used to scale with minimum friction in order to reach a critical mass of participants. Advertising can still act as a 'cost' on users (e.g. a type of 'friction') by detracting from the user experience. Therefore, these free, advertising sponsored models are not necessarily the panacea, and the relevance of the ads served is key to minimizing the negative effects of this source of financing.

Charging a subset of platform participants using 'premium' services

Another way to minimize friction is to only charge a small set of customers for advanced features while offering basic access for free. These so-called freemium models are, however, highly dependent upon the balance between free features and premium ones. If the platform withholds too many features in order to incentivize premium membership, it may see its growth stall. That's why the design of both free and premium value propositions require careful thinking about the trade-off between the free features (usually conducive to scaling) and the take-up of the premium version (usually conducive to revenues). While a difficult balance to strike, this model has been used by a number of fast-growing platforms such as SoundCloud. Platforms such as LinkedIn, now owned by Microsoft, also have a freemium model that is targeted at various segments of users. For example, jobseekers can join the premium subscription model in order to have increased visibility of job offers, while established professionals can join a premium networking option where they will be able to see the identity of the people who viewed their profile.

It is worth noting that a number of classified websites also use some form of price discrimination, depending on whether or not you are a business user and/or which section you want to place your adverts in. Gumtree, owned by eBay, offers free posts to private individuals in most second-hand goods sections, while businesses have to pay. In some sections of the site, such as property, all posters have to pay. In some cases, more visibility can be gained within a category ('featured ad') for a small fee as well.

Charging only when a transaction occurs on the platform

Transaction fee models have been used to encourage participants to join platforms as they are only charged when the participants receive some significant value from the platform (e.g. eBay charges transaction fees to sellers when items are sold). This approach works best when the platform seeks to offer a wide selection of 'inventory' with minimal friction. It may, however, increase 'search costs' for users if the platform is then inundated with low-quality listings. This search cost can be reduced through enhanced matching, searching and curation activities by the platform (to make sure most relevant results are displayed first).

Charging a membership fee irrespective of transactions on the platform

Where platforms seek reliable participants who will conduct a high volume of interactions, they may charge joining or membership fees. This can help with 'liquidity' on the platform as there is an incentive to use it frequently once membership has been paid. This is the case at Artfire, a marketplace for handmade products, which offers a monthly fee in exchange for a reduced transaction fee of 3% (instead of 9% for non-members).[2] Ruby Lane, an antique marketplace, also uses membership fees rather than transaction fees.

In addition, some platforms have used joining fees on the merchant side to fund a strong referral program (e.g. Alibaba). This method can drive growth when the joining fees are relatively small compared to the potential savings on transactions.

Charging a listing fee

In some cases, platforms decide to charge for listing a product or service. Such a fee is quite common, and well-known platforms – such as Amazon and eBay – use them. These fees generate revenue, but they also allow the platforms to use the friction generated (e.g. payment of the listing fee) as a filter in order to enhance the quality of its listing inventory. In some cases, the listing fee is deployed for specific categories of listings where the bottleneck is not the supply, but the 'quality of supply'. It is, however, rare to find platforms that *only* charge a listing fee. Listing fees are generally used in combination with other charging mechanisms. In the case of classified sites such as leboncoin in France, listings are often free but visibility can be enhanced by paying extra. These sites, however, tend to generate the bulk of their revenues through advertising.

Charging for a number of different things

The above-mentioned pricing models are not mutually exclusive, and many mature platforms have combined several pricing levers to achieve their objectives. eBay charges both listing fees and transaction fees to deal with inventory quality concerns while minimizing friction. Some platforms have a membership fee and a transaction fee (e.g. Artfire) to both encourage recurrent purchases and get some volume-related revenues. The interplay between the various pricing levers needs to be carefully considered by the platform owner as it represents an opportunity to balance supply and demand, as discussed below.

How to balance supply and demand on the platform through pricing?

Why balance is important

Balancing supply and demand ensures that both sides benefit from sufficient cross-network effects. A marketplace seller who receives few bids will be concerned that they're not achieving the best price. Likewise, a marketplace buyer who finds goods that are constantly sold out will be frustrated. Since the two sides of the platform are interdependent, price signals on one side will have an impact on the value of the platform for the other side (for example, the introduction of a listing fee may reduce the inventory of a platform and undermine buyers' ability to find what they are looking for). Platform balancing is therefore key to maximizing the number of relevant transactions and ensuring that the platform can find an equilibrium in matching supply and demand.

Imbalance can occur for a number of reasons. Often it's easier to sign up members on one side of the platform than the other(s) because the benefit of transactions is higher for one side. Sometimes the ancillary and time costs of joining a platform make one set of customers more likely to align with a single platform while members on the other side join many different platforms (e.g. they 'multihome'). This is important since one side ends up with fewer options than the other side. In gaming, many households decide to commit to a single platform (be it an Xbox, PlayStation or Nintendo), while few developers commit to a single platform (or if they do, they ask for additional fees for exclusive games).

Pricing strategies to achieve balance

Platform pricing should seek to balance the value received by participants in a way that optimizes the cross-platform network effects. This is generally done by setting higher prices for the side that receives the most value from the transaction (for example, if men are finding it more difficult to find girlfriends than the opposite, then they may be willing to pay more to join a dating platform). One side of the platform may be provided free (or even be sponsored if women get a free drink). This occurs if the value of their involvement and the elasticity of their demand are high enough that cross-subsidizing their participation becomes worthwhile (e.g. the cost of attracting women on the platform is more than made up by the revenues generated by men joining the platform). Nightclubs didn't wait for economists to realize that they could effectively sometimes operate on a platform model and make more money by offering free drinks and free entry to women . . . while men have to pay a hefty sum to get in and buy drinks.[3]

Early-stage platforms may be eager to offer a free service to all customers in order to scale quickly. They may, however, grow faster – and in a more balanced way – by charging one side and investing in extra services and incentives for the customers that provide the most value to the network or where there is a significant gap in the network.

Conversely, some platforms' business models may rely so much on scale that pricing either side of the platform (e.g. producers and consumers, or women and men in our previous example) may be difficult unless extra value is created. In addition, just because one side gains significant value from the platform does not mean that value can be readily captured (for example, if a platform competes on the basis of its exhaustive selection, having sellers leave as a result of a price increase would undermine the promise at the heart of its value proposition). In these cases, revenue may need to be generated from complementary value-added services (see below).

Many platforms use a range of charging techniques in order to balance supply and demand. By selecting the right pricing models, platforms are able to deal with different objectives and priorities at the cost of some increased complexity. Etsy charges a small listing fee as well as a reasonable transaction fee (3.5%), while eBay only charges its US customers for listing after 50 listings per month but takes a 10% transaction fee in most categories. The mix of fees applied by platforms tends to be dynamic and changes over time and across geographies. Table 11.1 illustrates the various fees applied by a number of marketplaces in the US.

While comparing the US pricing policies of a number of platforms to illustrate supply and demand management, we note that the same platform may be at different stages of development (and face different competitors) in different geographic markets. This means that many platforms will need to adapt their

Table 11.1 Seller fee examples

	Listing fee	Final value fee	Membership	Fees if no sale	Total sale fees	Amount seller keeps
Bonanza	–	$1.05	–	–	$1.05	$28.95
Etsy	$0.20	$1.05	–	$0.20	$1.25	$28.75
Ruby Lane	$0.19	–	$69 per month	$1.35	$1.54	$28.46
eBay	$0.30	$3.00	–	$0.30	$3.30	$26.70
Amazon	$0.99	$4.50	–	$0.99	$5.49	$24.51

Note: Fees have been calculated for an item selling at $30. The seller has sold 50 other items in the month.
Etsy: Basic fees for selling on Etsy (no pattern site).
Ruby Lane: There is a $100 one-time setup fee, inclusive of free listings for the first 10 items. The monthly maintenance fee of $69 is for the first 80 items, with a corresponding charge per item in excess of 80 listings.
eBay: Basic fees for auction style and fixed priced listing. Insertion fees are free for the first 50 listings per month, $0.30 thereafter.
Amazon: Individual seller pricing, with 15% final value fee (most categories).

Source: Bonanza, Etsy, Ruby Lane, eBay and Amazon websites, Launchworks analysis, September 2016

pricing strategy to their local market environment – to ensure sides are balanced – ideally while staying within an overall global pricing framework.

How to enhance the quality of customer interactions and experiences

Sophisticated pricing strategies can enhance the overall value proposition of the platform by improving the quality of customer interactions, without adding too much friction. For example, by helping to solve a commitment or signalling problem between platform participants (e.g. if payment is made on the platform, it shows parties are committed and price is final). This is the approach that car-sharing start-up BlaBlaCar adopted with great success, by introducing upfront online prepayment of rides, after having tried a number of other models. The number of drivers not showing up for pickups was significantly reduced (from about 35% down to 3%!) almost overnight. BlaBlaCar was simultaneously able to monetize its service and capture real data about ride-sharing. This critical enabler, to help arbitrate potential disputes, was not possible when the financial transaction happened off-platform.

Platforms can also use such pricing strategies to differentiate their customer community vs other platforms based on the 'average value' of users. Apple promotes its users as higher-value customers to app developers, and Amex its cardholders as high-value diners to restaurants.

The monetization of value-added features of the platform can also enhance the quality of platform interactions when they help participants improve their offering. For example, offering (and charging for) data insights and service-enhancement tools can help platform participants improve the marketing and quality of their product offering on the platform.

Ensuring that the additional services monetized on the platform are having a positive impact on the overall customer experience is critical for a successful value-added pricing strategy. Some platforms have damaged trust in their communities by, for example, allowing sellers to buy their way to the top of listings. While evidence suggests that some well-known platforms have been able to recover from those pricing mistakes, it is always important for the platform owner to consider the impact of pricing on the platform as a whole, as opposed to just the segment being charged.

How to avoid disintermediation

Leakage is a risk for many platforms. Customers make initial contact using the platform but then form an ongoing transactional relationship outside of the platform. This makes it difficult for the platform to capture and share the value created by these interactions. Many platforms suffer from some level of leakage,[4] so it needs to be managed carefully, especially if the value capture is done at the transaction stage. This is why some platforms have tried different pricing for first and subsequent transactions between participants. TaskRabbit, a service platform, takes 30% on the first transaction with a producer, and 15% subsequently. Other service platforms, such as Thumbtack, simply monetize the lead/introduction to avoid leakage when participants connect.

The more direct the connection between participants, the greater the risk of disintermediation. Transactions requiring face-to-face meetings, for example, may lead to off-platform transactions, while anonymous mediated communication is likely to be more conducive to on-platform transactions.

Pricing structures such as one-off joining fees can negate this risk, but they may conflict too heavily with the goals of rapid growth and frictionless pricing. In these cases, a strategy of monetizing value-added and complementary products and services may be appropriate.

The key is to understand the most valuable additional services provided by the platform, in addition to searching/matching, and offer them as stand-alone products. For example, additional services could include insurance, reference checking, dispute and remediation services, simple safe payment systems and emergency on-demand services (e.g. a nanny platform may offer and monetize fully accredited and endorsed emergency nannies in addition to providing a free 'regular' nanny marketplace).

How to transition from one pricing model to another

A common platform strategy is to offer services for free and then seek to introduce new pricing structures once a critical mass of customers is reached. Many successful or promising platforms have failed in part because they managed this transition poorly (e.g. Myspace). While platform managers may not want to charge fees early on, they should have a coherent transition strategy in mind from the beginning.

Pricing transitions are particularly challenging for platforms because:

- cross-platform network effects can compound any negative impacts from the price change;
- platforms are often moving from a 'price of zero', which is the most difficult pricing transition to make; and
- customers may invest significant time into a platform community and may view the initial pricing as a type of 'social contract' promising a long-term return on their investment.

Of course, these challenges also provide opportunities. Positive network effects will amplify the benefits of effective price changes (e.g. improvements in average user 'quality'). Finally, users' investment of time into the platform makes them 'stickier' customers who are prepared to pay so as not to lose that investment.

While the lessons on these transitions are still being learned, some patterns are emerging:

- Customers can be highly sensitive to unexpected price changes (especially when free platforms start charging). For example, Meetup lost 95% of its listings after introducing fees (although this was not necessarily detrimental).[5] Customers may only invest time into a platform community because they expect the current fee structures to continue. Clarity on whether a platform's initial pricing is an 'introductory offer' or a long-term strategy is important to ensure that user growth and the monetization model are sustainable.
- Where new fees are introduced, the platform should seek to provide new value to its customers as well. This will help balance out the 'long-term equation' for the customer and avoid the feeling that they've been 'duped'.
- Offering highly relevant but optional fee-based services can enhance the value of the platform and provide revenue without upsetting the 'social contract' linked to the core interaction.
- Platform switching costs must be understood clearly, specifically how much investment users have made in the platform. Does this investment provide permanent value or must additional time/energy be spent to maintain it? And are users multihoming?
- Pricing transitions can be focused on one side of the platform or one customer segment at a time to avoid large shocks to the platform. For example, Facebook has placed constraints on commercial pages to assist its paid advertising business, but personal users remain free from direct fees.

In general, it is risky to unexpectedly alter the pricing or scope of the core interaction of a platform. Only platforms with extremely high value compared to competitors are able to suddenly change the price of the core interaction with limited impact, and even then they may choose to limit the change to specific customer segments. It is, however, possible for a platform to pivot and change its business model by starting to charge, especially once it reaches critical mass. The new resulting equilibrium can however be significantly different from the previous one (e.g. Meetup).

Transitional pricing strategies can be designed to leverage the core value proposition of the platform and build complementary businesses. Such approaches also open the door to the monetization of the wider platform-powered ecosystem. For example, LinkedIn introduced a number of premium subscriptions giving access to enhanced functionalities for people with specific requirements (e.g. looking for a job, keen to be able to reach out beyond their direct network, etc.), but still doesn't charge 80% of its users for its basic services.

Conclusion

Platform pricing has unique challenges. Many platform pioneers who have learned through trial and error have provided us with useful insights into the effects of various pricing models. This has allowed us to identify patterns and infer high-level pricing principles for new platform businesses. When poorly designed, pricing may stifle positive network effects and slow growth. However, the right pricing strategy can generate tremendous value while supporting the strategic objectives of the platform. BlaBlaCar is an excellent illustration of the growth that can be unlocked once the right platform pricing model is found. Platform pricing can sometimes be more an art than a science, and experimentations to test high-level hypotheses remain key. As illustrated in Table 11.2, it is important for pricing levels and structure to support the objectives of the platform at a given point in time.

Table 11.2 Matching platform objectives with pricing levers and examples

Objective	Possible levers and examples
Rapidly grow platform membership	Freemium (SoundCloud) Transaction fees (Airbnb)
Encourage members to transact frequently	Membership fees with unlimited use (Match.com) Subscription for reduced fees (Ruby Lane)
Balance growth on each side of the platform	Credit card rewards (Amex issuing) Surge pricing (Uber)
Generate revenue for profit and cross-subsidization	Credit card merchant fee premium (Amex acquirer) Value-added features for reduced fees (OpenTable)
Embed loyalty and discourage disintermediation	Discounts for ongoing use (TaskRabbit) Lead generation fee only (Thumbtack)
Differentiate/attract the most valuable customers	Ecosystem strategy (iPhone premium customers drive App Store spending)
Improve inventory quality	Listing fees (SpareRoom) Super seller discounts (eBay top-rated sellers)

Source: Launchworks

Notes

1 See http://qz.com/687231/people-are-more-likely-to-take-uber-at-2-1x-surge-pricing-than-2x/.

2 See www.artfire.com/ext/sell/join_now for terms and conditions. Also, we note that the membership fee gives access to added 'premium' services, such as higher caps on number of listings or enhanced tools to sell on the marketplace.

3 Interestingly, such a pricing approach has been banned on the basis of gender discrimination in a number of US states. The California Supreme Court, for example, ruled that it violated California's Unruh Civil Rights Act. See, for example, *Angelucci v. Century Supper Club* (2007). Attempts to circumvent the law by having 'free drinks for people wearing skirts' have apparently been tried as a result.

4 Typical examples include platforms introducing cleaning ladies to clients or even some product categories sold on marketplaces such as eBay where some sellers clearly try to get the connection with the buyer before selling the full service direct. This may explain why some firms are selling single planks of wood in the 'wood flooring' section as opposed to square metres . . .

5 See G. Parker, M. Van Alstyne and S. Choudary, *Platform Revolution*, New York: W. W. Norton & Company, 2016, Chapter 6, for a discussion on how price increases at Meetup actually strengthened the platform.

Chapter 12

Trust, governance and brand

Why trust matters

> Trust is the glue of life. It's the most essential ingredient in effective
> communication. It's the foundational principle that holds all relationships.
>
> Stephen Covey

What made people suddenly comfortable with the idea of sharing their flats with strangers (Airbnb), buying second-hand goods from people on the other side of the planet (eBay) or renting their cars while they are away (Turo)?

The answer is *trust*. Understanding how platforms have been able to build trust between participants of their ecosystem is key to understanding their success. Unlike traditional businesses – where trust must be established between the firm and its customers – platforms need a more holistic approach where trust has to be built between the platform and its participants as well as between the participants themselves. You not only need to trust the Airbnb brand, but also the person you are going to rent your flat to. Without a sufficient level of trust, perceived risks may outweigh the possible financial gains of using the platform. In fact, one of the key issues for platforms is that the producer has more information about what is being exchanged, sold or traded than the users. Using the example of cars, famous economic Nobel Prize winner George Akerlof wrote a very insightful paper titled 'The Market for Lemons'. In it, he explains that if some sellers are selling cars in working order while others are selling broken cars (so-called 'lemons', presumably because they leave a bitter taste in the mouth of buyers) and that buyers have no way of knowing which is which, then the price of all the cars will converge towards the price of the worst possible car. Without a well-thought-out trust framework and relevant information exchange between participants, a platform offering second-hand cars would therefore simply fail.[1]

So how do platforms build trust?

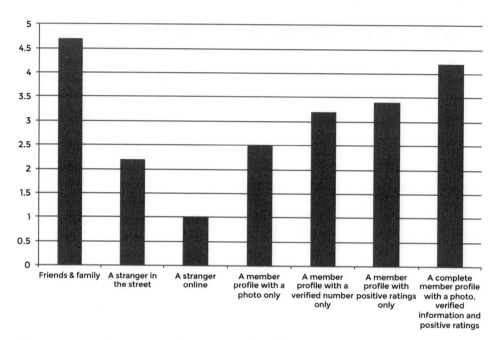

Figure 12.1 **Trust survey: responses to the question, 'On a scale of 0–5, how much do you trust . . . ?'**

Source: BlaBlaCar, Chronos

A fascinating study commissioned by BlaBlaCar[2] gives us some insights into the new unique tools available to platforms to help build enough trust for people to be comfortable transacting. In this study, the participants are asked to which extent they trust friends and family, strangers in the street, and a number of different online profiles.

As expected (see Figure 12.1), close friends and family are the most trusted (4.7/5), while online strangers are the least trusted (1/5). What is fascinating is the extent to which adding a picture and having a validated identity, as well as positive reviews on a platform, can make a total stranger almost as trusted as a family member (4.2/5). BlaBlaCar and NYU Stern Professor Arun Sundararajan also carried out an extensive study in 2016 over 18,000 BlaBlaCar members in 11 European countries. It validated earlier survey results across all countries, showing the universality of new online trust tools.[3]

The ability to create a trusted online profile is a very recent phenomenon that is partly linked to the ubiquitous availability of social networks and the unique ability for platforms to collect and display relevant data that increase trust between participants.[4]

Establishing trust between participants is therefore one of the foundational pillars of platforms and critical to their successful scaling. But as trust expert

Rachel Botsman explains, before participants trust each other, they need to trust the idea. It can be a challenge when this idea is new, couch-surfing for example. Then they need to trust the platform.[5] For someone to list their car on Turo, they need to know they're insured in case something bad happens. Finally, participants need to trust each other. While this applies to all platforms, the required threshold of trust for transactions to occur will vary depending on the type of transaction enabled by the platform. Marketplaces enabling simple transactions such as product purchases will need a basic level of trust between buyers and sellers. But the minimum trust threshold required also depends upon the type of platform. Service platforms with high-stakes transactions, such as Sittercity.com, which matches babysitters with parents, or medical sites, such as Doctolib, that match you with health practitioners, will require a high trust threshold. More mundane services, and more standardized lower-value items, typically have a lower trust threshold.

The building blocks of trust

First, it is important to understand the nature of trust. Trust is not a static concept, but grows over time as a result of accumulated experiences and interactions with the platform. Trust requires constant nurturing. It works like the reservoir shown in Figure 12.2: actions that build trust accumulate, but trust can be also be eroded. Finally, trust is more effectively built by repeatedly demonstrating, rather than asserting, one's strengths and values.

But what are the actions that can build trust, and what can erode it?

To answer these questions, it is useful to have an overall trust framework in place to identify, at least directionally, trust-enhancing and trust-eroding inter-

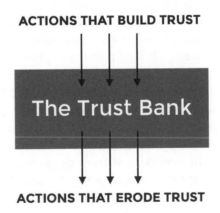

Figure 12.2 The trust bank

Source: Adapted from Hitendra Wadhwa, *Driving Strategic Impact*, Columbia Business School Teaching Material

actions. The trust framework can be used as a high-level guide to assess platform governance principles to ensure that new rules do not drain the trust bank.

Some academics have tried to unpack the key underlying drivers of trust to derive a simple formula for a trust quotient.[6]

The formula for the trust quotient is: $\quad TQ = \dfrac{C + R + I}{S}$

With the following definitions for the fundamental building blocks:

- Credibility (C), or the perceived capabilities of a person or an organization.
- Reliability (R), or how consistently experiences of kept promises have been repeated.
- Intimacy (I), or how enjoyable to interact with.
- The inverse of self-orientation ($1/S$). It can also be described as benevolence, empathy and the ability to hold the other party's interest over one's own.

The formula states that the sum of credibility, reliability and intimacy are key positive drivers of trust and that the effect of these three building blocks is magnified when combined with high empathy or, conversely, diminished when exhibited by a 'selfish' individual or organization.

This generic trust formula is said to be applicable to a range of situations, from professional relationships to social interactions.

We know that trust can be enhanced or eroded based on experiences and interactions, so platforms need to design a user experience that encourages interactions and activities that enable trust rather than limit it.

Many surveys and studies show the type of behaviours that are conducive to trust and those that undermine it. A World Economic Forum survey on trust in 2014 showed that the characteristics or behaviours most damaging to people's trust were when people were: 'not doing what they say' (45% of respondents), 'self-interested' (28%), 'secretive' (11%) and 'arrogant' (8%). A platform could look at the interactions it enables and seek to develop governance principles to ensure that the above issues are addressed. For example, when BlaBlaCar introduced its online pre-payment feature, as described in the previous chapter, it started to monetize its ride-sharing platform, but more importantly it solved a key trust issue that had been undermining the growth of the platform. When the service was free, the cost of not showing up for a ride (either to pick up or to be picked up) was very low. Since money had not changed hands, people were not always fully committed. This was consistent with the very high 'no-show' rate prior to the online payment feature being introduced. Enabling online payment on the BlaBlaCar platform was therefore a key trust-enhancing move that directly contributed to the subsequent exponential growth of the platform.

The trust framework and the 7Cs of trust in a platform environment

Digital platforms can incorporate the general principles presented earlier by developing online tools and processes that create the foundation and environment for communities to develop high levels of trust.

While the trust quotient equation is a helpful starting point, we find that platforms often benefit from a more granular approach of the key levers available to enhance trust. BlaBlaCar's co-founder Frédéric Mazzella believes trust is fundamental to the company success. His excellent DREAMS framework (declared, rated, engaged, activity-based, moderated, social)[7] has facilitated the mapping and enhancement of key trust levers for peer-to-peer ride-sharing. From our experience, we have found that a more generic framework, as illustrated by the 7Cs in Figure 12.3, can be applied to and adapted for most types of platforms, from marketplaces, social networks, payment platforms, operating systems and app stores. Let's have a look at each part in more detail.

Figure 12.3 The 7Cs of trust

Source: Launchworks

Credibility

Credentials of participants and/or products/services provided should include the relevant information needed for trust to be built. As we saw from the trust survey, a picture, a verified email and mobile phone number, and positive feedback scores are all critical components of platform participants' online trust profiles.

Companies such as eBay, Airbnb and BlaBlaCar all offer useful information on the profiles of their members. In many cases, the information is supplemented by some form of platform ranking (Ambassador in Figure 12.4), as well as relevant preferences (e.g. likes to talk during trips, non-smoker, etc.) to maximize the chances of positive interactions on – and off – platform.

In our experience, the link between the quality of the profile and likelihood to transact is very strong. There is ample evidence that, with all other things being equal, sellers with complete profiles and verified information sell significantly more than others. Big high-resolution product pictures and clear

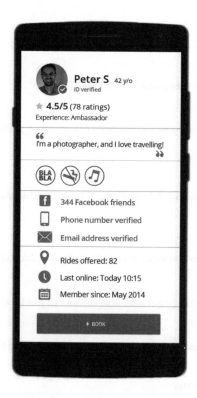

Figure 12.4 BlaBlaCar driver profile
Source: BlaBlaCar

detailed descriptions also have a higher conversion rate. To come back to our opening example of Airbnb, the poor quality of pictures for homes being advertised in the early days was indeed a limiting factor, and dealing with this proved to be a key contributor to the exponential growth that ensued.

While we have been focusing on trust aspects on the producer side of the platform, it is worth remembering that the credibility principle also applies to the user side. On Airbnb, hosts can check potential guests before accepting a rental.

Higher-credential participants not only do better, but they also benefit the entire community and the platform itself. This is why Upwork, the talent platform, has developed hundreds of proprietary skill tests for freelancers to assure clients that the freelance contractors are certified. Upwork also recently launched its 'Pro' status, which requires that freelancers go through a rigorous vetting process, including technical skill evaluations and behavioural interviews. LinkedIn's acquisition of online certification company Lynda for $1.5 billion in April 2015 can also be seen in that light.

Contribution

Showing participants' activity on the platform can be a good indication of their level of contribution, engagement and proficiency in using the platform. BlaBlaCar displays an activity box on driver profiles showing the day they joined the platform, the number of rides given, how long ago they were active on the platform, when they last logged on, and how responsive they are. Quora provides the number of questions and answers a user has contributed to. Twitter shows how many tweets people have posted and liked. Upwork displays the number of hours freelancers have worked for clients through the platform.

Consistency

As we've seen from the trust equation, trust results from the accumulation of positive interactions and experiences. So it's not just the activity or contribution that counts, but also the consistency of experiences over time. Many marketplaces use rating and review systems to capture the quality of past experiences delivered by participants.

eBay was one of the first companies that managed to scale its review and rating system globally, and this has been instrumental in creating trust between buyers and sellers. Buyers can rate and review sellers on their overall experience (positive, negative or neutral), which results in a feedback score (percentage in parentheses next to a member's user ID in Figure 12.5).[8] Detailed seller ratings (item as described, communication, dispatch time, postage) are also

Feedback profile

Recent Feedback ratings (last 12 months) [?]

	1 month	6 months	12 months
● Positive	923	5347	10024
● Neutral	10	41	69
● Negative	9	56	96

Detailed Seller Ratings (last 12 months) [?]

Criteria	Average rating	Number of ratings
Item as described	★★★★★	8260
Communication	★★★★★	8815
Dispatch time	★★★★★	8398
Postage and packaging charges	★★★★★	8306

Figure 12.5 **eBay star system**
Source: eBay/Stuff U Sell

rated on a score of 1 to 5. eBay reports these ratings over time with one-, six- and 12-month averages in order to show consistency trends. Amazon has a similar reporting system for merchants on its platform.

eBay started with a reciprocal reputation system in the early years, where sellers could leave visible ratings for buyers. eBay, however, found that sellers with poor ratings often retaliated against buyers by also giving them bad ratings. Clearly, this 'tit for tat' approach gave the wrong incentives to platform participants and amplified issues instead of strengthening positive network effects. eBay therefore decided to carry on collecting ratings from sellers, in order to identify and weed out bad buyers, but that data is no longer visible to platform participants.

Platform rating and review systems are not perfect and can suffer from biases as Andrei Hagiu and Simon Rothman point out.[9] Some customers never leave ratings, and those who do so tend to be either very happy or very unhappy with the product or service. Rating and review systems therefore need to be calibrated to lessen the impact of biases. Airbnb has an advanced feedback system with the possibility of leaving confidential feedback directly to the host as well as the platform, in addition to public feedback. This is very useful to track changes, spot emerging issues or even capture suggestions that do not deserve a public mention but could help the host/platform adjust its offering. Airbnb, like many other platforms, also captures NPS scores for both guests and hosts, which provides better insights into the experiences of platform participants.

Community

Community building is at the heart of many platforms and plays a key part in encouraging positive interactions – leading to positive network effects – and reducing negative interactions. A moderation policy should be instituted early, especially for social platforms. It helps shape the community's culture and set the tone for the first 1,000 people. Once this early culture is set, it is harder to change later on.

Providing the right tools to platform participants

Tools for participants to interact are key, and can take many forms depending on the nature of the platform (upvotes, likes, posts, intermediated email systems, etc.). Tools to help participants understand how they relate to each other within the community (how they're connected/related, etc.) are also important to enhance trust.

The platform should supplement its own internal controls by harnessing the power of its communities to detect negative interactions and offensive content. The ability for participants to flag and report inappropriate content or behaviour and to file complaints is key to this process. Participants are usually happy to help 'police' the platform and recognize the role the platform plays in regulating the community.[10]

Platform community management

Many companies are using community managers to establish and maintain relationships with clients online. The role of community managers is even more critical for platform businesses since communities are the very source of value of the platform. Community management needs to support the scaling stage of the platform by securing user and producer engagement, identifying star customers and producers – as well as troublemakers – moderating content, and shaping the norms and behaviours that support a platform's ethos and brand. The influence of platform community managers shouldn't be underestimated since they play some of the roles that managers used to play in traditional companies (reward, praise, nudge, coach, etc.) with the community members who are effectively co-creating value with the platform. They can also ensure that they engage with their communities on issues of strategic interest to the platform itself. Airbnb community managers are very active in mobilizing its hosts and guests on the topic of rental regulations, for example.

Control

Platforms have significant power and responsibilities associated with their operations. To quote law professor Jeffrey Rosen, platforms such as Facebook have 'more power in determining who can speak and who can be heard around the globe than any Supreme Court justice, any king or any president'. It is certainly true that the monitoring of content contribution and sharing (automated or not) is a key activity for many platforms. While the exact numbers are not reported, some social platforms are thought to have up to a third of their entire staff involved in content monitoring.[11] When participant activity happens off-platform, monitoring tools may also be required to control the experience. In some places, Uber asks a driver to take and send a selfie when starting work. Uber then compares the image with the biometric data on record for an ID check. If it does not match, Uber suspends the account until an investigation takes place.[12]

As a platform scales, monitoring often needs to be extended beyond the platform itself. A more holistic type of 'client service' monitoring involving social platforms, corporate blogs, review sites, etc. can be instrumental in surfacing bad – or good – customer experiences. It can also help recognize VIP customers and influencers and monitor so called 'trolls', that are only there to provoke the community. This holistic monitoring function, sometimes called 'social listening', is often part of the customer service team and benefits greatly from strong analytics support (optimize function of the Launchworks rocket model) and feedback loops with most teams (trust, product, engineering, growth, marketing, pricing and legal) to drive meaningful calls to action.

Correction

Control and correct activities are closely linked. When platforms detect that some interactions or transactions are not carried out in a trust-enhancing way, or contravene governance principles, they have an opportunity to correct the outcome directly. As a platform matures, corrections may be automated by algorithms, with exceptions managed manually by employees from the trust and safety team.

Punish bad behaviour and incentivize good behaviour

Correction can go from taking down illicit content (YouTube) and banning a participant who displayed inappropriate behaviour (Twitter), to de-prioritizing a seller with low ratings in search results (eBay). The trust and safety team will need to constantly review and update rules and policies against governance principles, as new use cases and behaviours reveal themselves.

Following the 2016 US presidential election, Facebook and Twitter have been heavily criticized about their role in allowing 'bots' to spread misleading or fake information to voters.[13] Since then, Facebook has vowed to tackle hoaxes. Google has also blocked fake news from its ad network. Twitter, which by design is a more open platform, still faces challenging governance issues in this area.

Make it right

Inherently, platforms do not completely control the end-to-end customer experience. When something goes wrong, great customer service can help minimize the reputational damage. Airbnb has been known to book hotel rooms directly to make sure a guest who was let down by a host could have a place to sleep.

Conflict resolution and risk management

As mentioned earlier, many participants expect a platform to regulate its community. This includes resolving three different types of conflicts that may arise on the platform: between producers (for example, if a producer tries to undermine a competitor by giving bad reviews), between producers and users (say, if orders are not delivered) and between users (who may disagree about reviews of a product, etc.). To that end, the platform needs to understand how to mitigate the risks associated with producers or users not fulfilling their obligation. The platform should also decide who should bear the cost of failures from users and producers. Poor risk management led to the demise of peer-to-peer luxury car-sharing service HiGear. A criminal ring used stolen identities and stolen credit cards to bypass HiGear's security checks and stole several high-end cars. HiGear's insurance covered the thefts, but it made the economic equation unsustainable and HiGear had to shut down shortly after the incident.[14]

While conflict resolution should be fast, clear and fair, some platforms apply a correction bias on one side. Amazon will generally side with buyers if they have a dispute with a merchant on the platform. A refund is almost always given. Since both buyers and sellers are platform participants, it is important to make sure that the correction bias does not undermine one side of the platform too much. For example, very lenient policies biased towards buyers may result in legitimate sellers not being paid. In the long term, this may harm trust on the platform. Bad buyers therefore also need to be monitored and managed, even if a positive bias towards buyers is part of the platform governance framework.

Coverage: insurances as a trust device

At a basic level, trust is about making sure that things go as expected. If they don't, insurance is a helpful device to bring the final outcome closer to what was expected, even when something goes wrong. In that sense, insurance can be used as a trust-enhancing mechanism for platforms.

Platforms are often reluctant to secure insurance early on for a number of reasons, including price, the difficulty of finding suitable products and the perceived brand impact of signalling that the platform offering could fail. Yet offering insurance often results in enhanced trust and increased platform transactions.

An often-cited example is the one of credit card companies that were forced to offer insurances by regulators in the US in the 1970s.[15] While they reluctantly complied with the $50 consumer liability limit, this move ended up benefiting them commercially as increased consumer trust in cards led to significantly more transactions.

Similarly, despite an initial reluctance to cover its hosts and guests, Airbnb's introduction of its $1 million liability insurance was instrumental in growing its market share beyond the early adopters segments.[16]

BlaBlaCar's sharing model is largely covered by the existing insurance policies of drivers. This is because BlaBlaCar drivers are only able to recoup part of the costs associated with the ride and are not therefore offering a commercial service. The BlaBlaCar passengers are therefore covered under the driver's insurance policy, as if they were friends or family members of the driver. Yet Blablacar added an insurance provided by Axa to cover some other, very rare, use cases. The marketing impact of the insurance on trust, however, made the deal worthwhile irrespective of the real value of the additional coverage.

Insurance companies, historically organized domestically even when part of large international groups, are waking up to these developments and designing new insurance products for platform businesses. New insurance start-up companies such as Kasko have also entered the market with innovative products tailored to platform businesses and the sharing economy. Going forward, we have no doubt that new insurance products suited to platform needs will emerge.

Trust as a new currency

> It is trust, more than money, that makes the world go round.
> Joseph Stiglitz, professor of economics at Columbia
> University, Economics Nobel Prize winner (2001)

As participants get more familiar with one platform, research shows that they also become more willing to use other platforms. A recent study from Professor Arun Sundararajan showed that existing BlaBlaCar ride-sharers were more likely to use a peer-to-peer marketplace than non-ride-sharers.[17]

As interpersonal trust is being transformed from a 'scarce to an abundant resource',[18] a new digital trust ecosystem is emerging. Companies such as eRated or Traity are now aggregating ratings and reviews from various marketplaces, social networks and government sites in order to create a unified online trusted identity. This can be extremely valuable to new platforms since they may be able to leverage some of the trust that users have acquired somewhere else instead of only relying on feedback on the platform itself (often scant at ignition!). The need for a 'trusted online identity' is likely to increase in tomorrow's platform economy, and today's solutions are just the beginning.

Governance principles

Platform governance principles must enhance trust between the platform and its participants, as well as among participants. The trust framework principles should therefore be part of the overall governance framework of the platform.

Once the key features of a platform have been designed, the focus should be on the governance framework. This framework needs to set out the key principles that will drive the way the platform:

- allows participants to join and interact with the platform and other participants;
- shares economic and non-economic rewards among the platform itself and its participants; and
- deals with exceptions, conflicts and outside stakeholders.

We have to keep in mind that these governance principles have far-reaching consequences for platform participants. Some businesses may be excluded overnight and go bankrupt, while some participants may lose a needed source of income due to sudden rule changes. The economic importance of good platform governance can't be overemphasized, especially since some platforms are now larger than countries.[19]

Filtering platform participants

In order to maximize trust, a platform needs to ensure that its participants are trustworthy, and that those engaging in trust-eroding interactions and behaviour are marginalized or excluded.

The first step for building a platform is attracting relevant participants. This will partly be a function of the positioning of the platform in terms of brand and acquisition channels used to recruit participants. In some cases, the platform is designed in such a way that unsuitable participants are simply discouraged to join. Before a seller or a shop can get started selling items, vintage marketplace Ruby Lane conducts a prescreening to see if they meet predetermined standards. There is also a $100 one-off setup fee to be paid to discourage uncommitted sellers.[20] Dating platforms such as Tinder seem to be doing all they can to keep their user bases 'young' and 'cool'. Tinder markets predominantly to teens and young adults, and offers users the option to use age filters to exclude older singles. Tinder even decided to charge more – up to four times more in the UK – when users are above 30.[21]

Checking that participants are who they say they are is also a key trust-enhancing feature of many platforms. This can be done in a number of ways, from checking email addresses at a very basic level (date of account creation, account activity) to full ID checks on individuals. For example, companies like Onfido, Sift Science or Checker provide these types of services. Facebook has had a major impact on the scaling of new platforms and marketplaces thanks to the Facebook Connect API,[22] which helps reduce friction at user registration and login but also enables trust building as people register/log in using their real identity. Prior to social media, the main way to register on eBay was to create a new user ID, which was a real impediment to increasing trust since it said very little about who was behind the account.

Finally, the continuous monitoring of participants' behaviour and the identification of trust-eroding actions as they emerge will be key to trust-enhancing governance of the platform. Based on feedback, complaints and pattern analysis, platforms should be able to marginalize participants that are not following the rules or even exclude them from the platform.

Fairly rewarding participants

To be trusted, the platform also needs to ensure that the right kind of behaviour is encouraged and rewarded. Rewards can be monetary and act as an incentive to participate in the platform. But more subtle recognition cues, or privileges, can be bestowed upon its 'good citizens'.

Many platforms have a super user programme whereby the platform itself can award special status, points or karma, to its most active/best participants. In some communities, such as Wikipedia, these super users are even entrusted with curating privileges and controls over the platform content and operations.

Dealing with exceptions and conflicts

The extent to which a platform is involved in dispute resolution depends on how it is designed. For example, some 'thin' platforms with limited functionalities, such as Craigslist, have minimal conflict resolution capabilities since they simply provide a canvas for platform participants to transact directly among themselves.

However, platforms such as eBay, Airbnb or Uber need to carefully monitor the behaviour of their participants, drivers and clients alike to ensure they offer a safe and trusted environment for them to transact.

Platform governance through laws, norms and architecture

Unlike countries, which are built upon layers and layers of history, legal practices, memberships to various supranational bodies and deep cultural ties, digital platforms emerge from a blank slate. They have to comply with local laws and regulations and operate in various cultural contexts, but they are free to set their own internal governance principles. This is an opportunity to design fair and transparent models that will attract participants and ensure their success but also an immense challenge to ensure that the platform minimizes 'collateral damages' that changes in governance may trigger.

The starting point of many platforms is simply to rely on market mechanisms. As we have seen, the platform has to create the basic conditions for participants to join (attract), find what they are looking for (match), and exchange relevant information (connect) before they are able to make a deal (transact). In some cases, platforms are able to succeed with a very light governance structure, but markets are not always efficient and governance principles need to deal with market failures.

The platform owner is, however, not neutral in the platform market in which it operates and may be tempted to design governance principles that capture disproportionate value for itself.

Platform architects need to ensure that good behaviours are encouraged while negative behaviours are minimized. In order to achieve this, platforms have a number of levers available to them, including[23] sets of governance rules, which – in a similar way as countries use laws – are aimed at strengthening incentives for good behaviours, such as rewards for loyalty, increased status for participation, monetary incentive for good referrals, etc. The same applies for rules that undermine bad behaviours and prevent fraud, misrepresentation, bullying, etc. This should be done as overtly as possible. While it is important to clearly set out generic policies and objectives, it is often useful to keep their detailed implementation hidden so that participants punished for bad behaviour cannot easily bypass the exact rule that was invoked.

Sometimes the softer rules of platforms are conveyed through the behaviour of existing platform participants, community leaders or even through coaching examples chosen to explain the on-boarding process to new participants. A 'like' on a Facebook post from Mark Zuckerberg will do wonders to your online credentials and shows other platform participants that whatever you are doing is consistent with what Facebook expects from its users. The behavioural norms that emerge over time in many platforms help shape the future behaviour of new joiners and the platform ecosystem as it scales.

Lastly, the platform itself should embed some of the intelligence required to enforce governance principles. Many automated algorithms and rules help ensure that the right information is captured, that it is internally consistent, and that the parties are who they say they are (if anonymous participation is forbidden). Going forward, new technologies, such as distributed database models like blockchain, will open the door to 'self-enforcing smart contracts' between platform participants and further strengthen the legal certainty of core transactions. This will be a formidable enabler for platform businesses since it will further lower friction between transacting parties.

Platform branding

The other side of trust is brand recognition. Brands still play a very important part in the buying decision, and this is likely to hold true for many years. This is because we still draw trust from familiar and recognizable names.

The development and management of a relevant platform brand is therefore a key strategic enabler of reaching mass-market position and long-term success. Typical branding strategies, however, need to be adapted to the fact that the platform has unique relationships with its users and producers, and that they themselves will interact with one another. That's why the brand strategy needs to not only ensure that the brand conveys trust in the idea and the platform itself, but also that the brand is conducive to enabling transactions between users and producers.

Getting participants over the fear barrier

Dealing with the potential fears of platform participants head-on should be one of the brand-building missions of platform marketing executives. In the case of Airbnb, there are three fear barriers. First, peer-to-peer home sharing is safe. Second, people using Airbnb can be trusted. And third, Airbnb will look after both hosts and guests if something goes wrong. The chief marketing officer of Airbnb and former senior Coca-Cola executive Jonathan Mildenhall identified the fear barrier early on and deliberately cast a single white female who wanted to travel the world alone as the lead protagonist in the company's global TV campaign, 'Never a Stranger'.[24]

Serving both sides

While branding efforts are often focused on building trust on the user side – especially in B2C markets – success is also dependent on acquiring and retaining producers. Platforms should therefore champion a set of clear and powerful values and a design identity that resonate with both user and producer communities. Sub brands can be used to more effectively target specific segments on one side of the platform. eBay recognized this earlier as it rolled out its 'Powerseller Programme'. Not only did it reassure buyers that some sellers had a seal of approval from eBay and could be trusted more, but it also provided an evolution path and status recognition that sellers could strive for. Many platforms have followed suit: Upwork has Upwork Pro freelancers, Airbnb has Superhosts, Google has Android Certified developers, etc.

Brand co-evolution

At the launch stage, there is so much to do, from achieving platform fit, acquiring and retaining users and producers, to building technical capabilities, etc. that branding can be treated as a secondary concern. Airbnb co-founder Joe Gebbia talks about the first airbed and breakfast logo, and explains: 'Those brand identities were created in a matter of hours, for a short deadline, and only for temporary use'. Brian Chesky echoes that sentiment and continues: 'We were growing so fast, it became one of those things where you say you'll figure it out later, but then you never end up doing it because you're too busy.'[25]

Platforms introducing a new concept such as Airbnb may initially focus on describing simply and convincingly to both users and producers how interacting and transacting on the platform can help them create and capture value. But as the platform scales and its communities grow, a utility-driven and descriptive brand is unlikely to reach, inspire and reassure late adopters. Airbnb relaunched its website and mobile apps with a new brand identity in July 2014, with the new focus of expanding internationally and becoming a more inclusive hospitality brand. The year-long brand study included user research as well as interviews from guests and hosts in more than a dozen countries to capture the essence of the brand. It boiled down to one powerful concept: belonging. Brian Chesky explains: 'Airbnb is about belonging anywhere. The brand shouldn't say we're about community, or our international [reach], or renting homes – it's about belonging.'

It will be interesting to see how brands such as Airbnb will evolve over time and how their communities will influence this process. We believe that platform brands co-evolve with their communities and that participants contribute to shaping brand values through their interactions with the platform and other participants.

In the case of food delivery platform Deliveroo, the rebranding that took place in September 2016 resulted in significant changes to the brand identity. These changes were driven by the need to be more attuned to the expectations of not only users, but also producers of the platform. For example, the new identity now includes colourful jackets and jerseys for Deliveroo riders so that they can be better seen at night.

When platforms change their strategies, like eBay did when it introduced its 'Buy It Now' option, a brand refresh is often required. By the mid-2000s, eBay had attained nearly universal brand recognition in Western countries as the go-to marketplace for second-hand auctions, with vibrant seller and buyer communities. eBay was well known for auction-style listings, second-hand, quirky and unique items. It was so ingrained in the popular psyche, and existing buyers and sellers were so passionate about the old eBay, that the transition to being known as the destination for buying brand-new items – as well as second-hand ones in auctions – took many years. A new branding redesign in 2012 encapsulated this evolution of continued innovation, combining eBay's history of the unique, the vintage and its vibrant communities with the new.

Notes

1 For an accessible summary of the argument and its implications for platforms, see R. Fisman and T. Sullivan, *The Inner Lives of Markets: How People Shape Them – and They Shape Us*, London: Public Affairs/John Murray Learning, 2016.

2 Betrustman Report, Chronos & BlaBlaCar, December 2012.

3 See BlaBlaCar, NYU Stern, Entering the Trust Age, 2016. In this study, respondents were asked to rank on a scale from 0 to 5 the level of trust they gave to different types of relationships, from a social network contact through to friends or family. A BlaBlaCar member with a full online profile was then included in the mix. Looking at the percentage of respondents that gave a high level of trust (4 or 5 out of 5), the results revealed that 88% of respondents had high trust in a BlaBlaCar member. This percentage is largely above the percentage of people who highly trust their colleagues (58%) or neighbors (42%), and close to the percentage of people who highly trust their friends (92%), revealing that trust built by online platforms can supersede offline relationships.

4 Arun Sundararajan, *The Sharing Economy*, Cambridge, MA: MIT Press, 2016, p. 61.

5 Rachel Bostman, the Trust Stack, www.rachelbotsman.com.

6 D. H. Maister, R. Galford and C. Green, *The Trusted Advisor*, London: Simon & Schuster, 2 January 2002.

7   BlaBlaCar, NYU Stern, Entering the Trust Age, 2016.

8   This feedback profile example is from StuffUSell, the UK's leading trading assistant. This popular merchant helps people who don't have the time or don't have enough positive feedback to efficiently sell on eBay.

9   H. Hagiu and S. Rothman, 'Network Effects Aren't Enough', *Harvard Business Review*, 94(4), 2016, https://hbr.org/2016/04/network-effects-arent-enough.

10 Survey from BlaBlaCar showed that 75% of participants believed in the importance of the platform in regulating the community. Betrustman Report, Chronos & BlaBlaCar, December 2012.

11 See www.theverge.com/2016/4/13/11387934/internet-moderator-history-youtube-facebook-reddit-censorship-free-speech.

12 See http://venturebeat.com/2016/09/23/uber-selfies-security-photos-drivers/.

13 See www.thedailybeast.com/articles/2016/11/17/how-pro-trump-twitter-bots-spread-fake-news.html. By election day, automated pro-Trump activity outnumbered pro-Clinton activity by a 5:1 ratio.

14 See https://techcrunch.com/2012/01/01/luxury-car-sharing-service-higear-shuts-down-due-to-theft/.

15 G. Parker, M. Van Alstyne and S. Choudary, *Platform Revolution*, New York: W. W. Norton & Company, 2016, p. 175.

16 www.airbnb.co.uk/host-protection-insurance

17 BlaBlaCar, NYU Stern, Entering the Trust Age, 2016. Interestingly, the results were even higher for millennials.

18 Frédéric Mazzella, *Ouishare* magazine interview, 14 January 2013.

19 Apple itself is roughly the size of Slovakia. See http://ftalphaville.ft.com/2015/01/28/2103622/if-apple-were-a-country/.

20 Ruby Lane fees effective 1 May 2016, www.rubylane.com/kb/question.php?ID=36.

21 See www.bloomberg.com/news/articles/2015-03-03/how-tinder-gets-away-with-charging-people-over-30-twice-as-much.

22 Facebook Connect was launched in 2009.

23 These governance principles are borrowed from Lawrence Lessig, who formulated them in the context of governments. See G. Parker, M. Van Alstyne and S. Choudary, *Platform Revolution*, New York: W. W. Norton & Company, 2016, p. 164.

24 See www.adweek.com/news/advertising-branding/how-airbnbs-cmo-transformed-company-super-brand-just-18-months-167620.

25 See www.fastcompany.com/3033130/most-innovative-companies/airbnb-unveils-a-major-rebranding-effort-that-paves-the-way-for-sh#8.

Chapter 13

Platforms, regulation and competition

Why should firms be regulated in the first place?

Governments are typically concerned about firms becoming 'dominant' because they can then abuse their market power to drive competitors away, before increasing their prices. Typically, such issues can be dealt with in two ways. The first one is to pre-emptively set rules for market participants. This approach is often called *ex ante* regulation – because it sets the rules at the outset – and is the domain of sector-specific regulators.[1] The second way to avoid abuse of market power is to intervene if evidence of anticompetitive behaviour emerges after the facts (*ex post*). These types of interventions are usually triggered by a complaint or an investigation and are the responsibility of competition agencies and the commercial courts.

Similar principles are applied in many jurisdictions around the world, including the US and Europe, where antitrust concerns are taken very seriously. As seen in Chapter 6, platform-powered companies such as Apple, Google and Amazon have been extraordinarily successful over the past decade and are now among the largest in the world. This has in turn attracted the attention of those in charge of policing markets to prevent firms from abusing dominant positions.

Much has been written on the various competition cases and regulatory challenges that have been launched against platforms. This chapter will summarize some of the main regulatory and competition arguments that have been made in favour of, or against, platforms. This will help us answer some of the key questions surrounding platform regulations:

- When is intervention warranted and what does good regulation look like?
- What are the characteristics of platforms that may cause economic harm?
- What should those in charge of policing markets, including governments, regulators and competition authorities, do?
- How should platforms deal with regulation and regulators?

When and how to regulate platforms

Platforms such as Uber or Airbnb are often accused of 'unfair competition' and of being in breach of a raft of regulations. Such accusations, which are often brought about by established firms disrupted by platforms such as taxi companies or hotel chains, have not been taken lightly by governments and regulators. Many cases against platforms have resulted in total or partial bans.

One of the central questions is whether or not successful global platform businesses are now able to behave in ways that reduce competition and innovation to the detriment of customers.

In this section, we will look at the two main dangers facing regulatory and competition interventions:

• Platforms end up being regulated when they shouldn't have been.
• Platforms end up not being regulated when they should have been.

It's worth remembering that both over-regulation and under-regulation result in bad market outcomes, including reduced choice, reduced innovation and higher prices. It is therefore important to understand what good regulation would look like and whether the biggest risk is to over-regulate or to under-regulate.

If it becomes apparent that over-regulation seems to be happening, it may be because the regulations are not fit for purpose, or the wrong tools are being applied. If it also appears that the value creation potential of platforms is very significant, then over-regulation runs the risk of preventing the benefits brought about by platforms from being realized. To take the example of the taxi market, forcing the status quo and preventing platforms such as Uber or Lyft from operating, as advocated by many, may result in enshrining the position of existing taxi firms, reducing choice and convenience, and keeping prices high while discouraging future innovation.

If, however, platforms end up being under-regulated, then they may be able to drive out competition and abuse their market power in the longer term, ultimately to the detriment of consumers.

One way to avoid this trade-off is to ensure that the right tools are available to minimize both under- and over-regulation. In the absence of perfect regulation, however, it is useful to understand how 'less harm' could be done.

First do no harm: intervention and market failure

While markets have shown how efficient they are at allocating resources under a wide range of conditions, they can also fail to promote efficient outcomes. This does not mean that markets do not work at all, but that they do not *always* work properly.

These market failures are the basis of intervention for many governments and regulators, since without external intervention and 'remedies' to correct these failures, some markets may result in suboptimal outcomes for society.[2]

Typically, economists associate the source of market failures to one of the following three categories:

- The market consolidates and only a small number of firms (or even one) are left with significant market power (or monopoly).
- The market under consideration has strong externalities (such as pollution), and those are by definition not factored in the decisions of the firm.
- The good being traded is a 'public good' (such as street lighting) where consumption cannot be denied and people can't be excluded.

One of the first issues platforms are facing is that it is unclear how some of the 'historic' regulations would pass the current market failure tests. This suggests that these regulations, which often date back decades, sometimes centuries, may in fact prevent the market from functioning rather than correcting market failures. Many of the regulations that create barriers to entry in markets where there is no market failure fall into this category. The question for regulators and policymakers is then how to change these regulations to ensure that the market is not artificially distorted. In some cases, regulators seem to have been 'captured' by the firms they are meant to regulate.

Competition authorities tend to be more independent and therefore often argue that many regulations need to be updated and shouldn't be used to prevent innovation. They also remind us of a very important principle: 'the purpose of competition law is to ensure that consumers are not harmed, not to ensure that inferior competitors are protected from disruption'.

To be clear, that doesn't mean that new entrants should be allowed to do anything they want, including not carrying out checks on their drivers, not providing insurance and not paying taxes. But it means that shielding specific interest groups from competition should only be done after careful considerations have been given as to why this should be the case and why society would be better off as a result. Granting regulatory protection without tangible welfare benefits would simply represent a tax on consumers in the form of increased prices and reduced innovation.

This is a case where platforms risk being 'over-regulated' and prevented from operating efficiently, and the regulations being applied to a sector are aimed more at protecting corporations than enabling fair competition. It is worth noting that in such cases, platforms are simply the catalyst for the disruption and any other innovative entrant would create similar tensions. We will illustrate how the above dynamics play out in the taxi industry later in this chapter.

Big platforms are not necessarily dominant

As we have seen, platforms benefit from network effects, which means that they are often more valuable the more people use them[3] (e.g. imagine Airbnb with one flat, or Tinder with only your profile!). When successful, these platforms gain scale and achieve critical mass to become market leaders – this is the 'winner takes all' principle. This is why securing the capital to acquire more users and scale-up quickly is often the name of the game for platform businesses.

This is not an abuse of market power, but simply a feature of the economics of platform businesses. Yet scale can still create some market issues, and any market with few competitors is bound to attract scrutiny. If competition is really only a click away, the platforms are unlikely to be able to exploit their market power. But in some circumstances, if switching is particularly difficult, or if 'multihoming' (using similar platforms such as Uber and Lyft at the same time) is for some reason not possible, it could become a concern.

Platforms have far more flexible pricing options

By virtue of the fact that platforms attract and market to different customer groups in order to enable them to transact, they benefit from enhanced pricing flexibility that is not available to traditional businesses. If you sell to only one customer group, you need to price above the costs associated with this product for the company to be sustainable in the long term.[4] If you are a platform, you may be able to offer the platform service for free to one side of the platform (say, the producers) and charge the other side (say, the clients). We illustrated the complexity and range of pricing models available to platforms in Chapter 11, and showed that offering free entry to women in night clubs – or dating platforms – in order to attract paying men is a rational pricing strategy.

Some judges and lawyers seem to still be assuming that platforms offering services for free are necessarily behaving in a predatory manner. Since it is perfectly legitimate for platforms to price below cost *on one side* of the market for profit motives, rather than anticompetitive ones, traditional predation tests are not fit for purpose in the context of platforms.

Who do platform participants work for?

While this chapter focuses on competition issues, it is also important to mention the tension between labour laws in many countries and many platforms' use of self-employed or independent contractors.

When the California Labor Commission suggested that an Uber driver could in fact be considered an employee, rather than an independent contractor, it sent shockwaves throughout the industry. Similar judgments have been reached in UK courts,[5] where the self-employed status of Uber drivers has been called into question. Such findings, under appeal by Uber at the time of writing, would have far-reaching consequences since they would undermine many platform business models that are predicated on the participation of self-employed workers. It is clear that platforms shouldn't be allowed to circumvent labour laws, yet we find the argument that platform participants should be considered full employees of the platform quite difficult. Unlike traditional employees, platform participants have the flexibility of working only when suitable, can switch off at any time, are able to work for other platforms (multihoming) at the same time, and have no notice to serve if they decide to leave the platform. Yet we understand that the current labour laws, designed primarily for the business models of the Industrial Revolution, are struggling to cater for the new fluid reality of the platform economy. One of Uber's arguments is that is it a technology platform company offering a service to both drivers and passengers, but some judges believe that Uber is a transport company instead. Many legal practitioners believe that new types of contracts, and agreements, will emerge as a result of this tension. In the meantime, the legal uncertainty resulting from these labour regulations are seen as a major risk by platform businesses and investors alike.

Are platforms ignoring regulations?

Platform-powered businesses such as Uber have been forced to change their business model in several countries in order to comply with domestic regulations and laws.[6] In some cases, platforms have been fined[7] or even banned.[8] In the UK and France, regulatory authorities even proposed that their service be degraded in order to 'level the playing field' with traditional taxi companies. For example, Transport for London (TfL) proposed that a five-minute delay be added as a regulatory requirement before a trip can be accepted by the Uber platform, while the French Government passed a law adding 15 minutes to online bookings of taxis in 2013. The real-time display of cars on a map, a valuable and innovative feature of Uber and other digital entrants, was also in the cross hairs of taxi companies that were seeking a ban on such disruptive new technologies. On both occasions, it is interesting to see that the domestic competition authorities, in charge of enforcing competition law, have strongly criticized these proposals. The Competition and Market Authority (CMA) made its point known in no uncertain terms:

> A number of TfL's (Transport for London) proposals will harm competition and, by extension, consumers. This will take the form of harm to competition between Private Hire Vehicles (PHVs), through regulations which is disproportionate and/or reduces incentives for entry, expansion or innovation.[9]

It further added:

> The CMA is concerned that some of TfL's proposals will create barriers to innovation in particular. Hampering innovation results in inefficient business models, services of a lower quality than could otherwise be the case, and dissatisfied consumers.

Ultimately, these proposed regulations were not retained by TfL. Following a petition organized by Uber that attracted in excess of 200,000 signatures in only a few days, it became clear that TFL's proposals were not seen favourably by consumers. Under pressure, the regulator decided to back down, although black cabs are now seeking other legal options to block Uber. In France, l'Autorité de la Concurrence (the French Competition Authority) argued that the mandated delay was not necessary, that it would distort competition between taxis and private hire vehicles, and that it should be removed. The rule was subsequently struck down on technical grounds in December 2014. Uber's own lobbying efforts seem to be paying off in a number of US states as well as other countries, and traditional taxi companies have not managed to get the app banned (although court cases are still likely to be launched in many jurisdictions).

Taxi companies have used regulations as a barrier to entry and have been able to keep supply constrained for many years. That is to say by not allowing more taxis on the streets – through so-called *numerus clausus* policies – they have been able to increase their prices significantly above what happens in other competitive markets. For example, the number of cab drivers in NYC between 1937 and 1996 was exactly 11,787. Not one more and not one less, despite a structural increase in demand over the 60-year period.

In fact, the value of such a monopoly model is directly enshrined in the value of the 'licence' – a taxi medallion in this case. In other words, the economic returns the taxi owners receive above what would be a fair return in a competitive market is captured in the price of the medallion (which exceeded $1 million in NYC in 2013). Incidentally, economists will tell you that this value also represents the lifetime super profits or – in other words – money taxis make by charging above market price that would otherwise be retained by clients.

However, since new potential buyers are now anticipating more competition from platforms such as Uber going forward, the price of medallions is dropping, and quickly, as shown in Figure 13.1.[10]

Taxis are not the only sector to be impacted by the disruptive entry of platforms. The hotel lobby has also mounted a global war on Airbnb, arguing that taxes were not collected in the same way and that security regulations that hotels are subject to didn't apply. This resulted in a number of legal moves against Airbnb,[11] with partial or total bans in a number of cities (e.g. Barcelona). In many cases, the legal position is not directly targeted at Airbnb, but clearly aimed at reducing the number of people letting their property on the site. While it is important for Airbnb and its hosts to pay the relevant taxes, it is sometimes difficult to justify the proportionality of the regulations proposed

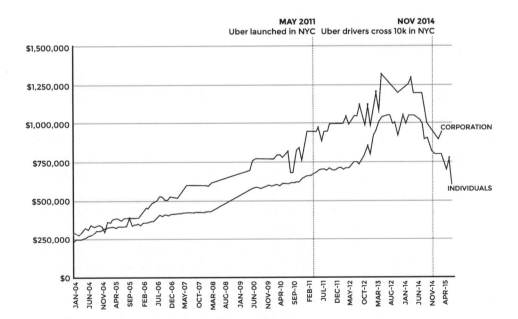

Figure 13.1 **NYC taxi medallion prices (2004–2015)**

Source: NYC Taxi and Limousine Commission

or passed in some countries. Clearly, it is important to prevent unscrupulous businesspeople from circumventing legitimate hotel regulations by setting up entire buildings as Airbnb rental properties rather than hotels, but should private individuals be forced to implement hotel regulations when they rent their own place?

Like Uber, Airbnb is now actively lobbying and its public policy teams have been hard at work over the past couple of years to ensure consumers can carry on participating in its platform.

It is, however, true that platforms often fail to prioritize these regulations and requirements as they enter their international scale-up phase and tend to negotiate 'after the fact'.[12] While the tension between compliance at a local level and the need to gain scale for network effects to kick in is understandable and may lead to a 'bias towards action' rather than compliance, it is clear that this needs to be remedied quickly and that consumer protection regulations shouldn't be overlooked simply because services are provided by platforms. In fact, it is clear that some platforms also impose negative externalities – such as increased visits in formerly secure shared areas of buildings in the case of Airbnb – that need to be factored in.

We also understand that it may be politically difficult for government to suddenly remove previously granted exclusivity rights (especially if your entire country can be locked down by angry taxi drivers as a result) and transition measures may well be warranted. We, however, do not believe that seeking to preserve the status quo by preventing innovation is either a practical or desirable long-term option.

Could platform ecosystems abuse their market power?

Leaving behind the misguided 'unfair competition' argument we previously discussed, it is important to ask whether or not some platforms, especially very successful ones, are in a position to abuse their market power.

While we have seen that below-cost prices or even a large market share are not enough to accuse platforms of abusing platform participants (users and/or producers), it remains important to ensure that platforms are not in a position to harm consumers in other ways.

When a platform becomes very successful, it gains significant market power and may be tempted to use that power to colonize adjacent markets (e.g. Google could bias search results in order to support its own music, finance, etc. services to the detriment of competitors). While this presents clear advantages for Google and allows the company to further develop its platform-powered ecosystem, it may also undermine competition in a way that is harmful to customers in the long term. As one of the largest companies in the world in terms of market capitalization, Google is a prime candidate for market power accusations. We'll illustrate the type of competition issues that platform-powered ecosystems can give rise to using Google as an example.

Google cases linked to 'search favours' for its own services

At the time of writing, Google is the second largest company in the world in terms of market capitalization[13] and its influence has not escaped competition authorities and competitors alike.[14] Google didn't face much criticism as it grew its superior search engine and displaced some of its early competitors such as Alta Vista. However, things started to change once it became a market leader. Its leadership position in search, combined with entry into new markets, were often deemed to provide Google with the means and incentives to discriminate against competitors, which in turn led to a wave of competition cases.

Indeed, Google has developed a number of vertical services over the years, and has sometimes been accused of giving them favourable treatments, especially in terms of search display (and without informing end users). Table 13.1 lists some of Google's services and their direct competitors at time of launch.

Table 13.1 Selected Google services and some competitors' services by year of launch

Year	Google service	Competitors' services
2002	Froogle (now Product Search)	Amazon, eBay, Shopzilla
2005	Google Maps	MapQuest, navX, Bing Maps
2006	Google Finance	Yahoo Finance, MSN Money, AOL Money
	YouTube	Dailymotion, Veoh, Go Fish
2009	Google eHealth	WebMD, Mayo Clinic
	Google Compare	Bankrate, LendingTree
	Google Place (now Google Local)	Yelp, TripAdvisor, Citysearch
2010	Google's Boutiques.com	eBay, Amazon
2011	Google Travel and Flights	KAYAK, Expedia, TripAdvisor
	Google+ (formerly G Wave)	Facebook, LinkedIn
2013	Google Helpouts	Duolingo, Hired, Fiverr

Source: Google, Inc., Fairsearch.org, Launchworks analysis

The first type of legal cases are linked to claims that Google discriminates by favouring the rankings of its own services. Marissa Mayer, former Google senior VP, commented in 2007 during a conference:

When we rolled out Google Finance, we did put the Google link first. It seems only fair right, we do all the work for the search page and all these other things, so we do put it first . . . That has actually been our policy, since then, because of Finance. So for Google Maps again, it's the first link.

The above statement would suggest that Google's search results may have been biased in favour of the ranking of its own ecosystem properties vs those of its competitors.[15]

Google cases linked to tying and bundling

Google also has an incentive to bundle the services it offers as part of its ecosystem in order to increase overall penetration, and in turn the value of its platform. In September 2013, Google started to require that users of YouTube open a Google+ account in order to be able to post comments (on YouTube). The strategic rationale for trying to boost Google's new social network was clear, but led some observers to highlight the possible anticompetitive nature of such ties.[16] The fact that users of Google search services do not pay for the platform doesn't mean that Google doesn't have incentives to extend its market power in some service markets (e.g. YouTube) to other apparently free services (Google+) in order to later monetize these through advertising contracts. But since bundling can also be useful to consumers, such tying and bundling issues need to be approached on a case-by-case basis. Conventional competition methods and bundling analysis guidelines[17] are based on prices set by traditional firms and need to be adapted, since many of these services are free and offered by platforms.

Google's tying strategies are not only happening on the end user side (as per Google+ and YouTube), but also on the content producer side.

The testimony of Jeremy Stoppelman,[18] CEO of Yelp, in front of the US Senate in 2011 provides some further insights into these allegations:

Websites typically allow search engines like Google to crawl and index their sites so that links to their sites can appear in response to relevant search engines queries . . . In 2010, Google began incorporating the content it indexed from its competitors into Google Local without permission. Although Google had previously acknowledged that it needed a license to use Yelp's content, it was now using it without permission to prop up its own, less effective, product. In some instances, Google even presented this content to its users as if it were its own . . . In response to our objections, Google informed us that it would cease the practice only if we agreed to be removed from Google's Web search index, thereby preventing Yelp from appearing anywhere in Google Web search results. This of course was a false choice . . . it is a choice between allowing Google to co-opt one's content and not competing at all.

Google's comments about delisting Yelp from its Web search results in a retaliatory move if Yelp didn't accept to license its content for free suggests that Google may have been trying to abuse its market power. Other academics have highlighted a number of potentially problematic linkages within Google's ecosystem.[19]

Google cases linked to exclusion and innovation deterrence

Google can also exclude competitors offering services overlapping with those offered by its own ecosystem.

In 2011, Microsoft accused Google of preventing rival search engines, including Microsoft's Bing, from indexing YouTube and therefore voluntarily degrading the quality of the service that other competitors could offer. This is typically a case where some of Google's own services were given a preferential treatment compared to third parties, and the case would not have arisen had Google not invested in its own video portal and associated advertising offering.

The FTC also investigated allegations that Google was: (i) using proprietary Application Programming Interfaces (APIs) in a way that hampered advertisers willing to switch from AdWords (Google's advertising service) to competing providers; and (ii) stifling innovation by erecting barriers to entry through unfair licensing of essential patents.[20] Google agreed to legally binding commitments in lieu of a full investigation. This directly led to a change in its APIs so that transfer to other advertising platforms would be easier, and a new fair licensing regime for any 'essential' Intellectual Property (IP) owned by Google.[21]

Recent Google cases in Europe

In 2014, the Directorate of the European Commission in charge of competition (DG Comp) expressed the following four concerns:

(a) Search results of Google services (hotel, restaurant, flight search, etc.) are displayed more favourably than competing services and users are unaware of this favourable treatment;

(b) Google uses content from competing search engines on its own site against their express will and without payments;

(c) Publishers are asked to sign exclusive advertising agreements with Google which risk reducing competition in the market for internet ads; and

(d) Google is actively preventing the development of technology that would facilitate the switching of ad campaigns from its own AdWords service to competing ones (such as Microsoft's AdCentre).

Instead of going to court, Google responded by proposing several legally binding undertakings,[22] including an agreement to inform its users about sponsored shopping results and to provide links to competitors (as illustrated in Figure 13.2). The Commission decided *in fine* to reject Google's offer, and

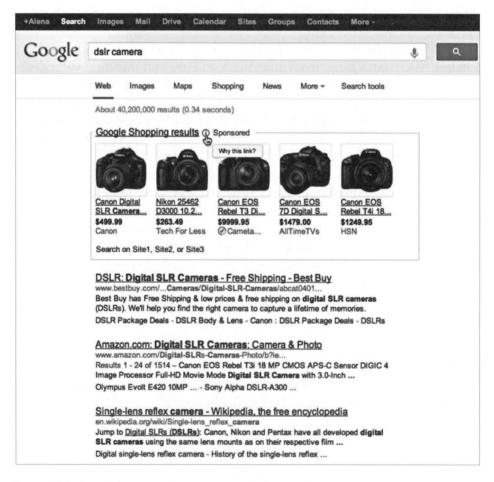

Figure 13.2 **Google's proposed search page during negotiations**

Source: EU Commission

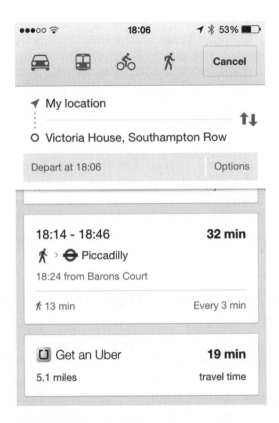

Figure 13.3 **Uber banner appearing in Google Maps mobile searches**

the EU is reviewing the evidence, but still believes that Google may well be favouring its own comparison shopping service.

Google also started showing the Uber option on the results of its mobile mapping application in June 2014 (see Figure 13.3). This is an interesting twist since Google is also a large shareholder of Uber,[23] and may therefore be in a position to offer favourable terms to Uber. However, in March 2016, Google announced that new partners would be added to its service, including 99Taxis in Brazil, Ola Cabs in India, Hailo in the UK and Spain, mytaxi in Germany and Spain, and Gett in the UK.

Google also came under scrutiny for its Android operating system and the extent to which handset partners, such as Samsung and HTC, were forced to pre-install Google apps[24] – and whether or not such a practice distorts competition. This again illustrates the extent to which Google can leverage parts of its ecosystem (in this case, its operating system platform) to secure prime 'real estate display' and default usage settings in order to favour its own services. The US lawsuit was dismissed in early 2015, but EU antitrust commissioner Margrethe Vestager also focused on Google's Android, and recently declared, 'Google's behaviour denies consumers a wider choice of mobile apps and services and stands in the way of innovation'.

In fact, Google is now being accused by the European Commission of using the Android operating system to tie together its own search engine, maps, Gmail and YouTube video services (among others) in order to leverage its position and increase its advertising revenues. The Commission's concerns, communicated to Google in July 2016, are likely to be the beginning of another protracted negotiation that may lead to a fully fledged regulatory and legal battle. We are of course only focusing on antitrust and competition matters, but Google, and other platforms, have also raised concerns about their tax affairs and their management of data privacy (and compliance with the 'right to be forgotten' principle) from the EU and member states.

What should governments, regulators and competition authorities do?

Our goal in the previous section was to distinguish between potentially legitimate competition concerns levied against platforms and misguided arguments rooted in bad regulations or due to a lack of understanding of platforms as business models. While we have used Google as an example to illustrate some of the potential ways in which platform-powered ecosystems may behave strategically to maintain their market power, we are not accusing Google – or indeed any other platforms – of systematically behaving anticompetitively. Each case is different, but we have highlighted specific areas where platforms may have the means and incentives to reduce competition. The purpose of this chapter was to provide a balanced view as to what may or may not constitute anticompetitive conduct in a platform world, and dispel some of the more self-serving arguments sometimes deployed by 'protected firms' while focusing on more relevant competition concerns.

We would, in particular, like to attract the attention of governments and competition authorities on the confusion around the notion of 'unfair competition' and encourage them to distinguish between regulatory provisions that platforms need to embrace in order to provide the quality of service and security expected and regulations aimed at preventing entry and innovation.

We, however, believe competition authorities should remain vigilant when dealing with platform-powered ecosystems able to leverage their market power across business models and product categories.

But most of the debates we've followed have been about trying to apply traditional regulatory instruments and thinking to the new world of platforms. This has often been a forced process, and few policymakers seem to have been able to truly grasp what platforms really are and how a new type of regulation could harness their power to flexibly embed regulatory requirements into the platforms themselves.

We believe that a new type of regulatory approach is warranted, and that public policy objectives should be reviewed in light of today's innovations. While the thinking around what some call Regulation 2.0 is only emerging, it sketches a way forward to provide a sustainable answer to the challenges brought about by platform-powered business models.[25] Regulations based on the need for pre-authorizations were often predicated on the fact that information was scarce and therefore an independent body needed to check and centralize it. Today, platforms could leverage their analytics to monitor who is doing what in near real time. Companies such as PayPal have engaged with regulators and encouraged such iterative approaches leveraging new data analytics tools to deal with the regulators' concerns. Platforms, since they mediate markets, generate both new types of market failures (around consumer safety, privacy and fraud, for example) and unique ways of addressing them (through data capture, analytics and governance). Professor Abbey Stemler even suggests setting out policy objectives, such as 'user feedback on platforms must be authentic' or 'services, spaces, and assets offered must be provided by legitimate and trustworthy users' to ensure that relevant data are gathered and analysed by platforms and governance iteratively updated until these objectives are met and good long-term regulatory outcomes secured.[26]

How should platforms deal with regulation and regulators?

It may be tempting for platforms to ignore regulations, and the 'ask for forgiveness rather than ask for permission' approach has been a guiding principle for many start-ups. The inherent iterative approach of new innovative firms trying to find a product/market fit is arguably not well suited to traditional regulations. However, we would strongly advise platform firms to engage with regulators, government officials and policymakers at the earliest opportunity in order to explain the value they bring to the market and what regulations hamper their development, if any. Frank and early engagement, with a cogent articulation of their value proposition and economic contribution, would allow them to shape the debate. Without engagement, disrupted companies, who often already have the right contacts within the media and government, are able to control the narrative. Being able to communicate and explain what the company does and its economic contribution, in terms of jobs, taxes generated and value added, is important for policymakers. It is also worth articulating benefits that are often ignored because they are not captured by traditional economic indicators such as gross domestic product. These include time saved by platform participants and increased convenience provided by the platform, enhanced choice and selection on the platform, as well as lower cost of products.[27]

Simple case studies showing how the platform is used help regulators to understand the benefits. For example, a traditional approach to planning holidays often required numerous visits to a travel agent, significant research to ensure that the destination will turn out as expected, that the hotel is suitable, and the flights selected are the most convenient and cost-effective. Using a platform such as TripAdvisor is easier, cheaper, less time-consuming, offers more choice and minimizes the risk of disappointment through the extensive use of real-time feedback on countries, hotels, restaurants and flights. The articulation of these benefits should help frame the debate with policymakers.

Platforms rely on both producers and users to market themselves. This co-creation effort can extend to regulation aspects. Airbnb and Uber have successfully encouraged their communities to engage with local authorities to promote the benefits of their services.

Successful platforms should also provide regulators with data on their activities in order to alleviate concerns. Existing regulations are often designed for data-poor environments and therefore seek to enforce rules *ex ante* in order to secure public policy objectives of reduced fraud, consumer protection, etc. If platforms are able to demonstrate that they have both the means and incentives to achieve the same objectives through their analytics, governance rules and trust frameworks, this will significantly alleviate many regulatory concerns.

Finally, platforms may be able to engage with policymakers to change and improve regulations. When current regulations impede innovative practices, it may be helpful to return to the original public policy objective that under-pins these regulations. The very innovations that platforms bring to the market could quite possibly be used to efficiently solve public policy concerns that led to the need for regulation in the first place. By focusing on market outcomes – rather than simply compliance and legacy regulations – regulators may be able to harness the power of platforms in the pursuit of their public policy objectives.

Government regulations for cars, when they were introduced in the 1910s, stipulated that cars were not allowed to go faster than horse carts, at around

5 mph. This limit, which had been suggested by horse cart drivers, was not very efficient. Incidentally, it also made it very difficult for cars not to stall. In England, the law even required that the automobilist had to notify a village constable of his arrival, so that officials could walk in front of the car waving two red warning flags while the driver followed slowly behind. Road regulations have moved on quite a bit since then. For platforms, however, the regulatory challenges ahead are still very significant and, as with the early days of cars, some regulations are likely to be more focused on the protection of the status quo rather than aimed at improving the lives of consumers.

Notes

1   Such regulators typically exist in sectors where monopoly provision used to be the norm before a transition towards a more competitive market structure was decided as part of a liberalization programme, such as in telecoms, energy, water, transport, post, etc.

2   We note that some renowned economists, such as George Stigler, have argued that regulators could be 'captured' by market participants and that regulation may in some cases lead to a worse outcome than market failures. There is, however, a broad consensus around the importance of regulation to deal with market failures.

3   Note that this is a significant departure from many traditional models driven by 'scarcity'. The more a traditional company sells its products, the less stock it has, and it needs to spend money to manufacture new products, often at a significant marginal cost, while with many platforms the more their services are used (often with a marginal cost close to zero), the more valuable they become.

4   Temporary promotions resulting in some products being sold below costs are of course possible, but cannot be systematic and across all product categories, since this would generate cumulative losses, preventing the firm from being sustainable.

5   See *Mr Y Aslam, Mr J Farrar and Others -V- Uber*, UK Employment Tribunal, Case Numbers: 2202551/2015, 28 October 2016, available at www.judiciary.gov.uk/ judgments/mr-y-aslam-mr-j-farrar-and-others-v-uber/.

6   'Uber Suspends UberPOP in France Following Turmoils and Arrests', *TechCrunch*, 3 July 2015, http://techcrunch.com/2015/07/03/uber-stops-uberpop-in-france-following-turmoils-and-arrests/.

7   'Tourist-Heavy Barcelona is Cracking Down on Airbnb', *Atlantic Citylab*, 25 December 2015, www.citylab.com/housing/2015/12/barcelona-airbnb-tourism/421788/

8   'Here's Everywhere Uber Is Banned Around the World', April 2015, www.business insider.com/heres-everywhere-uber-is-banned-around-the-world-2015-4?IR=T.

9   See Competition and Markets Authority response to Transport for London's private hire regulations proposals: www.gov.uk/government/uploads/system/uploads/attachment_ data/file/481450/CMA_response_to_TfL.pdf.

10   This chart shows how Uber is devastating New York's taxi business: www.goldman sachs.com/our-thinking/pages/2015-10-favorite-charts.html.

11   See Zaw Thiha Tun, 'Top Cities Where Airbnb Is Legal or Illegal', *Investopedia*, updated 30 October 2015, www.investopedia.com/articles/investing/083115/top-cities-where-airbnb-legal-or-illegal.asp.

12   See insightful piece from Richard Feasey, 'Compliance Is for Winners', Remarks at
     Cullen BITS Seminar on Platforms, Brussels, 16 July 2015, www.fronfraithltd.com/
     home/articles.

13   With a market capitalization of $529 billion as of 11 September 2016, just behind
     Apple.

14   We note that Google's search business is not always seen as a pure platform, since
     advertisers, rather than users, are the main source of revenues. We consider that Google
     directly connects information producers and information consumers. Irrespective of
     the approach used for the search market, Google is undeniably an ecosystem combin-
     ing different business models, including some with clear platform characteristics (such
     as its app store and operating system).

15   See Measuring Bias in 'Organic' Web Search, by Benjamin Edelman and Benjamin
     Lockwood from HBS: www.benedelman.org/searchbias/.

16   B. Edelman, *Leveraging Market Power Through Tying and Bundling: Does Google Behave
     Anti-Competitively?*, self-published, 2014, for a discussion of potential tying and bundling
     issues within Google's ecosystem, www.benedelman.org/publications/google-tying-
     2014-05-12.pdf.

17   See, for example, the European Commission's 2009 Guidance Paper proposing the
     following test: 'If the incremental price that customers pay for each of the dominant
     undertakings products in the bundle remains above the LRAIC of the dominant firm
     from including this product in the bundle, the Commission will normally not intervene
     since an equally efficient competitor with only one product should in principle be able
     to compete profitably against the bundle.' December 2008, OJ C45/7,§60.

18   The power of Google, Serving consumers or threatening competition? Hearing before
     the Sub Committee on Antitrust, Competition Policy and Consumer Rights of the Sub
     Committee on the Judiciary, 112th cong. 247 (2011). Submission of Jeremy Stoppelman,
     cofounder and CEO of Yelp! Inc and quoted by H. Shelanski, 'Information, Innovation,
     and Competition Policy for the Internet', *University of Pennsylvania Law Review*, 161,
     2013, 1664–705.

19   B. Edelman, *Leveraging Market Power Through Tying and Bundling: Does Google Behave
     Anti-Compettively?*, self published, 2014, identified eight different families of products
     and services that Google is linking to one another.

20   Including the 24,500 patents acquired as part of the Motorola Mobility acquisition in
     May 2012.

21   The binding settlement ('consent decree') signed by Google and the FTC in February
     2013 states that: 'Google has agreed to remove restrictions on the use of its online search
     advertising platform, AdWords, that may make it more difficult for advertisers to
     coordinate online advertising campaigns across multiple platforms. [This decision was
     taken] following concerns from some FTC Commissioners that Google's contractual
     conditions governing the use of its API made it more difficult for an advertiser to
     simultaneously manage a campaign on AdWords and on competing ad platforms.'

22   See: Commission obtains from Google comparable display of specialized search rivals,
     EU Memo/14/87, 5th February 2014.

23   Google Ventures invested $258 million in Uber's August 2013 round. See http://
     techcrunch.com/2013/08/22/google-ventures-puts-258m-into-uber-its-largest-deal-
     ever/.

24 See https://uk.finance.yahoo.com/news/smartphone-suit-against-google-plays-101909548.html, 18 July 2014.

25 White Paper: Regulation, the Internet Way: A Data-First Model for Establishing Trust, Safety, and Security, Nick Grossman, 8 April 2015.

26 See A. Stemler, 'Regulation 2.0: The Marriage of New Governance and Lex Informatica', Kelley School of Business Research Paper No. 16-25, March 2016.

27 See, for example, 'The Sharing Economy in the UK', report commissioned by Airbnb, Diane Coyle, 18 January 2016.

Chapter 14

Competing against platforms

We have seen how platforms are designed, ignited, scaled-up and defended once mature, but what about traditional businesses facing increased competition and disruptions from platform entrants?

How to deal with platform disruption is a question often asked by leaders of large established organizations. Traditional responses of established players to disruptive market entry often follow what we call the '5Ds' process (deny, deter, denigrate, delay and dollar!). Our experience, however, suggests that enlightened leadership may benefit from considering an alternative '5Es' pattern about engaging, enabling, enhancing, embracing and earning, to maximize value creation in an increasingly platform-powered economy. This is a significant shift in terms of mindset, and no one should underestimate the difficulty of the journey.

With this in mind, we note that since some of the most successful businesses out there are platform-powered ones, traditional firms may wish to leverage some of their key assets to add platform capabilities where relevant. As we saw previously, Apple is still generating more than 80% of all its revenues through the sale of hardware, but one of the key reasons why its hardware is so sought after is to be found in the strength of its overall app-based ecosystem.

In many cases, established firms looking to add platform capabilities already have a client base, which can constitute one side of a platform. Their priority should be to develop the other side – by inviting third-party producers – and enabling matching, connecting and transacting between the two sides. Starting from scratch is much more difficult since both sides need to be attracted at the same time. Traditional business models have strengths that pure platforms are unable to replicate. Therefore, markets where these strengths are key to success can remain relatively protected. Irrespective of the response to platform disruption, one thing is certain: the cultural shift required by many established players is significant. Denying markets are being disrupted or trying to undermine the innovation process brought about by platform entrants is a very risky long-term strategy indeed.

Traditional response to market disruption: 'the 5Ds'

The pattern of responses from firms in disrupted industries is quite consistent across geographies, sectors and even periods. Clearly some firms do behave differently and exceptions can be found, but the default response of established firms to disruptive entry usually follows some combination of the '5Ds' sequence described below.[1]

Deny: The first response of established market participants is to ignore that emerging competitors represent any form of threat. This is akin to the 'ostrich strategy', where individuals and firms decide to 'bury their heads in the sand' and ignore bad news rather than deal with the new information and adapt their strategy. In the words of Richard Tedlow, denial is 'the unconscious calculus that if an unpleasant reality were true, it would be too terrible, so therefore it cannot be true'. Sigmund Freud described denial as the combination of 'knowing with not knowing', while George Orwell called it bluntly 'protective stupidity'.[2] This response does not only apply to platforms, but change and disruption in general. For many years, firms such as Polaroid, IBM and Blockbuster were in denial. Today, many established companies challenged by platforms behave simply as if this was a temporary phenomenon that will go away, as illustrated in Figure 14.1.

Denigrate: Trying to downplay – or even undermine – what competitors are doing is a traditional reflex for established firms and industries that are being disrupted. Living in London, we often use black cabs[3] and sometimes indulge in discussions with their drivers. While we are big fans of black cab drivers and are always amazed at their unparalleled knowledge of London, their kind demeanour changes abruptly when competition is mentioned. In fact, mentioning Uber is an invitation to a diatribe about 'uninsured drivers', 'often without a driving licence', 'criminals that were not ID checked', 'not paying a cent in tax', etc. We would, of course, expect Uber and its drivers to be in serious legal trouble if all these accusations were true. Yet creating the doubt in the minds of potential customers by denigrating the platform-based competition is still seen by many as a worthwhile approach, at least in the short term.

Deter: When disruptive entrants can no longer be ignored and it is self-evident that markets are under threat, then traditional firms conclude that something

"What if we don't change at all ...
and something magical just happens?"

Figure 14.1 **Denial**
Source: Cartoonresource/Shutterstock.com

drastic has to be done. A strong signal needs to be sent to the enemy, a credible
threat, or even in some cases a physical one, as in the case of French taxi
drivers turning on Uber drivers and their passengers. The ultimate objective
of deterrence is to make entry costly (and bias the risk/reward equation
underpinning the opportunity). This phase is usually associated with a strong
lobbying strategy in order to mobilize government agencies and policymakers
who can prevent disruptive entry through regulatory means. Public relations
campaigns are also often used during this stage to highlight the benefits of
the current market model and undermine the credibility of disruptors or
potential disruptors. From an economic perspective, the more protected the
incumbent business, the higher its incentives to invest in deterrence.

Delay: Delaying tactics are almost always used by established firms in order
to postpone disruption. In many cases, established firms operate within a broad
regulatory environment, and one of the most potent ways of delaying
disruptive entry is to use regulatory and legal arguments to prevent entrants
from being allowed to establish themselves. It is, however, important to also
highlight the fact that a number of global platforms may have been happy to
enter markets without first being fully compliant, and that testing legal
boundaries also comes at a price.

Dollar. Ultimately established companies often try to get some form of compensation, to make up for what they would have earned had their markets not been disrupted, through the courts, from the government or even from consumers (through raised prices). An example is taxi companies asking for their 'medallions' or 'licence' to be repurchased by the government at full price.[4] This is predicated upon the belief that their income should be guaranteed by somebody and that they should not bear any economic risk. It is understandable that a driver would feel cheated after buying a licence at peak price – on the understanding that she is buying monopoly protection – and subsequently finding out that there is in fact increasing competition in the market. Going forward, it is therefore important for buyers of such licences to factor in the risk of disruption and to negotiate prices accordingly. Governments and regulators should also come clean about the fact that they are unlikely to be able to shield drivers from more efficient and innovative competitors forever. This stage can be particularly difficult since disrupted firms try to be compensated at the time when their value proposition is seriously undermined by disruptive new entrants.

New response to market disruption: 'the 5Es'

We have observed the pattern of the '5Ds' in a number of sectors and geographies. While we understand the temptation to fight for the status quo, we believe that relying on such strategies is unlikely to be optimal in the long term. Usually, platform disruption means that key elements of the value proposition can be provided in much more efficient and innovative ways.[5]

Ultimately, we propose a range of alternative approaches, some more difficult to implement than others, but all focused on the root causes of the problem rather than its symptoms.

Embracing market disruption and trying to understand the nature of the business models and value propositions that are emerging is a far more valuable activity than denial. It is the key to having a baseline for action. Dispassionate insights into the nature of the threat being faced, as well as the existing capabilities and assets that can be leveraged, is a first essential step for a strategic response. It is key to a culture of experimentation, either directly, through partnerships or investments. It is also about the ability of established firms to read weak market signals and capture them in market development scenarios against which they can test their generic strategies and the (preferably unique) value they can bring to the market going forward. These 'sensing' and 'seizing' skills are key dynamic capabilities required to fully embrace new opportunities.

Enabling clients *and* relevant market participants is often a way of carving out a sustainable market position. Instead of trying to protect existing equilibria and market structures at all costs, it may be more effective to engage with disruptors – while still from a position of strength – in order to find ways to deliver superior market value. Platforms are very unique businesses that face serious challenges before they reach a critical mass, and existing firms can therefore find partnership opportunities. Of course, fear of cannibalization has to be dealt with, and a simple strategy of enablement without value capture is unlikely to be sustainable. However, it is important to recognize how the formidable strengths of existing players in terms of brands, distribution channels and access to finance can be combined with innovative platform entrants to offer superior products and services. When Reed Hastings, founder of Netflix, a new start-up at the time, approached Blockbuster's CEO in 2000 to discuss a potential partnership, he was apparently 'laughed out of the office'.[6] A few years later, Blockbuster filed for bankruptcy. Both firms could have probably benefited from a deal at the time, though apparently Blockbuster more so than Netflix. Now partnerships and ecosystem management may involve application programming interfaces (APIs) that firms can develop to give access to some of their capabilities.[7]

Enhancing capabilities and value propositions rather than simply investing large sums in deterrence strategies is likely to pay better dividends in the long term. As we have seen, above-average economic value is only fundamentally created in one of three ways: (a) by being more innovative than competitors; (b) by being more efficient than competitors; and (c) by being able to abuse a position of market power. Since (c) is not legal in most jurisdictions, and assuming that ultimately competition authorities will be efficient at enforcing competition law, investments in efficiency and innovation capabilities are key to profit generation.

In the case of taxis, it is pretty obvious that offering a real-time app with location information and accepting credit cards instead of cash would be an obvious commercial response to reduce the competitive gap between taxis and Uber. Being even more welcoming, knowledgeable about their city and friendly with clients would also further enhance their value proposition and help differentiate them from alternatives. Yet despite a number of announcements, there is little evidence that all taxis are embracing this view at the moment.

Encouraging those who are a force for change internally – and externally – in order to develop new organizational capabilities rather than support the status quo will, in most cases, be more effective than simply delaying the entry of competitors. Plenty of individuals and groups within traditional businesses are well aware of the competitive threats and understand the potential for disruption of these new platform business models. Often these people even have ideas and projects to respond and compete effectively against new entrants, but they struggle to get their voices heard. Unable to get the attention of top management in order to harness the resources required to implement their recommendations, they become disillusioned and resentful towards those who try to maintain the status quo at all cost. The most adventurous ones may even leave and provide valuable knowledge and expertise to the very start-ups that are taking on their former employers. These departures are significant losses for established firms, and further reduce their ability to respond to the threats in a timely manner.

Earning their keep instead of asking for compensation is the best way for firms to develop a sustainable long-term position. This doesn't mean that disrupted companies should not invest in a robust regulatory defence, but the ultimate objective should be to support a winning business strategy delivering a relevant value proposition to the market rather than prevent competition from altering the status quo. Betting the ranch on long-term regulatory protection from innovation and more efficient entrants is a risky gamble.

Some practical options to manage platform disruptions

Arguably, the '5Ds' and '5Es' above are highly simplified and very generic descriptions of possible responses to platform disruption. In some cases, the two lists are not mutually exclusive. Mounting legal challenges in order to 'delay' the entry of some new disruptive competitor that may not comply with local legislation could be a legitimate course of action for established companies keen to buy time to adapt their business. But our experience suggests that established firms often waste valuable time and resources by going through their 'Ds' instead of strategically investing to address the platform challenges ahead. With this in mind, we believe established non-platform companies can deploy a range of strategies to deal with the challenges of platform competition. Here are a few suggested areas:

Understand platform market dynamics

Benjamin Franklin once said that 'an investment in knowledge pays the best interest'. We agree with this maxim and believe that the single most dangerous pitfall for many established firms in the next decade would be a failure to grasp the underlying economic models that are disrupting so many markets. The key to competing against platforms – or becoming one – is to understand the way they operate and what it means for the industry and for the business – both in terms of opportunities and threats. At a macro level, industries characterized by relatively high transaction costs, asymmetry of information and regulatory protection are now ripe for disruption by innovative digital entrants. In many cases, these entrants have proven that customers can be more efficiently served and transactions better coordinated through a platform business model. Even if parts of an industry are not directly impacted (for example, car production), the firms operating in this industry may see that platforms are disrupting their market (for example, by undermining car ownership and therefore depressing demand). Some traditional platforms, such as lenders, estate agents or recruiters, also need to realize the threat for them not to embrace a digital platform strategy. They operate in markets that are particularly open to disruptive entry and cannot afford to rely on legacy management systems, technology and processes.

If not a leader . . . develop real 'fast follower' capabilities

Innovation may be a rewarding game, but it is also a very difficult one, and there is increasing evidence suggesting larger organization are finding it more difficult to innovate.[8] But not being the first out of the starting blocks doesn't mean that the race is lost. In fact, established companies often have valuable assets and capabilities that can help new ideas scale faster. This opens a strategic option sometimes called 'fast follower' that is predicated upon the ability to scale an idea rather than come up with it. In the words of Reid Hoffman, being the 'first to scale' rather than the first to launch a product is now the name of the game.[9] Many traditional firms talk about being 'fast followers', and while this a laudable strategy (rooted in solid research),[10] it only works if the company focuses on developing the capabilities to be able to identify market niches and business innovations, and quickly scale their new value proposition. Such a fast follower strategy relies on a superior ability to identify and seize opportunities before scaling them. This in turn requires investments in dynamic capabilities, described below.

Develop dynamic capabilities to see, seize and harness opportunities

It is worth noting that while traditional firms often develop 'ordinary' capabilities and focus on efficiency improvements, firms embracing platform-powered business models tend to master higher-level capabilities, enabling them to better 'orchestrate' resources, within and outside the firm. In fact, harnessing the power of communities, such as users and producers, while managing complementary business models as part of a platform-powered ecosystem, requires strong 'dynamic capabilities'. Using David Teece's framework, it can be said that the advent of platform firms makes the need for dynamic capabilities more salient. Platform firms need the sensing skills required to spot market changes, the seizing skills required to address new opportunities and the transforming skills needed to ensure the overall organization, and its ecosystem, remain relevant. We note that while it is difficult to attribute precisely to what extent a given firm may display these capabilities, all the platform-powered ecosystem companies in our case studies have displayed inordinate sensing, seizing and transforming skills to get where they are today. These skills are at the heart of the dynamic capabilities framework.[11]

Develop your own platform-powered ecosystem

As we have seen, a platform-powered ecosystem is made up of a combination of business models and has been an extremely successful organizational form for companies such as Apple, Google, Microsoft, Facebook and Amazon. Without necessarily trying to emulate the scale of these giants, it is possible to introduce platform capabilities to an existing business model in order to benefit from its characteristics. Ideally, this needs to be done on the back of a strategic review of the markets the firms operate in, and based on the identification of market niches where platform characteristics (e.g. long tail, community involvement, etc.) are highly valued. The permutations and synergies between existing business models and platforms can then be assessed in light of these opportunities and experiments launched to validate the proof of concept. Online retailer Zalando[12] decided to proactively open its traditional retail model further to create a fashion ecosystem. Today, shoppers can already be matched with fashion stylists with Zalon, Zalando's curated shopping service, but Zalando's co-founder Robert Gentz's vision for the future is to go far beyond: 'to connect every stakeholder in the fashion world: retailers, stationary stores, advertising agencies, logistic services, app developers and many more'.[13]

It may also pay off to partner with – or invest in – young platforms before they scale in order to benefit from their expertise while helping them to realize their true potential. Established firms may not be as nimble as new entrants, but they often benefit from valuable assets and capabilities that can be harnessed in the context of a competitive response. The recent acquisition of Onefinestay – a UK-headquartered premium start-up offering access to luxury accommodations in London, Los Angeles, New York City, Paris and Rome – by the Accor Group can be seen in that light. Accor's CEO Sébastien Bazin told its investors they had missed an early opportunity to invest in Airbnb, that Accor would have needed between two and three years to develop a competing offer, and that it would have been a 'terrible idea' for the group to do this internally.[14] Accor Group will help Onefinestay scale its offering to 40 new cities within the next five years. While details on how Accor may provide access to its client base and loyalty reward programme have not yet been announced, joint collaboration on these would be a logical next step for the group. Accor also announced that it would open its online booking service to independent hotels in order to counter the threat of increasingly powerful holiday booking platforms such as Expedia, Priceline.com or Booking.com. These initiatives may well help Accor become a fully fledged platform-powered ecosystem.

Make sure incentives don't get in the way

In some cases, the reward and incentive structure of top management doesn't help with decision-making in light of significant disruption. As a senior executive of a large established business that is starting to be disrupted by platform-powered entrants, would you rather:

(a) tell your board that all is fine – as your stock options vest quietly over the next two years; carry on managing the existing business on a quarterly basis and execute the current strategy – agreed by all – before moving on to your next role/retiring; or

(b) go to your board and explain that the current strategy is under threat, that the very basis of competition in your industry is changing, that you need to reorganize globally and that this will be hard and risky work and that dividends may need to be lowered over the next few years so that you can invest to transform the business?

The established organizations able to incentivize choice (b) over choice (a) have a significantly better chance to successfully deal with the kind of disruption brought about by platforms. Launching your own platform is likely to bring new challenges, such as potential cannibalization of the traditional model itself. A new reward and incentive system may also be needed. This is of course linked to the transformational aspects of the dynamic capabilities that firms need to build to be able to remain relevant.

Become an experienced platform user

Many of the efficiencies brought about by platforms can be captured simply by using them. Identifying the assets, processes and resources that are historically kept in-house but could be replaced by the use of disruptive platforms may generate significant savings while providing insights into the workings of platform businesses in general. Offices could be shared, temporary expertise could be hired, and new, efficient and cost-effective suppliers could be identified in ways that bypass and supplement traditional and (often cumbersome) in-house processes. Traditional firms may still need to keep many activities 'in-house' and tightly integrated – as they are at the heart of the unique value proposition that is offered – but the use of platforms in a client capacity can unlock significant value where the firm has no particular competitive advantage – or arguably is at a competitive disadvantage. For example, crowdsourcing ideas by using platforms such as Crowdicity or InnoCentive is an easy way for large established firms to tap into a global and diverse network of innovators.

Analyse platform disruption holistically and focus on 'non-Uberizable' markets

Some businesses are unlikely to be *directly* impacted by platform models. This is especially the case where end-to-end control of the value chain is a critical element of the production process. For example, a platform business is unlikely to be optimal for the mass manufacturing of cars. The coordination of the various production stages needs to be tightly controlled, and while car manufacturers increasingly need to manage a complex ecosystem of suppliers and technology, their core business model remains linear.

But does that mean new platform businesses are irrelevant in this industry and will not have any impact on car companies? Of course not. The rise of platforms enabling the sharing economy movement – both in terms of renting other people's cars or sharing rides with them – will no doubt have a profound impact on future demand for cars. Some observers are predicting a future where personal car ownership becomes a distant memory and an economic aberration. Recent moves by General Motors (who invested $500 million in Uber's competitor Lyft and is forging strategic alliances with other platforms) suggest that some companies are taking notice and trying to secure orders from companies that will be tomorrow's customers. Lyft is unlikely to become a car manufacturer and compete against GM, yet it is one of the companies disrupting the transportation market, which will definitely have an effect on demand for cars. These 'second order' effects can be missed if the assessment of possible platform disruption is too narrowly focused on the emergence of direct competitors.

But while platforms are formidable business models in many respects, they fail to deliver on a range of fronts. Many activities require tight control over the value chain to ensure high quality and consistency, and platforms are not good at enabling this. By focusing on markets where these characteristics are prominent, it is possible to strengthen a competitive position that a platform would struggle to undermine. It still leaves the business open to traditional competitors, but at least fundamental disruption can be avoided. Some large groups have just started to review their portfolio of activities in this light and to consider disposing of assets in markets likely to be disrupted while reinvesting in businesses less exposed to platform disruption.

Notes

1   We note a loose parallel between the organizational 5Ds we are using to describe firms' responses to disruption and the Kubler-Ross model of grief that suggests a very personal pattern starting with denial, anger, bargaining, depression and acceptance.

2   Richard S. Tedlow, *Denial: Why Business Leaders Fail to Look Facts in the Face – and What to Do About It*, New York: Penguin Portfolio, 2010.

3   Black cabs in London are a good example of strong established market participants who, while being among the best in the world in terms of market knowledge, security and efficiency, are fighting hard to keep new entrants at bay. Their approach very much matches the 5Ds described above, while we believe they would be a formidable force if they were to embrace the 5Es instead.

4   It is worth noting that in France, taxi licences are given for free by the government but subsequently traded by taxi drivers and taxi companies for substantial sums.

5   We agree with Peter Thiel when he says that markets where companies are able to gain market power based on their innovations are a lot more attractive than markets where undifferentiated companies compete on low margins to survive. See Peter Thiel, 'Competition Is for Losers', *Wall Street Journal*, 12 September 2014 (based on *Zero to One: Notes on Startups, or How to Build the Future*).

6   Source: CNET, 9 December 2010, Greg Sandoval. https://www.cnet.com/uk/news/blockbuster-laughed-out-at-netflix-partnership-offer/

7   Recent research by Seth Benzell, Guillermo Lagarda and Marshall Van Allstyne from Boston University and MIT (12 July 2016) seems to suggest that firms adopting APIs become more profitable than those who don't. See http://questromworld.bu.edu/platformstrategy/files/2016/07/S4-Seth-Benzell-Guillermo-Lagarda-role-apis-economy-7-12.pdf.

8   M. Wessel, 'Why Big Companies Can't Innovate', *Harvard Business Review*, September 2012, https://hbr.org/2012/09/why-big-companies-cant-innovate.

9   See, for example, *Wired* article by Cade Metz dated 14 September 2015 titled 'Silicon Valley Success Goes to the Fastest, Not the First'.

10 P. Geroski and C. Markides, *Fast Second: How Smart Companies Bypass Radical Innovation to Enter and Dominate New Markets*, San Francisco, CA: Jossey-Bass, 2005.

11 David Teece, 'The Foundations of Enterprise Performance: Dynamic and Ordinary Capabilities in an (Economic) Theory of Firms', *Academy of Management Perspectives*, 8(4), 2014, 328–52.

12 Zalando generated €3.6 billion in 2016, with a growth rate of 23%, 17 January 2017, Zalando's corporate website.

13 'How Zalando Is Becoming the Online Fashion Platform for Europe', 1 June 2016, https://blog.zalando.com/en/blog/how-zalando-becoming-online-fashion-platform-europe.

14 Murad Ahmed and Adam Thomson, 'Accor to Acquire Online Home Rental Site Onefinestay', *Financial Times*, 5 April 2016.

Chapter 15

The future of platforms

As we have seen, platform-based business models are having a profound impact on the business world. In the words of Ray Fisman and Tim Sullivan, in their insightful book *The Inner Lives of Markets*:

> Not even the market designers themselves have all the answers: economics is an inexact science, and every time we participate in a market innovation – each time we hail a ride via a smartphone or download a song via iTunes – we're part of a massive social experiment whose ultimate consequences are unknown.

While, like them, we remain optimistic and see the potential for good, we are acutely aware that the long-term consequences of the current platform revolution are unclear. Society will need to apply judgement and common sense to ensure that the potential negative side effects of these innovative business models are minimized. Platforms are likely to change the way people work, are managed, get paid, share and collaborate, interact with others – humans and 'robots' – generate insights from data, and organize themselves to deal with world issues. We discuss these changes in turn in this final chapter.

The future of work

The way people work and interact with one another in an increasingly platform-based economy will be vastly different from the traditional work relationships of the past. In fact, a recent study[1] of all drivers of change affecting our economies by the World Economic Forum singles out 'the changing nature of work and talent platforms' as the most important trend.[2]

Platforms provide a unique degree of flexibility, transparency and trust to their participants. They organize markets that would have otherwise been very difficult for individuals to participate in. Being able to work specific time shifts around one's own life constraints (picking up kids from school, looking after elderly relatives, etc.) can in some cases make the difference between being able to work and having to stay at home, possibly relying on state benefits. While some will no doubt see this flexibility as another form of alienation,[3] we can't help but see it as an opportunity to unlock job creation and economic growth. And we're not alone. A recent McKinsey report on talent platforms[4] suggests that $2.7 trillion of value could be created by talent platforms alone by 2025. This is equivalent to the GDP of the UK. That amount could be generated simply by increasing labour force participation for existing workers, reducing unemployment through better job matching and raising productivity through better coordination of work through platforms. In fact, the countries currently struggling with the most inefficient labour markets are the ones that would benefit the most from the development of talent platforms.[5] Upwork now has more than 12 million freelancers globally who can help with coding duties, graphic design, financial planning, etc. and over 10,000 sign-ups every day.

Firms can tap into these platforms in order to supplement their own capabilities or develop their own internal platforms to flexibly secure the skills and capabilities they need. Eden McCallum, a successful management consulting firm headquartered in the UK, uses a hybrid model of full-time analysts and partners supplemented by hundreds of part-time consultants who are members of its platform. Launchworks, our own advisory business, uses some of the same principles to develop its global network of platform experts.

And this is just the beginning. Existing platforms are still very much version 1.0 of talent platforms. While existing models focus on connecting companies with individual contributors, new generations of platforms will allow entire teams to coordinate projects and offer turnkey solutions. HoneyBook, for example, is a platform connecting event managers, creative professionals and clients. It provides tools to coordinate a team of producers (caterers, photographs, venue rental, make-up, event planning, etc.) to manage events throughout their entire life cycle, from the proposal to invoicing stages.

However, the transition from a traditional labour market to a platform-powered one is unlikely to go smoothly for all. As the physical location of platform workers is increasingly irrelevant for some jobs, the cost of work can be driven down significantly. This has been happening for years in the manufacturing sector, with China becoming the world's factory. Platforms are now enabling this for services. Entire businesses now rely on externalized flexible workforces for a range of activities. Amazon's Mechanical Turk,[6] for example, provides 'businesses and developers access to an on-demand scalable workforce', while 'workers can select from thousands of tasks and work whenever it's convenient'. Tasks are called HITs (human intelligence tasks) and can be posted – and carried out – by anybody. Testing features of a website, transcribing a recording, tagging content of pictures, answering questions of a survey, and moderating content of a blog are some of the *hundred of thousands* of tasks posted on the site at any point in time. In fact, some companies outsource entire processes, such as the 24/7 monitoring of comments on a blog or the tagging of images before their publication, to the Mechanical Turk. Since these tasks can be carried out globally, unless a specific expertise is required, such as language or coding skills, the pricing is quite low by US or European standards. This means that many 'low-level' tasks can now be efficiently and flexibly outsourced to a platform, and that therefore 'high-cost' workers are increasingly unlikely to be able to compete for these activities. You don't need to have offices everywhere to arbitrage labour market rates anymore. Knowledge workers are now a click away, and this is understandably one aspect of globalization that is increasingly worrying employees and governments.

The future of management

Platform companies will change the way we work, and leading these new organizations successfully will require very different management skills. As we have seen, platform business models, and their cousins, platform-powered ecosystems, have unique organizational models. All the key management disciplines, as taught in business school and learned on the job, are impacted by these changes. We have, for example, observed a number of differences in areas such as strategy development, organizational design, finance and talent management. We also believe that these differences will increase, as many platforms that started off using the same tools as traditional firms are now adapting these management principles to the new challenges they are facing. Many of these approaches are new and therefore still in a state of flux, but we highlight some of the patterns we see emerging.

We see the yearly strategic planning process of traditional firms superseded by more organic and iterative models where portfolios of experiments and hypothesis have to be tested over a short time frame before the strategy is reviewed in light of new available data.

In terms of organizational design, while many platforms started off with traditional hierarchical structures, we have witnessed an increasing drive to create communication channels across business areas to avoid the silo mentality and truly enable coordination across the various sides of the platforms. This is important since having a structure where different sides of the platforms are managed independently – with a distinct business unit leader in charge of the performance of his 'side' – would almost always result in a suboptimal market outcome unless the CEO constantly arbitrates between 'side owners' in order to ensure that the platform is balanced. For example, rewarding the head of one side of the business with additional resources based on his success, something seen as natural in a traditional firm, may result in increased imbalance on the platform and undermine its overall success. We are increasingly seeing calls for more flexible organizational forms allowing iterative resource allocation decisions between sides, depending upon which one is a bottleneck for the growth of the platform at a given point in time. This requires management able to internalize and orchestrate more holistic success metrics. Platforms typically need employees and leaders who understand and are able to harness dynamic network effects rather than staff who can optimize static processes.

Financial management is also drastically different, with some platforms being able to largely outsource some of the risks of trading physical stocks and associated cash flow requirements onto platform participants. That's why marketplaces such as eBay or Alibaba have been able to scale-up quickly with a huge inventory without incurring these costs. Alternatively, platforms are able to reduce risk through data analytics to more effectively deploy their own capital. Deliveroo, the restaurant delivery marketplace, knows so much about areas lacking quality food, that it recently announced it would partner with restaurants and invest in setting up dedicated kitchens – so-called RooBoxes – in order to further stimulate the growth of the platform.

Lastly, platforms themselves increasingly require specific talents. The necessity to manage an ecosystem often requires technology-savvy individuals, comfortable with ambiguity and fluid networks, to help design and grow the platform. Generally, we see talents with advanced degrees and more international outlooks attracted to, and successful at, the kinds of challenges that potentially global platforms throw up. Lastly, we see significant transferable skills from one platform to another, even across industries, and we are starting to see talents able to build on their experiences with 'platform careers' spanning multiple firms. Our own corporate and consulting experience at Launchworks strongly points to the importance of having senior individuals able to build and deploy cross-industry platform knowledge.

The platform-powered 'sharing economy'

Platforms powering sharing economy activities will undoubtedly continue their expansion. Today, they can be classified into five broad categories:

- The sharing of goods, from recirculation of second-hand goods (eBay or Craiglist) to shared usage (Drivy and Turo for peer-to-peer car rentals,

BlaBlaCar for car-sharing trips, Airbnb for home rentals, Love Home Swap for home exchanges).

- Knowledge sharing, such as massive open online course (MOOC) platforms connecting students all over the world with universities (edX, FUN, Coursera).
- Money sharing, where projects can be financed through crowdfunding or crowd-lending platforms (Kiva, Kickstarter, Lending Club).
- Time/service sharing, where people can share their time and expertise, on an ad hoc or regular basis with others in need (Stootie, TaskRabbit, Thumbtack).
- Content sharing, from music platforms connecting amateur artists and listeners (SoundCloud) to user-generated content platforms (Reddit).

Many of the platforms that we have talked about in this book are for-profit private companies, often backed by sizeable VC investments. Their business model is designed to maximize the value that they can capture and reward their shareholders accordingly. When successful, platforms can indeed return very significant sums to their backers, as early shareholders of the GAFAMs (Google, Apple, Facebook, Amazon and Microsoft) will testify. Even when platform participants are not allowed to make a profit themselves,[7] the platform owner can generate significant profits as a result of the service provided. While this has enabled the development of successful large-scale transformative platform companies, bringing much-needed efficiency to numerous markets, many now believe that the promise of platforms powering the 'sharing economy' is flawed. The initial dream of green 'co-creation' and 'co-consumption' enabled by platforms and shared by many early platform enthusiasts seems to have been replaced by a platform-powered capitalist market economy more able to extract value from both its workers and its assets.

The arguments that have been raised against such platforms include:[8] (i) they are for-profit and therefore concentrate rather than redistribute wealth; (ii) they aim at becoming dominant and driving out other market participants; (iii) they are not really green as they stimulate consumption; (iv) they replicate discrimination biases rather than solve them; (v) they exploit labour by breaking/circumventing existing laws; (vi) they shift the risk of production from the company to the participants; and (vii) they are managed privately top-down rather than by their participants bottom-up.

Many of these arguments are not without merit, and privately owned platforms do indeed seem to accumulate wealth for their shareholders – like most successful businesses. Platforms also reflect some discriminatory biases already present in society. Everything else being equal, a study showed that

African–American hosts on average charge 12% less renting their homes on Airbnb than white hosts.[9] When platforms stimulate consumption (e.g. make people travel more because Airbnb is cheaper than alternatives), they increase the carbon footprint rather than lower it.

In many ways, platforms still reflect many of the issues affecting our society, but the question is whether or not platforms can demonstrate that they have a positive impact overall. Since platforms have both positive and negative impacts, the question is really about the net effect of the disruption. On one side of the argument, many established providers and associated jobs are at risk, but on the other end, like other innovations, platforms create jobs and result in lower prices, increased convenience and greater choice for millions of users. And that's probably why the views on platforms are so polarized; some stakeholders are negatively impacted while others are winning out.

The increased productivity brought about by platforms – and other innovative companies – may magnify some imbalances in our economies and require government intervention. For example, the prospect of having to deal with increased levels of unemployment is leading many policymakers and economists – of all persuasions – to call for an unconditional basic income to be put in place.[10]

Platforms themselves may be able to adopt more collective governance models, such as modern forms of 'cooperatives'. While the concept of sharing value between contributing members is appealing, cooperatives may find it more difficult to raise funds (since shares are often fixed at their nominal value) and to reward stakeholders with different motivations. This makes it more difficult for these models to scale.

We are also likely to see the emergence of hybrid models where the platform is co-owned by the communities using it. Some platforms have toyed with such models in the past and Reddit went as far as to announce its intention of sharing 10% of new equity with members when raising $50 million in September 2014.[11] However, the lack of regulatory clarity, combined with the legal and tax issues associated with shared ownership, have hampered progress for the time being.

Given that these issues affect so many countries, we believe that governments and lawmakers have a significant role to play in shaping platform friendly policies. This could enable the emergence of more flexible platform-based organizations, where value and equity are shared in a simple and effective way with their contributing participants and the wider ecosystem.

A few sharing economy platforms have recently taken a stance to address the profit conundrum. Benefit Corporations include Etsy, Juno, and Kickstarter, which reincorporated as a benefit corporation in 2015.[12] Kickstarter's mission is driven first by how well they bring creative projects to life before the size of their profits. Kickstarter measures project success rates (typically only 9% of projects fail to deliver results)[13] as a key driver of added value.

It is also very possible that more open, decentralized platforms, with shared governance models, as advocated by many within the sharing economy movement, are able to scale and offer successful alternatives not controlled by large corporations. Sites such as OpenBazaar, while in their infancy at the time of writing, are proposing totally open, not-for-profit, peer-to-peer platform functionalities to buy and sell a wide range of goods and services. Underground platforms that have existed on the Dark Web for years, such as Silk Road, have also shown that organic bottom-up platform models could succeed (and even reach a critical mass of buyers and sellers of illegal goods and services!).

Platforms will increasingly power complex ecosystems

Traditional business models have significant strengths that platforms are finding difficult to match (and vice versa). Firms such as Amazon that have managed to combine both business models have been able to create incredibly powerful companies. We believe this trend will carry on, and that while many markets will be successfully served – and disrupted – by pure platforms, the number of firms effectively combining traditional and new business models will increase. Firms will increasingly look at parts of their value creation processes that could be replaced or supplemented by platform models (or new entrants will show them). Many firms will then try to introduce these capabilities to their operations while pure platforms will also develop non-platform business models. Large retailers (including 'digital ones' such as Zalando) are now realizing that being online is not enough and are looking at ways to supplement their e-commerce operations with platform models. Hotel chains such as Accor are adding new platform capabilities. Car manufacturers have started making partnerships with ride-sharing companies. The answer of established firms is still a bit chaotic, but the direction of travel is clear.

Platform of things

Automation

Platform ecosystems will increasingly include automated 'sides'. If the future that GM is preparing for materializes soon, we will have the option to hail (or pre-book) a self-driving car from an app in just a few years' time.[14] This is not as far-fetched as many people think, and since the disruptive entry of Tesla, Uber and Google in the race for self-driving capabilities, the pressure has been mounting for traditional car manufacturers to get their act together. It is relatively easy to imagine a platform model where one side is entirely automated. There may still be a market for hand-driven rides (like handmade suits) for many years to come, but self-driving cars certainly have the potential to replace cab – and truck – drivers within a generation. In fact, parts of platform business models are likely to become automated in the near future.

Home automation is now around the corner with a range of controllable devices, from thermostat to audiovisual equipment, representing entry points for companies keen on developing their ecosystems. Google acquired Nest and Dropcam to extend the reach of its platform-powered ecosystem into the home; Amazon has its innovative, always-on Alexa speaker; Microsoft is trying to leverage the role of its Xbox and Windows 10, etc. Many of the connected devices that will appear over the next few years will be able to interact with various apps within, or even across, different platform-powered ecosystems. The development of cross-platform IoT enabling Web services such as If This Then That (IFTTT.com) or Yonomi – which allow users to connect and control devices from different manufacturers – is testimony to the growth potential of these applications.

Technology underpinning platform businesses is improving everyday

Current platform business models are powered by technologies such as relational databases, instant Internet-based communications and matching algorithms. To start with, all of these technologies benefit from regular hardware performance improvements.[15]

But more fundamental innovations in these areas, such as blockchains, which are effectively distributed ledgers, also contribute to the development of key building blocks able to further unlock the potential of platforms as business models. By lowering the friction for securely registering time-stamped *transactions*, blockchain technology can provide a global, scalable, low-cost registrar for contracts and commitments between platform agents. This has the potential to strengthen and broaden platforms' *transaction* capabilities globally.

The Internet provides connectivity, with quasi ubiquitous coverage, and enabling platform business models in an increasing number of countries. Emerging platforms of things even have dedicated operators such as Sigfox vying for their attention.

Other software building blocks, such as matching algorithm – increasingly powered by artificial intelligence models – and instant messaging solutions are also evolving at an unprecedented pace, and enabling increasingly efficient and frictionless *matching and connection* of platform participants. Analytics and big data provide unique ways of monitoring platforms in real time and *optimizing* their architecture.

In fact, the availability of core software-powering platforms – often through the software as a service model (SaaS) – is now making basic technical development of a platform proposition very easy.[16]

Platforms to save the world

Lastly, we think platforms also have the potential to help us deal with some of the global issues of our time, including inequalities, diseases, food and water supply, and global warming. Governments have shown the limits of existing domestic bureaucratic systems in dealing with many of these global challenges. Non-governmental organizations have sought to fill this void with some success, but the overall system remains woefully inadequate in light of the challenges we face. The allocation of money and resources is often very inefficient, their matching inadequate, and the connection between those who can help and those who need help is often heavily mediated if not simply absent from the altruistic process.

The best progress made in recent years may well have been achieved by rich philanthropists who decided to apply business thinking to the world's largest problems. These donors are prepared to give vast sums of money. However, they need to know that their capital is efficiently deployed according to clear strategic objectives, with projects carefully selected, tracked and closely monitored on the ground. Yet even the most sophisticated and advanced programs, such as the ones run by the Bill and Melinda Gates Foundation, recognize that there is much to do and that even good management techniques and technology may not be sufficient.

There is still a huge imbalance between the issues that cause the most suffering in the world and the ones that attract money because they are popular with donors. In a recent 'Ask Me Anything' online session on well-known social platform Reddit, Bill Gates's answer to a question about what is yet to be done was the following:

> So far we have not been able to use technology to connect people to the needs of the poorest in countries that are [too] far away to tap into their empathy. I think this can be done but it needs some missing creativity.

Jeremy Rifkin also describes how important an emphatic civilization is going to be to solve the world's problems.[17] Platforms have many of the characteristics required to help with the issues mentioned above. It should be possible to find ways to create this empathic connection that Jeremy Rifkin is so keen on. For example, an app – maybe a role-playing game – where the character being played is randomly generated – using real-world statistics – and has to overcome real-life challenges could help with this. Once the character 'dies' in the virtual world, the money generated by the game (either directly or through sponsorship) gets paid to the most relevant charity for that particular cause of death. This simple example would provide a platform business model with gamers on one side and charities on the other side, and the money allocated would go to these while creating a strong empathic experience between the virtual character and the player.

In fact, we believe such models are so worth exploring that we decided that we would dedicate all the royalties generated by this book to support such non-profit platform projects. There is no reason the power of communities that underpins the private platform businesses discussed in this book cannot be replicated to deal with some of the world's greatest challenges.

After all, everybody needs a platform strategy . . . what is yours?

Notes

1   World Economic Forum, Future of Jobs report, January 2016.
2   WEF Future of Jobs report, January 2016. With 44% of respondents, mainly human resources representatives from organizations representing more than 13 million employees in total, the topic of the changing nature of work was far ahead of all other strategic considerations, including growth of the mobile Internet and cloud technologies (with 34%) or increased processing power and big data (with 26%).
3   For a full Marxist analysis of these developments, see Nick Dyer-Witheford, *Cyber-Proletariat: Global Labour in the Digital Vortex*, 15 May 2015, or Ursula Huws, *Labor in the Global Digital Economy: The Cybertariat Comes of Age*, 10 December 2014.
4   A Labor Market That Works: Connecting Talent with Opportunity in the Digital Age, McKinsey Global Institute, June 2015.
5   The McKinsey report mentions that Spain, Greece, Portugal, Italy and France would benefit the most in Europe, while South Africa, Colombia, the Philippines, Egypt and Russia would be the emerging economies benefiting the most. The US would also benefit significantly through increased participation and faster matching of jobs.
6   See www.mturk.com/mturk/welcome.
7   Such as in the case of BlaBlaCar where only a contribution to the costs of driving from A to B can be levied by the driver, or charity-enabling platforms such as JustGiving that connect givers and good causes.
8   See, for example, Juliet Schor, 'Debating the Sharing Economy', October 2014, for a good summary of the debate: www.greattransition.org/publication/debating-the-sharing-economy#sthash.wjx6WQ6c.dpuf.
9   11 December 2015, CNN, http://money.cnn.com/2015/12/11/technology/airbnb-bias-harvard/. It is worth noting that Airbnb has since implemented robust anti-discrimination provisions that are aimed at improving this.

10 See, for example, Bloomberg article dated 2 May 2016 on universal basic income: www.bloombergview.com/articles/2016-05-02/a-basic-income-should-be-the-next-big-thing.

11 www.theverge.com/2014/9/30/6874353/reddit-50-million-funding-give-users-10-percent-stock-equity and www.reddit.com/r/AskReddit/comments/2moyiz/serious_how_should_reddit_inc_distribute_a/.

12 21 September 2015, Kickstarter blog, www.kickstarter.com/blog/kickstarter-is-now-a-benefit-corporation?ref=charter.

13 Kickstarter fulfilment report, www.kickstarter.com/fulfillment.

14 At the time of writing, the Singapore Autonomous Vehicle Initiative (SAVI) is running live trials of autonomous cars.

15 Moore's law states that computer processing power doubles every two years.

16 Sharetribe promises to have your platform business running in a few minutes without the need for a developer . . . give it a go at www.sharetribe.com/.

17 J. Rifkin, *The Empathic Civilization*, New York: Jeremy P. Tarcher, 2010.

A word from the authors

We hope you enjoyed reading *Platform Strategy* and learned a thing or two about platforms along the way.

Platform business models are changing many areas of our lives at an unprecedented pace. When we started writing this book, very little had been written about the practical principles of platform management. Now we see new platform businesses being launched every day and, increasingly, established businesses launching or acquiring their own platforms. We also come across a range of useful studies, conferences, reports and books touching upon platform strategy and related topics.

If you're interested in keeping track of these developments you may want to check the book's companion web site: www.platformstrategy.co, where you will find additional resources on how to design, ignite and scale your own platform.

Also we are always interested in hearing about platforms so feel free to drop us a line at benoit@platformstrategy.co and laure@platformstrategy.co.

Index

Taylor & Francis eBooks

Helping you to choose the right eBooks for your Library

Add Routledge titles to your library's digital collection today. Taylor and Francis ebooks contains over 50,000 titles in the Humanities, Social Sciences, Behavioural Sciences, Built Environment and Law.

Choose from a range of subject packages or create your own!

Benefits for you

» Free MARC records
» COUNTER-compliant usage statistics
» Flexible purchase and pricing options
» All titles DRM-free.

Benefits for your user

» Off-site, anytime access via Athens or referring URL
» Print or copy pages or chapters
» Full content search
» Bookmark, highlight and annotate text
» Access to thousands of pages of quality research at the click of a button.

REQUEST YOUR FREE INSTITUTIONAL TRIAL TODAY

Free Trials Available
We offer free trials to qualifying academic, corporate and government customers.

eCollections – Choose from over 30 subject eCollections, including:

Archaeology	Language Learning
Architecture	Law
Asian Studies	Literature
Business & Management	Media & Communication
Classical Studies	Middle East Studies
Construction	Music
Creative & Media Arts	Philosophy
Criminology & Criminal Justice	Planning
Economics	Politics
Education	Psychology & Mental Health
Energy	Religion
Engineering	Security
English Language & Linguistics	Social Work
Environment & Sustainability	Sociology
Geography	Sport
Health Studies	Theatre & Performance
History	Tourism, Hospitality & Events

For more information, pricing enquiries or to order a free trial, please contact your local sales team: **www.tandfebooks.com/page/sales**

 Routledge
Taylor & Francis Group

The home of
Routledge books

www.tandfebooks.com